~~Bus~~

Handbook

August 1993

British Bus Publishing

The Eastern Bus Handbook

The Eastern Bus Handbook is part of the Bus Handbook series that details the fleets of stage carriage and express coach operators. These are published by British Bus Publishing and cover Scotland, Wales and England north of London. Companion volumes, The North West Bus Handbook and The Yorkshire Bus Handbook are currently on sale with the The North East Bus Handbook scheduled to be published in September 1993 and the remainder during 1994. Together with the London Bus Handbooks, South East Buses and South West Buses published by Capital Transport, they provide comprehensive coverage of all the principal operators' fleets in the British Isles.

Livery and depot details are included in the fleet lists; more details of operators can be found in the Capital Transport book *Buses in Britain*, to be published in 1993.

Quality photographs for inclusion in these, and other areas covered by the series are welcome, though the publishers cannot accept responsibility of any loss. Details of changes to fleet information are also welcome.

More information on the Bus Handbook series is available from:

British Bus Publishing,
The Vyne,
16 St Margaret's Drive
Wellington
Telford,
Shropshire TF1 3PH

Series Editor: Bill Potter

Principal Editors for *The Eastern Bus Handbook*:
David Donati, Keith Grimes, Colin Lloyd and Geoff Mills

Acknowledgements:
We are grateful to Graham Ashworth, Mark Jameson, John Jones, Steve Sanderson, London Omnibus Traction Society, the PSV Circle and the operating companies for their assistance in the compilation of this book.

The front cover photo is by Geoff Mills
The rear cover and frontispiece photographs are by Ivor Norman, Michael Fowler and Colin Lloyd

Contents correct to July 1993
ISBN 1 897990 02 2
Published by *British Bus Publishing*
The Vyne, 16 St Margarets Drive, Wellington,
Telford, Shropshire, TF1 3PH
© British Bus Publishing, August 1993

Contents

Ambasador Travel	4		Jacksons	76
Amos Coaches	6		Lamberts	77
Anglian	7		Luckybus	78
Associated Coachways	8		Luton & District	79
B T S	9		Lutonian	90
Beeston	10		Milton Keynes City Bus	91
Blue Triangle	13		Morley's	95
Bordabus	17		Neave	96
Buffalo	18		Nibs	97
Busbybus	19		Northampton Transport	99
Buzz	20		Osbourne's	101
Cambridge Coach Services	21		Partridge Coaches	102
Cambus	22		Premier Travel	103
Caroline Seagull	27		Prestwood Travel	105
Cedar Coaches	28		R & I Buses	106
Cedric's	29		Red Rose	109
Challenger	30		Reg's Coaches	110
Chambers	31		Rover Bus Service	111
Coach Services	33		Rule's	112
Colchester Borough Transport	35		Sanders	113
Charles Cook	37		Seamarks	115
County	39		Semmence	116
District Bus	44		Simonds	117
Eastern Counties	45		Southend Transport	118
Eastern National	51		Sovereign	122
Emblings	55		Spratts	125
Enterprise	56		Stephensons	126
Felix	57		Stuart Palmer	127
Flying Banana	58		Thamesway	128
Fords Coaches	59		Towler	134
Galloway	60		United Counties	135
Golden Boy	62		University Bus	141
Graham's	63		Viceroy	142
Great Yarmouth Transport	64		Viscount	143
Harris Bus	67		West's	146
Hedingham Omnibuses	69		Whippet	148
Ipswich Buses	72		Yellow Bus	151
J B S	75			

AMBASSADOR TRAVEL

Ambassador Travel (Anglia) Ltd, James Watt Close, Gapton Hall Industrial Estate,
Great Yarmouth, Norfolk, NR31 0NX

100-108

Volvo B10M-61 — Plaxton Paramount 3500 III — C51FT* — 1989 — *104-6 C53F; 107/8 C49FT

100	F100BPW	104	F104CCL	106	F106CCL	107	F107CCL	108	G108HNG
101	F101BPW	105	F105CCL						

109	G109HNG	Leyland Tiger TRCL10/3ARM	Plaxton Paramount 3500 III	C53F	1990
110	F110CCL	Hestair Duple 425 SDAK1512	Duple 425	C37FT	1989
111	G111HNG	Leyland Tiger TRCL10/3ARM	Plaxton Paramount 3500 III	C53F	1990

112-117

Volvo B10M-60 — Plaxton Paramount 3500 III — C46FT — 1989

112	G512MNG	114	G870MAH	115	G125MNG	116	G481MVF	117	G380NAH
113	G609MVG								

118	H379TNG	Leyland Tiger TRCL10/3ARZM	Plaxton Paramount 3500 III	C53F	1990
119	H380TNG	Leyland Tiger TRCL10/3ARZM	Plaxton Paramount 3500 III	C51F	1990
120	G945JPW	Volvo B10M-60	Plaxton Expressliner	C46FT	1989
121	H381TNG	Leyland Tiger TRCL10/3ARZM	Plaxton Paramount 3500 III	C51F	1990

122-130

Volvo B10M-60 — Plaxton Paramount 3500 III — C46FT — 1990-91

122	H163EJU	124	H171EJU	126	H168EJU	128	H172EJU	130	H176EJU
123	H173EJU	125	H167EJU	127	H169EJU	129	H174EJU		

In recent years Ambassador Travel have undertaken an increasing amount of stage carriage work in both Great Yarmouth and Norwich in competition with Eastern Counties. No.878 (PIJ5751), a Leyland Leopard with Eastern Coach Works body and one of seven such examples, is seen working a circular service on Marine Parade, Great Yarmouth, passing typical seafront razzmatazz. *G R Mills*

131	H833AHS	Volvo B10M-60	Plaxton Paramount 3500 III	C46FT	1990	Ex Parks, Hamilton, 1993
132	J438HDS	Volvo B10M-60	Plaxton Première 350	C46FT	1991	Ex Parks, Hamilton, 1993
133	J437HDS	Volvo B10M-60	Plaxton Première 350	C46FT	1991	Ex Parks, Hamilton, 1993
134	J431HDS	Volvo B10M-60	Plaxton Première 350	C46FT	1991	Ex Parks, Hamilton, 1993
135	J432HDS	Volvo B10M-60	Plaxton Première 350	C46FT	1991	Ex Parks, Hamilton, 1993

878-886

Leyland Leopard PSU3G/4R   Eastern Coach Works B51   C51F   1982   Ex Eastern Counties, 1984

878	PIJ5751	882	PIJ9274	884	PIJ4317	885	CAH885Y	886	CAH886Y
881	PIJ3379	883	PIJ8513						

915	C915BPW	MCW Metroliner DR130/16	MCW		CH55/16DT	1986	
916	C916BPW	MCW Metroliner DR130/16	MCW		CH55/16DT	1986	
917	C917BPW	MCW Metroliner DR130/16	MCW		CH55/16DT	1986	
918	C918BPW	MCW Metroliner DR130/16	MCW		CH55/16DT	1986	
1001	JOX467P	Leyland Leopard PSU3E/4R	Plaxton Supreme III Exp	C49F	1977	Ex Midland Red West, 1992
1002	RDA670R	Leyland Leopard PSU3E/4R	Plaxton Supreme III Exp	C49F	1978	Ex Midland Red West, 1992
1003	XRR622M	Leyland Leopard PSU3B/4R	Plaxton Elite III Express	C53F	1974	Ex Barton, 1992
1004	GNN221N	Leyland Leopard PSU3B/4R	Plaxton Elite III Express	C53F	1975	Ex Barton, 1992
1005	PNN770M	Leyland Leopard PSU3B/4R	Plaxton Elite III Express	C53F	1974	Ex Barton, 1992
1006	ONN274M	Leyland Leopard PSU3B/4R	Plaxton Elite III Express	C53F	1974	Ex Barton, 1992
1007	ONN279M	Leyland Leopard PSU3B/4R	Plaxton Elite III Express	C53F	1974	Ex Barton, 1992

Liveries: White with various contract liveries.

Previous Registrations:

PIJ3379	CAH881Y		PIJ5751	CAH878Y		PIJ9274	CAH882Y
PIJ4317	CAH884Y		PIJ8513	CAH883Y			

Only four MCW Metroliners were supplied new into East Anglia, and all of them are still currently owned by Ambassador Travel. They are normally to be found on the National Express Rapide service between Lowestoft and London. No.918 (C918BPW) is seen in London on service 599. *Colin Lloyd*

AMOS COACHES

J Amos & Son, The Bungalow, Belchamp St Paul, Sudbury, Suffolk, CO10 7BS

HRT530N	Bedford SB5	Duple Dominant	C41F	1975	Ex Burton, Haverhill, 1990
SWO70N	Bedford YRQ	Plaxton Elite III Express	C45F	1975	Ex Davian, Enfield, 1990
NBJ462P	Bedford YRT	Willowbrook 001	B60F	1976	Ex Eastern Counties, 1991
YFT935T	Bedford YLQ	Duple Dominant II	C45F	1979	Ex Wright, Worthing, 1993
JAR484Y	Ford Transit	Ford	M12	1983	Ex private owner, 1993

Livery: Red and cream

East Anglia abounds with small operators working market day services from outlying villages into the nearest town. Typical of these is Amos of Belchamp-St-Paul, who has provided a link with Sudbury using Bedford built vehicles for over fifty years. SWO70N, a YRQ model, is seen with disembarking passengers on the regular Thursday arrival in Sudbury. *G R Mills*

NBJ462P, a large capacity Willowbrook-bodied Bedford bus has been serving the Suffolk community for most of its working life. New to Squirrell's of Hitcham for service into Ipswich, it later passed to Bickers of Coddenham, also serving the county town and Debenham. Subsequently the latter service, and the vehicle, passed to Eastern Counties, Partridges of Hadleigh and Amos where it was extensively refurbished. *G R Mills*

ANGLIAN

Anglian Coaches Ltd, Beccles Road, Loddon, Norfolk, NR14 6JJ

JBW497N	Ford R1114	Plaxton Elite III Express	C53F	1975	Ex Worth, Enstone, 1981
LOA176P	Ford R1114	Duple Dominant	C53F	1976	Ex Bowen, Birmingham, 1981
WDB551S	Ford R1114	Duple Dominant II	C53F	1979	Ex Phoenix Stowmarket, 1992
XHE753T	Ford R1114	Plaxton Supreme III	C53F	1979	Ex Davie's, Rye, 1984
OXK395	Ford R1114	Plaxton Supreme IV	C53F	1980	Ex Jenkins, Skewen, 1989
UVG846	Ford R1114	Plaxton Supreme IV	C53F	1980	Ex Horton, Ripley, 1984
KSU412	Ford R1114	Plaxton Supreme IV	C53F	1981	Ex Norfolk, Gt. Yarmouth, 1985
MJI4487	Ford R1114	Plaxton Supreme IV	C53F	1981	Ex Walker, Walsall, 1986
CSK282	Ford R1114	Plaxton Supreme IV	C53F	1981	Ex Wallace Arnold, 1987
NBX862	Ford R1114	Duple Dominant IV	C53F	1981	Ex Mullover, Bedford, 1992

Previous Registrations:

CSK282	PNW318W	MJI4487	PNB788W	OXK395	BCY249V
KSU412	SVF510W	NBX862	TND101X	UVG846	FTV546V

Livery: Red, white and blue

Anglian operations into Norwich are in succession to such well known names as Cullings and Red Car with an historic lineage of double decker useage. Nowadays the service is normally provided by UVG846 a Ford/Plaxton sporting a Norfolk registration which belies its true identity, an increasingly common practice. It is seen at rest in Rouen Road, Norwich before working service to Loddon. *G R Mills*

ASSOCIATED COACHWAYS

Associated Coachways Ltd, 30 The Service Bays, The Stow, Harlow,
Essex, CM20 3AB

LPB217P	Leyland National 10351/1R		B41F	1976	Ex County, Harlow, 1990
DCA31S	Leyland Leopard PSU3E/4R	Plaxton Supreme III	C53F	1978	Ex Hudson, Downley, 1992
BYW391V	Leyland National 10351A/2R		B36D	1979	Ex London Buses, 1991
DNK577Y	Leyland Tiger TRCTL11/3R	Plaxton Supreme V	C53F	1983	Ex Smith, Brenzett, 1992
IIL1640	Leyland Tiger TRCTL11/3R	Plaxton Paramount 3500 III	C53F	1987	Ex Shearings, 1992
F213NST	Freight Rover Sherpa 350	Aitken	B20F	1988	Ex Inverness Traction, 1992

Livery: Maroon, red and white.

Previous Registrations:
IIL1640   D585MVR

Associated Coachways have replaced their traditional Bedford coaches with Leyland Nationals for stage carriage workings in Harlow. LPB217P, new to London Country, is seen leaving the bus station. *Colin Lloyd*

B T S

Borehamwood Travel Services Ltd, Station Road, Borehamwood, Hertfordshire, WD6 1HB

L139-152

Leyland Olympian ON2R50C13Z4 Northern Counties Palatine H47/30F 1991

L139	H139GGS	L144	H142GGS	L145	H145GGS	L148	H148GGS	L151	H151GGS
L140	H140GGS	L143	H143GGS	L146	H146GGS	L149	H149GGS	L152	H152GGS
L141	H141GGS	L144	H144GGS	L147	H147GGS	L150	H150GGS		

S153-S158

Scania N113DRB   Alexander RH   H47/33F   1989

S153	F153DET	S155	F155DET	S156	F156DET	S157	F157DET	S158	F158DET
S154	F154DET							

T277	GYE277W	Leyland Titan TNLXB2RRSp	Leyland	H44/28F	1981	Ex London Buses, 1992
T620	NUW620Y	Leyland Titan TNLXB2RRSp	Leyland	H44/28F	1983	Ex London Buses, 1993
T706	OHV706Y	Leyland Titan TNLXB2RRSp	Leyland	H44/28F	1983	Ex London Buses, 1993
T777	OHV777Y	Leyland Titan TNLXB2RRSp	Leyland	H44/28F	1983	Ex London Buses, 1993

Livery: Red and yellow.

Recent arrivals with BTS are four examples of the Leyland Titan displaced by London Buses. Now converted to single door, T277 is seen in Elstree Way, Boreham Wood, white working LRT service 292. Noteworthy is the continued use of depot code holders, with BT transfers, and London Buses fleet numbers. *Colin Lloyd*

BEESTON

Beeston's (Hadleigh) Ltd, 21 Long Bessels, Hadleigh, Suffolk, IP7 5DB
Mulley's Motorways Ltd, Stowmarket Road, Ixworth, Suffolk, IP31 2HZ

Note: **M** = Mulleys Motorways. Depots: Long Bessels, Hadleigh; Stowmarket Road, Ixworth and Station Yard, Long Melford

	Reg	Chassis	Body	Code	Year	History
M	HGA637T	Leyland Leopard PSU3/4R	Plaxton Supreme IV (1979)	C53F	1967	Ex New Viscount, Witham, 1988
	PRG131J	Daimler Fleetline CRG6LX	Alexander L	H48/32D	1971	Ex Theobald, Long Melford, 1991
	PRG135J	Daimler Fleetline CRG6LX	Alexander L	H48/32D	1971	Ex Theobald, Long Melford, 1991
M	LJD922K	Leyland Leopard PSU3B/4R	Plaxton Elite	C53F	1972	Ex Thorpe, London, 1993
	PYJ456L	Daimler Fleetline CRG6LX	Alexander AL	H49/31D	1973	Ex Waddell, Lochwinnoch, 1988
	NEV678M	Leyland National 11351/1R		B52F	1974	Ex Thamesway, 1993
M	YVO281M	Bedford YRT	Duple Dominant Express	C53F	1974	Ex Barton, 1982
	PJI3670	Leyland National 11351/1R		DP48F	1975	Ex Wilts & Dorset, 1992
	PJI4084	Leyland National 11351/1R		B52F	1975	Ex Priory, Gosport, 1992
M	GVA388N	Bedford YRT	Duple Dominant	C53F	1975	Ex Baxter, Moggerhanger, 1976
M	KNP327N	Volvo B58-56	Plaxton Elite III Express	C53F	1975	Ex Frostways, Kennington, 1987
	LBJ65P	Bedford YRT	Duple Dominant	B55F	1975	Ex Theobald, Long Melford, 1991
M	NNN394P	Ford R1114	Willowbrook 001	B53F	1976	Ex Trent, 1980
	LNR87P	Bedford YMT	Plaxton Supreme III	C53F	1976	Ex Theobald, Long Melford, 1991
	PPV183R	Bedford YLQ	Plaxton Supreme III	C45F	1976	
	FIL4168	Bedford YMT	Plaxton Supreme III	C53F	1976	Ex Snowling, Shotley, 1986
	FIL4162	Bedford YMT	Plaxton Supreme	C53F	1977	
	FIL4163	Bedford YMT	Plaxton Supreme	C53F	1977	
	OJD212R	Leyland Fleetline FE30AGR	MCW	H44/24D	1977	Ex Davian, Enfield, 1991
	OBN502R	Leyland Fleetline FE30AGR	Northern Counties	H43/32F	1977	Ex Rossendale, 1992
M	WRO444S	Bedford YMT	Van Hool McArdle	C53F	1977	
	PJI5916	Leyland National 11351A/1R		B49F	1978	Ex Merseybus, 1991
	PJI5917	Leyland National 11351A/1R		B49F	1978	Ex Merseybus, 1991
	PJI5912	Leyland National 11351A/1R		B49F	1978	Ex Merseybus, 1991
	PJI5913	Leyland National 11351A/1R		B49F	1978	Ex Merseybus, 1991
	PJI5914	Leyland National 11351A/1R		B49F	1978	Ex Merseybus, 1991
	PJI4708	Leyland National 11351A/1R		B49F	1978	Ex Theobald, Long Melford, 1991
	XPV561S	Bedford YMT	Plaxton Supreme III Exp	C53F	1978	Ex Clarke, Elmswell, 1991
M	ATV535T	Ford R1114	Duple Dominant II	C53F	1978	Ex Millman, Buckfastleigh, 1991
M	EWR166T	Bristol VRT/SL3/6LX	Eastern Coach Works	H43/31F	1979	Ex United, 1991
	PJI4709	Leyland National 11351A/1R		B49F	1979	Ex Ipswich Travel, 1989
	YPB831T	Bedford YMT	Plaxton Supreme IV	C53F	1979	Ex AC, London, 1982
	FIL4167	Bedford YMT	Duple Dominant II	C53F	1979	
M	FIL4743	Bedford YMT	Plaxton Supreme IV	C53F	1979	
M	FIL4344	Bedford YMT	Van Hool McArdle	C53F	1979	
	LUA281V	Leyland Leopard PSU5D/4R	Plaxton Supreme IV	C57F	1980	Ex Ipswich Travel, 1989
	LUA283V	Leyland Leopard PSU5D/4R	Plaxton Supreme IV	C57F	1980	Ex Ipswich Travel, 1989
	GHB85W	Bristol VRT/SL3/6LXB	East Lancashire	H44/32F	1981	Ex National Welsh, 1992
	GHB86W	Bristol VRT/SL3/6LXB	East Lancashire	H44/32F	1981	Ex National Welsh, 1992
M	FIL4345	Bedford YMT	Duple Dominant II	C53F	1981	
	PNW296W	Leyland Leopard PSU5D/4R	Plaxton Supreme IV	C51F	1981	Ex Theobald, Long Melford, 1991
M	RUT684W	Volvo B58-61	Duple Dominant II	C53F	1981	Ex Brown, Crawley, 1993
M	TND134X	Volvo B58-61	Duple Dominant IV	C53F	1982	Ex Thorpe, London, 1993
	FIL4032	Leyland Leopard PSU5D/5R	Duple Dominant IV	C57F	1982	
	FIL4033	Leyland Leopard PSU5D/5R	Duple Dominant IV	C57F	1982	
	219GRA	Leyland Leopard PSU5D/5R	Duple Dominant IV	C57F	1982	
M	FIL4169	Leyland Leopard PSU5D/5R	Duple Dominant IV	C57F	1982	
M	FIL4741	Leyland Leopard PSU5D/5R	Duple Dominant IV	C57F	1982	
M	FIL4742	Leyland Leopard PSU5D/5R	Duple Dominant IV	C57F	1982	
M	ADC366A	DAF MB200DKTL600	Van Hool Alizée	C49FT	1982	Ex Caravelle, Felixstowe, 1992
	222GRA	Scania K112CRS	Jonckheere Jubilee P50	C51FT	1983	
	FIL8613	Volvo B10M-61	Van Hool Alizée	C49FT	1983	Ex Ellard, Princes Gate, 1989
	FHJ565	Volvo B10M-61	Van Hool Alizée	C49FT	1983	Ex Barratt, Nantwich, 1992
	FIL4145	Leyland Tiger TRCTL11/3R	Van Hool Alizée	C50FT	1984	Ex Thomas, Tonypandy, 1988
	FIL4146	Leyland Tiger TRCTL11/3R	Van Hool Alizée	C52FT	1984	Ex Thomas, Tonypandy, 1987
	FIL4164	Leyland Tiger TRCTL11/3R	Van Hool Alizée	C51D	1984	Ex Travellers, Hounslow, 1988
	FIL4165	Leyland Tiger TRCTL11/3R	Van Hool Alizée	C51D	1984	Ex Travellers, Hounslow, 1988
	FIL4166	Leyland Tiger TRCTL11/3R	Van Hool Alizée	C49FT	1984	Ex Travellers, Hounslow, 1988
	FIL8614	Leyland Tiger TRCTL11/3RZ	Van Hool Alizée	C52FT	1987	Ex Travellers, Hounslow, 1989
	FIL8615	Leyland Tiger TRCTL11/3RZ	Van Hool Alizée	C52FT	1987	Ex Travellers, Hounslow, 1989
	FIL8617	Leyland Tiger TRCTL11/3RZ	Van Hool Alizée	C52FT	1987	Ex Travellers, Hounslow, 1989
M	SXF615	Volvo B10M-61	Van Hool Alizée	C44FT	1984	Ex Crosville Wales, 1990
M	YRP371	Volvo B10M-61	Van Hool Alizée	C44FT	1984	Ex Crosville Wales, 1990

Theobalds of Long Melford first introduced double deckers when Corona Coaches of Sudbury went into liquidation. Many years later the former were also forced to call in the receivers. Currently providing the workings are Beestons of Hadleigh using two Bristol VRTs with East Lancashire bodied double decks that became available from National Welsh. GHB85W is one of the pair painted in duo brown with yellow and red bands. *G R Mills*

The last service bus delivered new to Theobalds Motor Services was LBJ65P, a Bedford YRT with Duple Dominant body. The vehicle was also the first of the fleet to be repainted into duo-brown when the fleet was acquired by Beestons of Hadleigh. It is seen at the old Long Melford rail station, freshly repainted a second time, about to work an afternoon schools trip. *G R Mills*

M	WSV555	Volvo B10M-61	Van Hool Alizée	C44FT	1984	Ex Berryhurst, London, 1986
	221GRA	Volvo B10M-61	Jonckheere Jubilee P599	C51F	1984	Ex Jalna, Church Gresley, 1992
M	FIL4034	Scania K112CRS	Jonckheere Jubilee P50	C50F	1985	Ex Crawford, Neilson, 1988
	PJI6394	Scania K112CRS	Jonckheere Jubilee P599	C51FT	1985	Ex Sunstar, London NW10, 1993
M	B711EOF	Volvo B10M-53	Jonckheere Jubilee P95	C54/13FT	1985	Ex Flights, Birmingham, 1990
M	B387UEX	Leyland Tiger TRCTL11/3R	Plaxton Paramount 3200	C57F	1985	Ex Rosemary, Terrington, 1992
M	B107NPY	Leyland Tiger TRCTL11/3R	Plaxton Paramount 3500 II	C48FT	1985	Ex Dredge, London SE18, 1992
	B989MAB	Scania K112CRS	Jonckheere Jubilee P599	C49FT	1986	Ex Brittains, Northampton, 1992
	D369JUM	Volkswagen LT55	Optare City Pacer	B25F	1987	Ex London Buses, 1992
	D371JUM	Volkswagen LT55	Optare City Pacer	B25F	1987	Ex London Buses, 1992
	D377JUM	Volkswagen LT55	Optare City Pacer	B25F	1987	Ex London Buses, 1992
	PJI4712	Toyota Coaster HB31R	Caetano Optimo	C18F	1988	Ex S S S, London NW1, 1992
	PJI6391	Volvo B10M-61	Van Hool Alizée	C49FT	1989	Ex Shearings, 1992
	PJI6392	Volvo B10M-61	Van Hool Alizée	C49FT	1988	Ex Shearings, 1993
	PJI6393	Volvo B10M-61	Van Hool Alizée	C49FT	1988	Ex Shearings, 1993
M	F880TNH	Toyota Coaster HB31R	Caetano Optimo	C20F	1989	Ex The Kings Ferry, 1991
M	F94CBD	Volvo B10M-61	Jonckheere Deauville P599	C51FT	1989	Ex Hill's, Tredegar, 1992
	F668DDO	Kässbohrer Setra S215HDI	Kässbohrer Tornado	C49FT	1989	Ex Highliner, Felixstowe, 1992
M	G468JNH	Volvo B10M-61	Jonckheere Deauville P599	C48FT	1990	Ex Antler, Rugeley, 1992
M	G973LRP	Volvo B10M-61	Jonckheere Deauville P599	C51FT	1990	Ex Hilo, Sandy, 1993
	PJI4713	Toyota Coaster HB31R	Caetano Optimo	C18F	1990	Ex Kingsman, Sheffield, 1992

Livery: Two-tone brown and orange (Beestons); cream and orange (Mulleys).

Previous Registrations:

219GRA	WGV861X	FIL4743	HDX666V
221GRA	B646OAY	FIL8613	A297RSU
222GRA	EBJ845Y	FIL8614	D229HMT
ADC366A	AGV260Y	FIL8615	D283HMT
B989MAB	B505CBD, RDU4	FIL8617	D284HMT
FHJ565	ODS464Y	HGA637T	JUA302E
FIL4032	WGV863X	PJI3670	GLJ677N
FIL4033	WGV866X	PJI4084	HWC83N
FIL4034	B510GBD	PJI4708	EPT883S
FIL4145	B332ANY	PJI4709	LUP898T
FIL4146	B331ANY	PJI4712	E174KNH
FIL4162	VGV445S	PJI4713	G138KKW
FIL4163	VGV446S	PJI5912	RKA872T
FIL4164	A143RMJ	PJI5913	RKA874T
FIL4165	A144RMJ	PJI5914	RKA876T
FIL4166	A145RMJ	PJI5916	RKA867T
FIL4167	FBM390T	PJI5917	RKA868T
FIL4168	MVN873P	PJI6391	E621UNE, WSV528, E489CDB
FIL4169	WGV862X	PJI6392	E620UNE, SPR124, E683CDB
FIL4344	HRO444V	PJI6393	E619UNE, XTW359, E684CDB
FIL4345	RRT111W	PJI6394	B701EOF
FIL4741	WGV864X	RUT684W	ODJ576W, VOI6874
FIL4742	WGV865X	WSV555	A623UGD

Since November 1992 Beestons have operated rival journeys to Chambers' long-established Bury St Edmunds to Sudbury and Colchester service using Leyland Nationals. PJI5917 (originally RKA868T) is one of five former Merseybus examples in the fleet, seen about to depart from Angel Hill on the thirty-five mile long route. *G R Mills*

BLUE TRIANGLE

R L Wright, Blue Triangle, 25 Lovell Walk, Rainham, Essex, RM13 7ND

RT2150	KGK959	AEC Regent III 0961	Weymann	H30/26R	1950	Ex preservation, 1988
RT2799	LYR969	AEC Regent III 0961	Weymann	H30/26R	1950	Ex preservation, 1988
RF401	MXX289	AEC Regal IV 9821LT	Metro-Cammell	B39F	1953	Ex preservation, 1990
	OPV47	AEC Regent V 2D2RA	East Lancashire	H37/28R	1962	Ex preservation, 1993
RCL2239	CUV239C	AEC Routemaster R2RH/3	Park Royal	H36/29RD	1965	Ex preservation, 1985
RMS49	NMY632E	AEC Routemaster R2RH2	Park Royal	H32/24F	1967	Ex preservation
RMS56	NMY651E	AEC Routemaster R2RH2	Park Royal	H32/24F	1967	Ex preservation, 1991
MCL218	FJY918E	Leyland Atlantean PDR1/1	Metro Cammell	O43/32F	1967	Ex Plymouth, 1987
MBS539	VLW539G	AEC Merlin 4P2R	MCW	B25D	1969	Ex London Transport, 1988
DMS404	JGF404K	Daimler Fleetline CRG6LXB	Park Royal	O44/24D	1972	Ex preservation, 1985
SMA8	JPF108K	AEC Swift 3MP2R	Alexander W	DP45F	1972	Ex preservation, 1992
DMS679	MLK679L	Daimler Fleetline CRL6	Park Royal	H44/29F	1973	Ex Nash, Enfield, 1990
DMS768	TGX768M	Daimler Fleetline CRL6	Park Royal	H44/24D	1973	Ex Grimsby-Cleethorpes, 1991
LC78	TPD178M	Leyland National 1051/1R/0402		B41F	1973	Ex Reg's Cs, Hertford, 1990
D1684	THM684M	Daimler Fleetline CRL6	MCW	O44/28D	1974	Ex Frontrunner, Dagenham, 1991
	GHV69N	Daimler Fleetline CRL6	Park Royal	H44/27D	1975	Ex Capital Citybus, 1992
DMS845	GHM845N	Daimler Fleetline CRL6	MCW	O44/27D	1975	Ex ??
DM1110	GHV110N	Daimler Fleetline CRL6	Park Royal	O44/27D	1975	Ex Evencost, Uffington, 1988
DM1133	KUC133P	Daimler Fleetline CRL6	Park Royal	H45/28D	1975	Ex Frontrunner, Dagenham, 1991
DM2391	OJD391R	Leyland Fleetline FE30AGR	Park Royal	H44/32F	1977	Ex London Buses, 1992
DMS2428	OJD428R	Leyland Fleetline FE30AGR	Park Royal	H44/32F	1977	Ex preservation, 1993
	OKW503R	Leyland Fleetline FE30AGR	MCW	H46/25D	1977	Ex Grey Green, 1993
LS174	THX174S	Leyland National 10351A/2R		B36D	1978	Ex London Buses, 1990
DMS2271	THX271S	Leyland Fleetline FE30ALRSp	Park Royal	O44/24D	1978	Ex London Buses, 1992
DMS2337	THX337S	Leyland Fleetline FE30ALRSp	MCW	H44/24D	1978	Ex London Buses, 1992
DMS2503	THX503S	Leyland Fleetline FE30ALRSp	Park Royal	H44/27D	1978	Ex London Buses, 1992
DMS2590	THX590S	Leyland Fleetline FE30ALRSp	Park Royal	H44/27D	1978	Ex London Buses, 1991
DMS2609	THX609S	Leyland Fleetline FE30ALRSp	Park Royal	H44/27D	1978	Ex London Buses, 1992
LS300	AYR300T	Leyland National 10351A/2R		B36D	1979	Ex London Buses, 1990
4015	GNF15V	Leyland Titan TNTL11/1RF	Park Royal	H47/26F	1979	Ex Bordabus, Abridge, 1992
RB130	EPM130V	AEC Reliance 6U2R	Duple Dominant II Exp	C49F	1979	Ex Yeoman's Hereford, 1991
	A758VAF	MCW Metroliner DR130/2	MCW	CH55/17DT	1984	Ex Western National, 1991

Livery: Blue and white or red and cream.

Rural Essex is linked to various larger towns by Essex County Council tendered operations on Sundays. LYR969, one of Blue Triangle's classic RT types, is seen at Gt Yeldham 'Oak', close by the Colne Valley Railway, on a Sunday working. *G R Mills*

Blue Triangle's fleet, mostly comprising former London vehicles, includes one of the very few former MBS class still working as a psv. VLW539G is in fine fettle as this view testifies. The vehicle is seen while working service 500 to Romford. *Roy Marshall*

Blue Triangle also operate weekday service 265 on behalf of Essex CC for which they introduced former London Leyland Nationals into the fleet. However, on this journey TPD178M, a former London Country example, was caught in St Edwards Way, Romford en route to Bulphan Church. *G R Mills*

BORDABUS

Bordacoach, 4 Highview Road, Thundersley Common, Benfleet, Essex,

Note: Bordabus and Dorayme Travel names are also used.

70	524FN	AEC Reliance 2U3RA	Plaxton Elite (1972)	C49F	1962	Ex East Kent, 1982
79	YPL91T	AEC Reliance 6U2R	Duple Dominant II Express	C49F	1979	Ex London Country, 1985
83	YPL96T	AEC Reliance 6U2R	Duple Dominant II Express	C49F	1979	Ex London Country, 1986
97	MED406P	AEC Reliance 6U3ZR	Duple Dominant	C57F	1976	Ex Baker, Weston-super-Mare, 1990
98	NMJ298V	AEC Reliance 6U3ZR	Duple Dominant II Express	C53F	1980	Ex Forest Coaches, London, 1989
103	OJD448R	Leyland Fleetline FE30ALRSp	Park Royal	H44/24D	1977	Ex London Buses, 1992
106	OHR190R	Leyland Fleetline FE30AGR	Eastern Coach Works	H44/30F	1977	Ex Thamesdown, 1993

Note: 106 is currently away on hire.
Livery: White and blue

Bordabus has mostly acquired vehicles which were formerly with major operators. YPL91T, an AEC Reliance new to the Green Line operation, is seen in Waltham Cross and is one of a pair of AEC Reliances formerly with London Country. *Colin Lloyd*

BUFFALO

Bornyard Ltd & Grouptravs Ltd, Enterprise Way, Maulden Road Industrial Estate, Flitwick, Bedfordshire, MK45 5BW

No	Reg	Chassis	Body	Code	Year	History
1	LXI2741	Volvo B58-56	Duple Dominant III	C53F	1981	Ex Classic, West Pelton, 1988
2	2583KP	Volvo B10M-61	Caetano Algarve	C53FT	1986	Ex Skills, Nottingham, 1988
3	UXI7897	Volvo B10M-61	Duple Dominant IV	C53F	1983	Ex Bere Regis & District, 1992
4	UXI5357	Volvo B10M-61	Duple Dominant IV	C53F	1983	Ex Bere Regis & District, 1992
5	2997HL	Volvo B10M-61	Caetano Alpha	C53F	1983	
6	KAF577W	Volvo B58-56	Duple Dominant IV	C53F	1981	Ex Brown, Horley, 1988
7	9349KP	Volvo B58-61	Plaxton Supreme III	C57F	1978	Ex Fountain, Twickenham, 1981
8	EAV810V	Volvo B58-56	Duple Dominant II Exp	DP53F	1980	Ex Brown, Horley, 1988
9	LXI2743	Volvo B58-61	Plaxton Supreme III	C57F	1978	Ex Silver Fox, Renfrew, 1984
10	RNK749M	Bedford YRT	Plaxton Elite III	C53F	1973	Ex Blackford, Isleworth, 1982
11	KKU835P	Bedford YRT	Duple Dominant	C53F	1975	Ex Sherborne, Andoversford, 1983
12	GTM155T	Bedford YMT	Duple Dominant II	C53F	1978	Ex Cedar, Bedford, 1992
15	WXI4357	Volvo B58-56	Plaxton Supreme III	C44F	1975	Ex Blunderbus, High Wycombe,
27	K447XPA	Dennis Dart 9.8SDL3017	Plaxton Pointer	B40F	1992	
28	K448XPA	Dennis Dart 9.8SDL3017	Plaxton Pointer	B40F	1992	
31	F151KGS	Volvo B10M-56	Plaxton Derwent II	B54F	1988	
32	F152KGS	Volvo B10M-56	Plaxton Derwent II	B54F	1988	
33	F153KGS	Volvo B10M-56	Plaxton Derwent II	B54F	1988	
34	F154KGS	Leyland Swift LBM6T/2RA	Wadham Stringer Vanguard II	B39F	1988	
35	F155KGS	Leyland Swift LBM6T/2RA	Wadham Stringer Vanguard II	B39F	1988	
36	F314RMH	Volvo B10M-56	Plaxton Derwent II	B54F	1988	
39	7178KP	Bedford YMQS	Lex Tillotson Maxeta	B37F	1981	Ex Rover, Bromsgrove, 1989
40	WNH50W	Bedford YMQS	Lex Tillotson Maxeta	B33F	1981	Ex Carriages, Fleetwood, 1981
41	H641UWE	Mercedes-Benz 814D	Europa Enterprise	B31F	1991	Ex Globe, Barnsley, 1992
42	H642UWE	Mercedes-Benz 814D	Europa Enterprise	B31F	1991	Ex Globe, Barnsley, 1992
43	RDS83W	Volvo B58-56	Duple Dominant	B53F	1980	Ex Irvine, Salsburgh 1990
44	RDS84W	Volvo B58-56	Duple Dominant	B53F	1980	Ex Irvine, Salsburgh 1990
45	HIL7467	Volvo B10M-61	East Lancs EL2000(1991)	B55F	1983	Ex Summerfield, Southampton, 1991
46	URY598	Volvo B10M-61	East Lancs EL2000(1992)	B55F	1985	Ex The Kings Ferry, Gillingham, 1991
47	NIB8459	Volvo B10M-61	East Lancs EL2000(1992)	B55F	1989	Ex The Kings Ferry, Gillingham, 1991
58	G58BEL	Mercedes-Benz 811D	Wadham Stringer Wessex	DP31F	1989	Ex Bournemouth, 1990
59	H231KBH	Mercedes-Benz 709D	Carlyle	B27F	1991	Ex Carlyle demonstrator, 1992
61	GSL895N	Daimler Fleetline CRG6LX	Alexander AL	H49/34D	1975	Ex Independent, Horsforth, 1988
62	GSL898N	Daimler Fleetline CRG6LX	Alexander AL	H49/34D	1975	Ex Independent, Horsforth, 1987
63	GHV979N	Daimler Fleetline CRL6	Park Royal	H45/32D	1975	Ex Ementon, Cranfield, 1988
65 w	THM706M	Daimler Fleetline CRL6	MCW	H44/27D	1974	Ex London Transport, 1983
67	HDB437V	Dennis Dominator DD110	Northern Counties	H43/32F	1980	Ex Whippet, Fenstanton, 1989
68 w	HDB438V	Dennis Dominator DD110	Northern Counties	H43/32F	1980	Ex Whippet, Fenstanton, 1989
69	TND439X	Dennis Dominator DD136	Northern Counties	H43/33F	1981	Ex Whippet, Fenstanton, 1989
70	TND440X	Dennis Dominator DD136	Northern Counties	H43/33F	1981	Ex Whippet, Fenstanton, 1989
73 w	OJD470R	Leyland Fleetline FE30ALRSpl	Park Royal	H44/32F	1977	Ex London Buses, 1992
74	WWJ771M	Daimler Fleetline CRG6LXB	Park Royal	O43/27D	1974	Ex South Yorkshire, 1984
75	HRU680E	Bristol FLF6G	Eastern Coach Works	H38/32F	1967	Ex City Fleet, Liverpool, 1983
78	A698EAU	Leyland Olympian ONTL11/1R	Northern Counties	H47/33D	1984	Ex Southend, 1990
79	A699EAU	Leyland Olympian ONTL11/1R	Northern Counties	H47/33D	1984	Ex Southend, 1990
	H668ATN	Toyota HB31R	Caetano Optimo	C21F	1990	Ex Wheadon, Cardiff, 1993
	PJI2451	Volvo B58-56	Plaxton Supreme III	C53F	1975	Ex McColl, Balloch, 1992

2583KP	C45OTV		LXI2743	DGD88T, 7178KP, HKX319T
2997HL	JNM55Y		NIB8459	E637NEL
7178KP	LCY302X		PJI2451	LUB514P
9349KP	CLC746T		URY598	B572AVW
H231KBH	CMN414C		UXI5357	ENF575Y
HIL7467	FUA387Y, 3408WY, NRV859Y		UXI7897	ENF562Y
LXI2741	DEC725W		WXI4357	LUB506P

Livery: White, yellow and red.

Buffalo's mixed fleet includes many examples based on Volvo chassis. Some of these ate fitted with coach bodies that are used to operate stage carriage services working alongside service buses. EAV810V, a Volvo B58 with Duple Dominant II Express bodywork, is now fitted with bus seats. This particular vehicle was new to Whippet. *Colin Lloyd*

A much travelled vehicle, especially for its age, is TND440X, a Dennis Dominator new to Greater Manchester Transport as one of its evaluation vehicles. All four of these have remained together having come to Buffalo from the Whippet fleet. *Colin Lloyd*

Buffalo has had three of its Volvo B10M coaches rebodied by East Lancashire with the EL2000 bus body for further stage carriage work. One of the trio, 47 (NIB8459), still displays the same private registration it wore when a Plaxton Paramount coach with The Kings Ferry. It is seen waiting at the Central Library terminus in Bedford. *G R Mills*

Buffalo has established numerous services in Bedfordshire and adjoining Hertfordshire such that a batch of new Volvo B10M/Plaxton Derwents were justified in 1988. One of the four, 31 (F151KGS), is seen in High Street, Dunstable on arrival from Bedford via Flitwick. *G R Mills*

BUSYBUS

Busylink Ltd, Bourne End Farm, London Road, Bourne End, Hemel Hempstead, Hertfordshire, HP1 2RH

SNB92	TPD192M	Leyland National 1051/1R/0402		B36D	1973	Ex NCP Stansted, 1991
LNC177	RBU177R	Leyland National 11351/1R		DP42F	1975	Acquired, 1993
DMS2321	THX321S	Leyland Fleetline FE30ALRSp	MCW	H44/24D	1977	Ex London Buses, 1992
	AFH389T	Bedford YMT	Duple Dominant II	C53F	1978	Acquired 1993
LD214	DAK214V	Leyland Leopard PSU5C/4R	Duple Dominant II	C50F	1980	Ex Burman, Mile Oak, 1993

Livery: Red, yellow and blue

Deregulation of bus services has promoted a host of new operations. Typical of these is Busybus whose TPD192M, a Leyland National at one-time with London Buses, is seen at St Albans City station. *Colin Lloyd*

BUZZ

Buzz Co-operative Ltd, Artic House, Riverway, Harlow, Essex, CM20 2DP

	Mercedes-Benz 609D	Reeve Burgess	B20F*	1988	*71 is DP25F
F71SMC	F73SMC	F75SMC	F77SMC		F79SMC
F72SMC	F74SMC	F76SMC	F78SMC		

FIL7253	Leyland Tiger TRCTL11/3R	Plaxton Paramount 3500	C49FT	1986	Ex Eastern Counties, 1993
F365BUA	Mercedes-Benz 811D	Optare StarRider	DP30F	1988	Ex Optare demonstrator, 1989
F678AWW	Mercedes-Benz 811D	Optare StarRider	B27F	1988	Ex Optare demonstrator, 1989

Livery: White and yellow;
Overall advert: F73SMC

Previous Registrations:
FIL7253   C913BMG

Although the bulk of the Buzz fleet consists of Reeve Burgess Beaver-bodied midi-buses there is also a pair of Optare StarRiders, both of which were originally employed as demonstrators. F678AWW reverses from the stands in Harlow bus station to work town service B1. *G R Mills*

CAMBRIDGE COACH SERVICES

Cambridge Coach Services Ltd, Kings Hedges Road, Impington, Cambridge, CB4 4PQ

350	D350KVE	Volvo B10M-61	Van Hool Alizée	C53FL	1987	Ex Premier Travel, 1990
351	D351KVE	Volvo B10M-61	Van Hool Alizée	C53F	1987	Ex Premier Travel, 1990
361	E361NEG	Volvo B10M-61	Plaxton Paramount 3200 III	C53F	1988	Ex Premier Travel, 1990
362	E362NEG	Volvo B10M-61	Plaxton Paramount 3200 III	C53F	1988	Ex Premier Travel, 1990
363	E363NEG	Volvo B10M-61	Plaxton Paramount 3200 III	C53F	1988	Ex Premier Travel, 1990
365	E365NEG	Volvo B10M-61	Plaxton Paramount 3200 III	C53F	1988	Ex Premier Travel, 1990
366	E366NEG	Volvo B10M-61	Plaxton Paramount 3200 III	C53F	1988	Ex Premier Travel, 1990
367	E367NEG	Volvo B10M-61	Plaxton Paramount 3200 III	C53F	1988	Ex Premier Travel, 1990
384	G96RGG	Volvo B10M-60	Plaxton Paramount 3500 III	C53F	1990	Ex Parks, Hamilton, 1991
385	G97RGG	Volvo B10M-60	Plaxton Paramount 3500 III	C49FT	1990	Ex Parks, Hamilton, 1991
386	G98RGG	Volvo B10M-60	Plaxton Paramount 3500 III	C53F	1990	Ex Parks, Hamilton, 1991
387	YIJ387	Volvo B10M-61	Plaxton Paramount 3200	C53F	1983	Ex Rover, Bromsgrove, 1991
388	F884RFP	Volvo B10M-61	Plaxton Paramount 3500 III	C53F	1989	Ex Bleach, Hetton-le-Hole, 1992
389	F424DUG	Volvo B10M-60	Plaxton Paramount 3200 III	C50F	1989	Ex Wallace Arnold, 1992
390	F425DUG	Volvo B10M-60	Plaxton Paramount 3200 III	C50F	1989	Ex Wallace Arnold, 1992
391	F421DUG	Volvo B10M-60	Plaxton Paramount 3200 III	C50F	1989	Ex Wallace Arnold, 1993
392	K392FEG	Toyota Coaster HDB30R	Caetano Optimo II	C18F	1993	

Livery: Silver and blue

Previous Registrations:
YIJ387   FUA393Y, TXI6342

Heathrow airport is the setting for this picture of Cambridge Coach Services F424DUG, a Volvo B10M with Plaxton Paramount coachwork. It features the frontal treatment of the Paramount III model and is one of three recently acquired from Wallace Arnold. The Airport provides much work for this and other coach operators. *Colin Lloyd*

CAMBUS

Cambus Ltd, 100 Cowley Road, Cambridge, CB4 4DN

Depots: Cowley Road, Cambridge and Depot Road, Newmarket.

65	OFB965R	Bristol LH6L	Eastern Coach Works	B43F	1977	Ex Prince Henry School, Otley, 1992
300	PEX611W	Leyland National 2 NL116L11/1R		B49F	1980	Ex Eastern Counties, 1984
301	PEX612W	Leyland National 2 NL116L11/1R		B49F	1980	Ex Eastern Counties, 1984
302	PEX618W	Leyland National 2 NL116L11/1R		B49F	1980	Ex Eastern Counties, 1984
303	PEX619W	Leyland National 2 NL116L11/1R		B49F	1980	Ex Eastern Counties, 1984
304	PEX620W	Leyland National 2 NL116AL11/1R		B49F	1981	Ex Viscount, 1990
305	PEX621W	Leyland National 2 NL116AL11/1R		B49F	1981	Ex Viscount, 1990
306	PEX622W	Leyland National 2 NL116AL11/1R		B49F	1981	Ex Eastern Counties, 1984
307	UVF623X	Leyland National 2 NL116AL11/1R		B49F	1981	Ex Eastern Counties, 1984
310	F167SMT	Leyland Lynx LX112L10ZR1S	Leyland Lynx	B49F	1989	Ex Miller, Foxton, 1992
311	F168SMT	Leyland Lynx LX112L10ZR1S	Leyland Lynx	B49F	1989	Ex Miller, Foxton, 1992
312	F171SMT	Leyland Lynx LX112L10ZR1S	Leyland Lynx	B49F	1989	Ex Miller, Foxton, 1992
500	E500LFL	Leyland Olympian ONLXCT/1R	Optare	DPH43/27F	1988	
501	E501LFL	Leyland Olympian ONLXCT/1R	Optare	DPH43/27F	1988	
503	UWW3X	Leyland Olympian ONLXB/1R	Roe	H47/29F	1982	Ex West Yorkshire PTE, 1987
504	UWW4X	Leyland Olympian ONLXB/1R	Roe	H47/29F	1982	Ex West Yorkshire PTE, 1987
505	UWW8X	Leyland Olympian ONLXB/1R	Roe	H47/29F	1982	Ex West Yorkshire PTE, 1987
506	B144GSC	Leyland Olympian ONTL11/2R	Alexander RLC	CH43/20F	1984	Ex Eastern Scottish, 1993
507	B145GSC	Leyland Olympian ONTL11/2R	Alexander RLC	CH43/20F	1984	Ex Eastern Scottish, 1993

512-517		Leyland Olympian ONLXB/1RH	Northern Counties	H45/30F	1988	
512	F512NJE	514	F514NJE	515	F515NJE	516	F516NJE	517	F517NJE
513	F513NJE								

The cantilever portal frame of Cambridge bus station provides a background for Leyland National 307 in the Cambus fleet. It was built to the lightweight specification, without the characteristic pod and other features. *Michael Fowler*

Originally introduced into the Cambus fleet via Ensignbus in an exchange for surplus Bristol VRTs and Leyland Nationals came three former West Yorkshire PTE Leyland Olympians with Roe bodywork. These were initially put to work at Peterborough. though with the formation of Viscount the trio were transferred to Cambridge. No.503 (UWW3X) is seen in the centre of the university city, heading for Cherry Hinton. *Colin Lloyd*

The Park & Ride service is an important aspect of Cambus operations in Cambridge. Following the absorption of all Millers workings on the previously competitive service, the three acquired Leyland Lynx have received a dedicated livery with bold signwriting, as shown on 311 (F168SMT), seen passing along Emmanuel Street. *G R Mills*

Different from any other double deckers in the Cambus fleet are the pair of former Eastern Scottish Leyland Olympians with Alexander's RLC-type coachwork. No.506 (B144GSC) leaves St Andrews Street in North Bury-St-Edmunds on a limited stop service back to Cambridge through Newmarket. *G R Mills*

Cambus provide the City Rail Link service using Optare City Pacers, featuring the large, angled, windscreen. Built on the Volkswagen LT55 base and new to the Taff Ely operations, 924 is seen in a cycle park. Pedal cycles are still a feature of Cambridge life. *Michael Fowler*

625	GNG711N	Bristol VRT/SL2/6LX	Eastern Coach Works	H43/31F	1975	Ex Eastern Counties, 1984
700	MCL937P	Bristol VRT/SL3/6LX	Eastern Coach Works	H43/31F	1976	Ex Eastern Counties, 1984
701	MCL942P	Bristol VRT/SL3/6LX	Eastern Coach Works	H43/31F	1976	Ex Eastern Counties, 1984
702	NAH137P	Bristol VRT/SL3/501	Eastern Coach Works	H43/31F	1976	Ex Eastern Counties, 1984
703	NAH138P	Bristol VRT/SL3/501(Gardner)	Eastern Coach Works	H43/31F	1976	Ex Eastern Counties, 1984
704	NAH140P	Bristol VRT/SL3/501	Eastern Coach Works	H43/31F	1976	Ex Eastern Counties, 1984
705	NAH136P	Bristol VRT/SL3/501(Gardner)	Eastern Coach Works	H43/31F	1976	Ex Eastern Counties, 1984

709-718

Bristol VRT/SL3/6LXB   Eastern Coach Works   H43/31F   1976-77   Ex Viscount, 1992
715 ex Eastern Counties, 1984

709	OPW179P	712	OPW182P	714	PEX385R	716	PEX386R	718	TEX405R
710	OPW180P	713	OPW183P	715	WPW200S	717	PVF353R		

719-729

Bristol VRT/SL3/6LXB   Eastern Coach Works   H43/31F   1978-79   Ex Eastern Counties, 1984
722 ex Viscount, 1991; 724 ex Green, Kirkintilloch, 1991

719	YNG209S	721	YNG212S	723	BCL213T	725	DEX228T	727	DNG232T
720	YNG210S	722	YWY830S	724	FRP905T	726	DEX231T	729	DNG234T

730-737

Bristol VRT/SL3/6LXB   Eastern Coach Works   H43/31F   1979-81   Ex York City, 1990

730	FWR216T	732	FWR218T	734	NUM341V	736	SUB794W	737	SUB795W
731	FWR217T	733	JUB650V	735	PWY37W				

738-755

Bristol VRT/SL3/6LXB   Eastern Coach Works   H43/31F   1979-81   Ex Eastern Counties, 1984
*741 is DPH41/24F; 751 is DPH41/29F; 747/8 are H39/31F and ex Green, Kirkintilloch, 1991

738	RAH260W	742	VEX295X	745	VEX303X	748	STW30W	753	VEX289X
740	RAH265W	743	VEX300X	746	VEX304X	751	VEX298X	755	VEX293X
741	RAH268W	744	VEX296X	747	STW24W				

756	KRE638P	Bristol VRT/SL3/501	Eastern Coach Works	H43/31F	1976	Ex Red Bus, Barnstaple, 1985
758	OFA644P	Bristol VRT/SL3/501	Eastern Coach Works	H43/31F	1976	Ex Red Bus, Barnstaple, 1985
759	OFA645P	Bristol VRT/SL3/501	Eastern Coach Works	H43/31F	1976	Ex Red Bus, Barnstaple, 1985
760	OFA646P	Bristol VRT/SL3/501	Eastern Coach Works	H43/31F	1976	Ex Red Bus, Barnstaple, 1985

Cambus has a selection of Bristol VRTs gathered from a wide variety of sources. A good example is 747 (STW24W), one of a pair that began life with Eastern National, later passing to Thamesway before returning to East Anglia via Greens of Kirkintilloch. It is seen leaving Cambridge for Gamlingay. *Michael Fowler*

761	PTT92R	Bristol VRT/SL3/6LXB	Eastern Coach Works	H43/31F	1976	Ex Red Bus, Barnstaple, 1986
762	XDV607S	Bristol VRT/SL3/6LXB	Eastern Coach Works	H43/31F	1978	Ex Red Bus, Barnstaple, 1986
763	YVV896S	Bristol VRT/SL3/6LXB	Eastern Coach Works	H43/31F	1978	Ex Green, Kirkintilloch, 1991
764	WWY130S	Bristol VRT/SL3/6LXB	Eastern Coach Works	H43/31F	1978	Ex Viscount, 1992
899	E814SUM	Volkswagen LT55	Optare City Pacer	B25F	1987	Ex Optare demonstrator, 1988
911	E911LVE	Volkswagen LT55	Optare City Pacer	B25F	1988	
912	E912LVE	Volkswagen LT55	Optare City Pacer	B25F	1988	
913	E913LVE	Volkswagen LT55	Optare City Pacer	B25F	1988	
922	E42RDW	Volkswagen LT55	Optare City Pacer	B23F	1987	Ex Taff Ely, 1988
923	E43RDW	Volkswagen LT55	Optare City Pacer	B23F	1987	Ex Taff Ely, 1988
924	E44RDW	Volkswagen LT55	Optare City Pacer	B23F	1987	Ex Taff Ely, 1988
925	E45RDW	Volkswagen LT55	Optare City Pacer	B23F	1987	Ex Taff Ely, 1988
926	E46RDW	Volkswagen LT55	Optare City Pacer	B25F	1987	Ex National Welsh, 1989
927	E750VWT	Volkswagen LT55	Optare City Pacer	B23F	1987	Ex National Welsh, 1989

960-975
| | | Optare MetroRider | Optare | B29F | 1992-93 |

960	J960DWX	964	K964HUB	967	K967HUB	970	K970HUB	973	K973HUB
961	J961DWX	965	K965HUB	968	K968HUB	971	K971HUB	974	K974HUB
962	J962DWX	966	K966HUB	969	K969HUB	972	K972HUB	975	K975HUB
963	K963HUB								

990	K390TCE	Optare MetroRider	Optare	B31F	1993
2030	C330SFL	Ford Transit 190	Carlyle	B16F	1986
2032	C332SFL	Ford Transit 190	Carlyle	B16F	1986
2033	C333SFL	Ford Transit 190	Carlyle	B16F	1986
2036	C336SFL	Ford Transit 190	Carlyle	B16F	1986

Livery: White, Cambridge blue and dark blue; Cream and red (Millerbus); Cream with light blue and dark blue (local coach).

Ely (Isle Hoppa):	2036.	Local coach:	500/1/6/7, 741/51
Millerbus:	302-6/10-2.	Newmarket Colts:	925/7
Rail Link:	922/3/4	Overall adverts:	515, 738, 926, 990.

On order: 14 Volvo B6/Marshall buses

Optare products have found great favour with Cambus for the past five years. Representing the 1993 intake is 971 (K971HUB), featuring a nearside route number display. It is seen attempting to cross Emmanuel Street among the normally congested city traffic. *G R Mills*

CAROLINE SEAGULL

Cobholm Hire Services Ltd, 59 Marine Parade
Great Yarmouth, Norfolk, NR30 2EJ

6544FN	AEC Reliance 2U3RA	Plaxton Elite III(1974)	C53F	1963	Ex East Kent, 1981
6546FN	AEC Reliance 2U3RA	Plaxton Elite III(1974)	C53F	1963	Ex East Kent, 1981
6539FN	AEC Reliance 2U3RA	Plaxton Elite III(1974)	C53F	1963	Ex East Kent, 1981
6545FN	AEC Reliance 2U3RA	Plaxton Supreme IV(1979)	C53F	1965	Ex East Kent, 1979
FEX817T	AEC Reliance 2U3RA	Plaxton Supreme IV(1979)	C53F	1965	Ex East Kent, 1979
JSC890E	Leyland Atlantean PDR1/1	Alexander L	O43/31F	1967	Ex Partridge, Hadleigh, 1982
GNM235N	Bristol LHL6L	Plaxton Elite III	C51F	1974	Ex H & M, Chasetown, 1992
531FN	AEC Reliance 6U3ZR	Plaxton Supreme III	C55F	1977	Ex Isle Coaches, Owston Ferry, 1992
ODL175R	Bedford YMT	Duple Dominant	C51F	1977	Ex Southern Vectis, 1988
ODL176R	Bedford YMT	Duple Dominant	C51F	1977	Ex Southern Vectis, 1988
TDL127S	Bedford YMT	Duple Dominant	C51F	1978	Ex Southern Vectis, 1988
TDL420S	Bedford YMT	Duple Dominant	C51F	1978	Ex Southern Vectis, 1988
535FN	Ford R1114	Plaxton Supreme IV	C53F	1980	Ex Norfolk, Great Yarmouth, 1984
522FN	Ford R1114	Plaxton Supreme IV	C53F	1981	Ex Norfolk, Great Yarmouth, 1984
523FN	Ford R1114	Plaxton Supreme IV	C53F	1981	Ex Norfolk, Great Yarmouth, 1984
526FN	Ford R1114	Plaxton Supreme IV	C53F	1981	Ex Norfolk, Great Yarmouth, 1984
536FN	Ford R1114	Plaxton Supreme IV	C53F	1981	Ex Norfolk, Great Yarmouth, 1984
538FN	Ford R1114	Plaxton Supreme IV	C53F	1981	Ex Norfolk, Great Yarmouth, 1984
6547FN	Bedford YNT	Plaxton Paramount 3200	C53F	1983	
6543FN	Bedford YNT	Plaxton Paramount 3200	C53F	1983	
EPW928Y	Mercedes-Benz L307D	Reeve Burgess	M12	1983	
537FN	Bedford Venturer YNV	Duple 340	C49FT	1987	
6541FN	Bedford Venturer YNV	Caetano Algarve	C53F	1988	
G469LVG	Dennis Javelin 12SDA1912	Plaxton Paramount 3200 III	C53F	1990	
G470LVG	Dennis Javelin 12SDA1907	Plaxton Paramount 3200 III	C53F	1990	
J652DVG	Toyota Coaster HB31R	Caetano Optimo	C21F	1992	

Livery: White, blue and orange

Previous Registrations:

522FN	TWX331W	537FN	D329LEX	6544FN	From new
523FN	TWX333W	538FN	SVF512W	6545FN	DJG631C, FEX818T
526FN	TWX329W	6539FN	From new	6546FN	From new
531FN	OKY66R	6541FN	E348TPW	6547FN	GEX631Y
535FN	LAH222V	6543FN	GEX632Y	FEX817T	DJG628C
536FN	SVF511W				

Originally one of a dozen Leyland Atlanteans with Alexander bodywork bought from Lothian by Partridge of Hadleigh, JSC890E was converted to open top for Caroline Seagull by Transport Techniques. It is employed on a seafront service and town tours during the schools summer holidays.
G R Mills

CEDAR COACHES

E J Reid, Arkwright Road, Bedford, Bedfordshire, MK42 0LE

1	WRR396Y	Dennis Falcon V DDA403	East Lancashire	H50/38D	1983	Ex Nottingham, 1992
2	XRA397Y	Dennis Falcon V DDA403	East Lancashire	H51/37D	1983	Ex Nottingham, 1990
3	HHT57N	Leyland Atlantean AN68/1R	East Lancashire	H47/35F	1975	Ex Hale-Trent, Clevedon, 1983
4	VRS152L	Daimler Fleetline CRL6	Alexander AL	H45/29F	1973	Ex Grampian, 1983
5	GSL907N	Daimler Fleetline CRG6LX	Alexander AL	H49/38F	1975	Ex Tayside, 1984
6	GSL908N	Daimler Fleetline CRG6LX	Alexander AL	H49/38F	1975	Ex Tayside, 1984
8	VET606S	Leyland Atlantean AN68A/1R	Roe	H45/29D	1978	Ex Ensign, Dagenham, 1991
9	PYJ458L	Daimler Fleetline CRG6LXB	Alexander AL	H49/34D	1971	Ex Gallagher, Waddington, 1987
	HOD55	Bedford OB	Duple Vista	C29F	1949	Ex Porter, Dummer, 1985
	OLN65P	Bedford J2SZ2	Caetano Sintra	C20F	1976	Ex Trollope, Salisbury, 1989
	NSJ3R	Seddon Pennine 7	Alexander AY	B53F	1976	Ex Western Scottish, 1987
	WRK20X	DAF MB200DKTL600	Jonckheere Bermuda	C57F	1982	Ex Victory Tours, Handley, 1989
	XTT5X	Dennis Lancet SD507	Wadham Stringer Vanguard	B52F	1982	Ex Tillingbourne, Cranleigh, 1988
	WSU368	Kässbohrer Setra S228DT	Kässbohrer Imperial	CH54/20DT	1984	Ex De Courcey, Coventry, 1989
	713WAF	Aüwaerter Neoplan N116	Aüwaerter Cityliner	C53FT	1985	Ex Swallow, Rainham, 1993
	D101PBM	Bedford Venturer YNV	Duple 320	C57F	1986	
	D102SPP	Bedford YNT	Plaxton Paramount 3200 III	C53F	1987	
	G103YNK	Leyland Swift ST2B44C97TS	Elme	DP39F	1990	

Previous Registrations:

713WAF	From new	HOD55	From new	WSU368	A263TYC

Livery: Red and cream

The mixed fleet of Cedar Coaches has included most chassis makes currently available, except Volvo. The first new vehicle for the fleet had an Irish built Wright Contour body while the latest new delivery was constructed in Portugal. G103YNK with Elme Orion coachwork on a Leyland Swift chassis is seen in Harpur Street, Bedford. *G R Mills*

CEDRIC'S

Cedric Garages (Wivenhoe) Ltd, Tudor House, The Avenue, Wivenhoe,
Essex, CO7 9AH

1	E199UWT	Mercedes-Benz 811D	Optare StarRider	C29F	1988	
2	F313TLU	Mercedes-Benz 811D	Optare StarRider	C29F	1989	Ex Wings, Uxbridge, 1992
3	KIW4389	Volvo B10M-61	Jonckheere Jubilee P50	C49FT	1985	Ex Len Wright, Isleworth, 1988
4	LIW9272	Volvo B10M-50	Van Hool Alizée	C49FT	1990	Ex Harry Shaw, Coventry, 1993
6	514FBP	Volvo B10M-61	Berkhof Everest 365	C53F	1982	Ex CharterCoach, Gt Oakley, 1985
7	KIW7813	Volvo B10M-61	Ikarus Blue Danube	C49FT	1987	
8	HIL6244	Volvo B10M-61	Ikarus Blue Danube	C49FT	1988	Ex Direct, Birmingham, 1990
9	PKE809M	Bristol VRT/SL2/6LX	Eastern Coach Works	H43/34F	1974	Ex Berrys, Taunton, 1992
10	LPF596P	Bristol VRT/SL3/6LXB	Eastern Coach Works	H41/31F	1976	Ex The Bee Line, 1992
11	NCD563M	Bristol VRT/SL2/6LX	Eastern Coach Works	H43/31F	1974	Ex Brighton & Hove, 1989
12	EIJ4016	Volvo B58-56	Caetano Alpha	C53F	1980	Ex JDW, Ipswich, 1982
13	GNJ574N	Bristol VRT/SL2/6LX	Eastern Coach Works	H43/31F	1974	Ex Brighton & Hove, 1989
14	KIW6416	Volvo B10M-61	Ikarus Blue Danube	C49FT	1987	Ex Boden, Dewsbury, 1991
15	HIL6245	Volvo B10M-61	Plaxton Paramount 3500 III	C48FT	1988	Ex Wallace Arnold, 1992
16	K878GOO	Iveco 49-10	Dormobile	M16	1993	
17	KIW4390	Volvo B10M-61	Jonckheere Jubilee P50	C53FT	1984	Ex Cantabrica, Watford, 1989
18	TWS905T	Bristol VRT/SL3/6LXB	Eastern Coach Works	DPH39/28F	1978	Ex Badgerline, 1992
19	7463RU	Volvo B10M-61	Jonckheere Bermuda	C57F	1981	Ex Ayres, Dalkeith, 1986
20	KIW4391	Volvo B10M-61	Jonckheere Jubilee P50	C51FT	1985	Ex Len Wright, Isleworth, 1988
21	KIW4392	Volvo B10M-61	Jonckheere Jubilee P50	C53FT	1984	Ex Cantabrica, Watford, 1989
22	KIW4388	Volvo B10M-61	Jonckheere Jubilee P50	C49FT	1985	Ex Cantabrica, Watford, 1990
23	KIW4981	Volvo B10M-61	Jonckheere Jubilee P50	C57F	1985	Ex Budden, Woodfalls, 1990
24	NTC571R	Bristol VRT/SL3/6LXB	Eastern Coach Works	DPH39/28F	1977	Ex Badgerline, 1992

Previous Registrations:

514FBP	CAR154X	HIL6245	E906UNW	KIW4392	A127XNH
7463RU	XNV142W	KIW4388	B493GBD	KIW4981	C408LRP
EIJ4016	LRT841V	KIW4389	B495GBD	KIW6416	D140SWL
F313TLU	F933AWW, WET590	KIW4390	A126XNH	KIW7813	D773WHJ
HIL6244	E499UOP	KIW4391	B491GBD	LIW9272	G600CVC, 1KOV

Livery: White, red orange and yellow (Coaches), red and yellow (buses).

Cedric's of Wivenhoe operated nine examples of the Gardner-engined Bristol VRT . GNJ574N, one of the six currently owned, originated with the Southdown fleet and is seen departing Colne High School, Brightlingsea, a location also served by Cedric's weekday bus service to Colchester. *G R Mills*

CHALLENGER

Challenger, 91/93 Sundon Park Road, Luton, Befordshire, LU3 3AA

Depot: Sundon Park Road, Luton

D127NON	Freight Rover Sherpa 365	Carlyle	B18F	1986	Ex Bee Line Buzz, 1991
D138NON	Freight Rover Sherpa 365	Carlyle	B18F	1986	Ex Bee Line Buzz, 1992
D140NON	Freight Rover Sherpa 365	Carlyle	B18F	1986	Ex Eagle, Bristol, 1991
D157NON	Freight Rover Sherpa 365	Carlyle	B18F	1986	Ex Bee Line Buzz, 1992
D161NON	Freight Rover Sherpa 365	Carlyle	B18F	1986	Ex Bee Line Buzz, 1991
D162NON	Freight Rover Sherpa 365	Carlyle	B18F	1986	Ex Bee Line Buzz, 1991
D164NON	Freight Rover Sherpa 365	Carlyle	B18F	1986	Ex Bee Line Buzz, 1992
D169NON	Freight Rover Sherpa 365	Carlyle	B18F	1986	Ex Bee Line Buzz, 1991
D173NON	Freight Rover Sherpa 365	Carlyle	B18F	1986	Ex Bee Line Buzz, 1991
D175NON	Freight Rover Sherpa 365	Carlyle	B18F	1986	Ex Bee Line Buzz, 1991
D188NON	Freight Rover Sherpa 365	Carlyle	B18F	1986	Ex City Fleet, Aintree, 1992
D192NON	Freight Rover Sherpa 365	Carlyle	B18F	1986	Ex Bee Line Buzz, 1991
D197NON	Freight Rover Sherpa 365	Carlyle	B18F	1986	Ex Arrowline, Knutsford, 1992
D213OOJ	Freight Rover Sherpa 365	Carlyle	B18F	1986	Ex C-Line, 1993
D218OOJ	Freight Rover Sherpa 365	Carlyle	B18F	1986	Ex Bee Line Buzz, 1991
D226OOJ	Freight Rover Sherpa 365	Carlyle	B18F	1986	Ex Bolton Coachways, 1991
D228OOJ	Freight Rover Sherpa 365	Carlyle	B18F	1986	Ex C-Line, 1993
D251OOJ	Freight Rover Sherpa 365	Carlyle	B18F	1986	Ex Bee Line Buzz, 1992
D111WCC	Freight Rover Sherpa 385	Carlyle Citybus	B18F	1987	Ex Midland Red North, 1992
D112WCC	Freight Rover Sherpa 385	Carlyle Citybus	B18F	1987	Ex Midland Red North, 1992
D116WCC	Freight Rover Sherpa 385	Carlyle Citybus	B18F	1987	Ex Owen, Oswestry, 1992
D128WCC	Freight Rover Sherpa 385	Carlyle Citybus	B18F	1987	Ex Crosville Wales, 1992
D131WCC	Freight Rover Sherpa 385	Carlyle Citybus	B18F	1987	Ex Crosville Wales, 1992
D134WCC	Freight Rover Sherpa 385	Carlyle Citybus	B18F	1987	Ex Crosville Wales, 1992

Livery: Yellow, red and black

Challenger of Dunstable has built up a number of services, using a fleet of Freight Rover Sherpas, competing with the existing routes of larger operators. D228OOJ is seen in St Albans working against Luton & District. *Colin Lloyd*

CHAMBERS

H C Chambers & Son Ltd, Knowle House, High Street, Bures, Suffolk, CO8 5AB

A211JDX	Bedford YMT	Duple Dominant	B63F	1984	
B792MGV	Bedford YNT	Duple Laser	C53F/C29FL	1984	
C668WRT	Bedford YMT	Duple Dominant	B63F	1986	
C808FMC	Leyland Tiger TRCTL11/3RZ	Plaxton Paramount 3200 II	C53F	1986	Ex Frames Rickards, Brentford, 1990
D642DRT	Bedford YMT	Duple Dominant	B63F	1987	
D211LWX	Volvo B10M-61	Duple 340	C53F/C31FL	1987	Ex Wallace Arnold, 1992
D212LWX	Volvo B10M-61	Duple 340	C50F/C20FL	1987	Ex Wallace Arnold, 1992
E87KGV	Leyland Lynx LX112L10ZR1R	Leyland Lynx	B52F	1988	
E633SEL	Volvo B10M-61	Van Hool Alizée	C49FT	1988	Ex Excelsior, Bournemouth, 1993
F246HNE	Peugeot-Talbot Pullman	Talbot	B22F	1989	Ex Pine, Stalybridge, 1992
F779LNB	Peugeot-Talbot Pullman	Talbot	B22F	1989	Ex Pine, Stalybridge, 1992
F243RRT	Leyland Olympian ONCL10/1RZ	Alexander RL	H47/32F	1989	
G760VRT	Leyland Olympian ONCL10/1RZ	Alexander RL	H47/32F	1989	
G864XDX	Leyland Olympian ONCL10/1RZ	Alexander RL	H47/32F	1989	

Livery: Red and cream (buses); red (coaches)

Previous Registrations:
E633SEL   E305OPR, XEL158

Chambers now provide a higher frequency facility on the route from Sudbury to Long Melford in competition with Beestons. Two Talbot Pullmans were acquired from Pine of Stalybridge to work the additional journeys. F779LNB is seen leaving Long Melford during the first week of the new operations. *G R Mills*

This Sudbury bus station scene *(above)* shows examples of Chambers' double and single deck intake of the eighties. G760VRT, departing for Bury St Edmunds, is one of a trio of new Leyland Olympians with Alexander bodywork, while C668WRT, one of a trio of surviving Duple Dominant-bodied Bedfords, waits to work the next journey to Colchester. Below is the newest of this trio, D642DRT, photographed as it passes through the village of Long Melford. *G R Mills*

COACH SERVICES

Coach Services Ltd, 14/16 Croxton Road, Thetford, Norfolk, IP24 1AG

Reg	Chassis	Body	Seats	Year	History
BTL49L	Bedford YRT	Duple Dominant	C53F	1973	Ex Petch, Hopton, 1991
PSX265V	Ford R1114	Plaxton Supreme V(1980)	C53F	1974	Ex APT Travel, Rayleigh, 1990
UNW36M	Bedford YRT	Duple Dominant	C53F	1974	Ex Petch, Hopton, 1991
HVD744N	Bedford YRT	Plaxton Elite III	C53F	1975	Ex Partridge, Hadleigh, 1987
HRR764N	Bedford YRT	Plaxton Elite III Express	C53F	1975	Ex Petch, Hopton, 1991
KVF853P	Bedford YRT	Duple Dominant I	C53F	1975	Ex Petch, Hopton, 1991
RUJ346R	Ford R1114	Plaxton Supreme III	C49F	1977	Ex Salopia, Whitchurch, 1980
PNK167R	Bedford YMT	Plaxton Supreme III	C53F	1977	Ex Petch, Hopton, 1991
VNT4S	Bedford YMT	Duple Dominant II	C53F	1978	Ex Petch, Hopton, 1991
ELA389T	Bedford YMT	Duple Dominant	B63F	1979	Ex Clarke, Swaffham, 1989
DJA551T	Ford R1114	Plaxton Supreme IV	C53F	1979	Ex Martin, Woking, 1989
MUY899T	Ford R1114	Plaxton Supreme IV	C53F	1979	Ex Woodstones, Kidderminster, 1988
DBA82T	Ford R1114	Plaxton Supreme IV	C53F	1979	Ex Silverdale, Nottingham, 1990
FVG667T	Ford R1114	Plaxton Supreme IV	C53F	1979	Ex Reynolds, Caister, 1990
EGT190T	Bedford YMT	Plaxton Supreme IV Exp	C53F	1979	Ex Petch, Hopton, 1991
100BGO	Ford R1114	Plaxton Supreme IV	C53F	1979	Ex Eagle, Basildon, 1989
GRT520V	Bedford YMT	Plaxton Supreme IV Exp	C53F	1979	Ex Squirrell, Hitcham, 1992
WDN295V	Ford R1114	Plaxton Supreme IV	C53F	1979	Ex Walker, Tadcaster, 1982
NLH288	Ford R1114	Plaxton Supreme IV	C53F	1980	Ex Partridge, Hadleigh, 1987
FUJ904V	Bedford YMT	Duple Dominant II	C53F	1980	Ex Petch, Hopton, 1991
MMJ538V	Bedford YMT	Duple Dominant II	C53F	1980	Ex Petch, Hopton, 1991
XNA337X	Ford R1114	Plaxton Supreme VI	C53F	1982	Ex Mayers, Manchester, 1984
WOD142X	Bedford YNT	Duple Dominant IV	C53F	1982	Ex Petch, Hopton, 1991
B345RVF	Bedford YNT	Duple Laser	C53F	1984	Ex Petch, Hopton, 1991
B23XKX	Bedford YNT	Plaxton Paramount 3200	C53F	1984	Ex Premier-Albanian, Watford, 1988
C815FMC	Bedford Venturer YNV	Duple Laser 2	C53F	1986	
D272HFX	Bedford Venturer YNV	Plaxton Paramount 3200 II	C53F	1986	Ex Excelsior, Bournemouth, 1988
E832EUT	Bedford Venturer YNV	Plaxton Paramount 3200 III	C57F	1987	Ex Wainfleet, Nuneaton, 1991
E222YTU	Quest J	Jonckheere Piccolo	C37F	1987	Ex Kerridge, Brighton 1992
F708ENE	Leyland Tiger TRCTL11/3R	Plaxton Paramount 3200 III	C53F	1988	Ex Shearings, 1992
F709ENE	Leyland Tiger TRCTL11/3R	Plaxton Paramount 3200 III	C53F	1988	Ex Shearings, 1992
F900RDX	Bova FHD12.290	Bova Futura	C53F	1989	Ex Petch, Hopton, 1991
H283TAH	Peugeot-Talbot Pullman	Talbot	B22F	1991	

Previous Registrations:

100BGO	EBU854T		NLH288	HFX419V	PSX265V	PUP504M

Livery: Cream and red

As the company title implies, coach-seated vehicles regularly work the stage services, as illustrated by WOD142X. This coach was one inhereted along with other vehicles together with the operations formerly worked by Petch of Hopton. It is seen on Angel Hill, Bury St Edmunds and features the less common Duple Dominant III body.
G R Mills

Colchester showed much enthusiasm for the Leyland Lynx from an initial pair supplied to the borough in 1986 through to the final Mark II version delivered in September 1992. The latest vehicle, 27 (K27EWC), is seen on Westlands Estate where a proportion of the residents petitioned against the introduction of the facility and, subsequently, objected to a reduced service.
G R Mills

Timings on route 7 from Colchester to West Mersea are frequently disrupted by the tides. Salt water regularly covers The Strood which is the only road onto Mersea Island. On this occasion Colchester 41 (C41HHJ), an Olympian, is crossing the saturated causeway having suffered a half-hour delay.
G R Mills

Colchester's fleet number 55 has always been allocated to a special bus. Maintaining the tradition, JHK495N is the only open topper in the fleet. Even when a conventional closed top bus the 1975 Leyland Atlantean with Eastern Coach Works was selected to receive special silver livery to commemorate the Queens Silver Jubilee in 1977. It is seen in High Street about to take up duty on the regular summer afternoon town tour.
G R Mills

COLCHESTER BOROUGH TRANSPORT

Colchester Borough Transport Ltd, 26 St Botolph's Street,
Colchester, Essex, CO2 7EA

27	K27EWC	Leyland Lynx LX2R11C15Z4S	Leyland Lynx II	B49F	1992	
28	H28MJN	Leyland Lynx LX2R11G15Z4S	Leyland Lynx	B49F	1991	
29	H29MJN	Leyland Lynx LX2R11G15Z4S	Leyland Lynx	B49F	1991	
30	H130LPU	Leyland Lynx LX2R11G15Z4R	Leyland Lynx II	B49F	1990	

31-40

				Leyland Lynx LX112L102R1*	Leyland Lynx	B49F	1986-89 *31/2 are LX112TL11FR1

31	D31RWC	33	E33EVW	35	E35EVW	37	E37EVW	39	G39YHJ
32	D32RWC	34	E34EVW	36	E36EVW	38	G38YHJ	40	G40YHJ

41-44

Leyland Olympian ONLXCT/1RH Eastern Coach Works H47/31F 1985-86

41	C41HHJ	42	C42HHJ	43	D43RWC	44	D44RWC

45	F245MTW	Leyland Olympian ONCL10/1RZ	Leyland	DPH43/29F	1988
46	F246MTW	Leyland Olympian ONCL10/1RZ	Leyland	DPH43/29F	1988
47	H47MJN	Leyland Olympian ON2R50C13Z4	Leyland	DPH43/29F	1991
48	H48MJN	Leyland Olympian ON2R50C13Z4	Leyland	H47/31F	1991
49	H49MJN	Leyland Olympian ON2R50C13Z4	Leyland	H47/31F	1991
55	JHK495N	Leyland Atlantean AN68/1R	Eastern Coach Works	O43/31F	1975

67-90

Leyland Atlantean AN68A/1R Eastern Coach Works H43/31F 1977-80

67	TPU67R	75	TPU75R	79	YNO79S	83	MEV83V	87	MEV87V
68	TPU68R	76	TPU76R	80	YNO80S	84	MEV84V	88	RVW88W
71	TPU71R	77	YNO77S	81	YNO81S	85	MEV85V	89	RVW89W
73	TPU73R	78	YNO78S	82	YNO82S	86	MEV86V	90	RVW90W
74	TPU74R								

93	ABN771V	Ford R1114	Plaxton Supreme IV	C53F	1979	Ex Ipswich, 1991
101	DHK101T	Leyland Leopard PSU3E/4RT	Duple Dominant II Express	C49F	1979	
102	DHK102T	Leyland Leopard PSU3E/4RT	Duple Dominant II Express	C49F	1979	
103	OHE274X	Leyland Tiger TRCTL11/3R	Duple Dominant IV	C53F	1982	Ex West Riding, 1987
104	OHE280X	Leyland Tiger TRCTL11/3R	Duple Dominant IV	C53F	1982	Ex West Riding, 1987
105	G105AVX	Dennis Javelin 12SDA1907	Duple 320	C52FT	1989	
106	G106AVX	Dennis Javelin 12SDA1907	Duple 320	C52FT	1989	
107	H107JAR	Volvo B10M-60	Ikarus Blue Danube 358	C49FT	1990	
108	H108JAR	Volvo B10M-60	Ikarus Blue Danube 358	C48FT	1990	
109	J109WVW	Leyland Tiger TR2R62C21Z68	Plaxton Paramount 3200 III	C53F	1991	

Livery: Cream and crimson (buses); white and blue (coaches)

Above A rare vehicle to find in a former municipal fleet is a Hungarian-built coach. CBT Coachways of Colchester has a pair which wears a livery of white and blue with gold lettering. No.108 (H108JAR) is seen among the shoppers coaches in Rouen Road, Norwich. The city still attracts large numbers of visitors despite rival facilities in other parts of East Anglia.
G R Mills

Right The oldest remaining of thirty Leyland Atlanteans with Eastern Coach Works bodies, supplied new to Colchester between 1976 and 1980 is 67 (TPU67R). This stalwart is seen passing St Leonards church on Hythe Hill bound for the large Greenstead housing estate.
G R Mills

CHARLES COOK

J C Cook, Cooks European, 59 High Street, Biggleswade, Bedfordshire, SG18 0LH

KRH411P	MCW Metropolitan BR111DH	MCW	H43/32F	1975	Ex Camm, Nottingham, 1991
KJD12P	Leyland Fleetline FE30ALR	MCW	H45/32F	1976	Ex Taylor, Morley, 1992
NVD328P	Leyland Leopard PSU3C/4R	Duple Dominant	C51F	1976	
OUC100R	MCW Metropolitan BR111DH	MCW	H43/29D	1976	Ex Reading, 1992
OBN503R	Leyland Fleetline FE30AGR	Northern Counties	H43/32F	1977	Ex Rossendale, 1992
XLW647X	Leyland Tiger TRCTL11/3R	Plaxton Viewmaster IV	C50DL	1982	Ex Winson, Loughborough, 1990
KBM533Y	Leyland Tiger TRCTL11/2R	Plaxton Paramount 3500	C50F	1983	
C441HHL	Leyland Royal Tiger RTC	Leyland Doyen	C49FT	1985	
HIL3474	Leyland Royal Tiger B54	Van Hool Alizée H	C49F	1986	Ex Eddie Brown, Helperby, 1991

Previous Registrations:
HIL3474   C51CWX

Livery: Red, gold and black

Charles Cook operate one of the all-Leyland Royal Tigers produced in the mid-1980s at the Lillyhall assembly plant in Cumbria. It is seen outside the depot in Biggleswade. *G R Mills*

The original of the Leyland Olympians with Roe bodywork that were supplied to London Country is LR1 (TPD101X), now painted in the latest Lea Valley scheme. The Roe body had much commonality with the Eastern Coach Works product, but is easily identified by the different shaped wind screen. LR1 is seen here passing through Waltham Cross. *Colin Lloyd*

The forerunner of the Leyland Olympian was the Atlantean, which provided the double deck requirement for London Country Bus Services for many years, with bodywork by MCW, Park Royal and Roe. AN248, seen here in Hornchurch, carries the a Roe body, one of twelve in the County fleet. *Colin Lloyd*

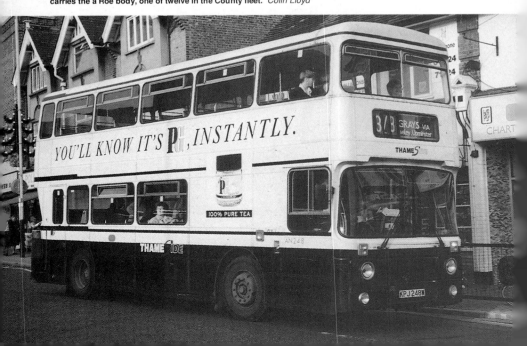

COUNTY

County Bus & Coach Co Ltd, Fourth Avenue, Harlow, Essex, CM20 1DU

Depots: Gibbs Road, Edmonton; Hogg Lane, Grays; Fourth Avenue, Harlow and Ware. A new depot will open in West Thurrock during 1993 when Grays will close.

AN110	MPJ210L	Leyland Atlantean PDR1A/1Sp	MCW	O43/29D	1972	Ex Premier, Cambridge, 1989
AN190	XPG190T	Leyland Atlantean AN68A/1R	Roe	H43/30F	1979	Ex Sovereign, 1989
AN194	XPG194T	Leyland Atlantean AN68A/1R	Roe	H43/30F	1979	Ex Sovereign, 1989
AN199	XPG199T	Leyland Atlantean AN68A/1R	Roe	H43/30F	1979	Ex Sovereign, 1989
AN238	KPJ238W	Leyland Atlantean AN68B/1R	Roe	H43/30F	1980	Ex Luton & District, 1993

AN244-256

Leyland Atlantean AN68B/1R   Roe   H43/30F   1980

244	KPJ244W	247	KPJ247W	249	KPJ249W	251	KPJ251W	254	KPJ254W
245	KPJ245W	248	KPJ248W	250	KPJ250W	252	KPJ252W	256	KPJ256W
246	KPJ246W							

BCL501	D851CNV	Bedford Venturer YNV	Caetano Algarve	C57F	1987	Ex Davian, Enfield, 1991
BP504	DDX741T	Bedford YLQ	Plaxton Supreme III	C45F	1978	Ex Davian, Enfield, 1991
BP507	SGS497W	Bedford YMT	Plaxton Supreme IV	C53F	1981	Ex Davian, Enfield, 1991
BTL6	B106KPF	Leyland Tiger TRCTL11/3RH	Berkhof Everest 370	C53F	1984	Ex London & Country, 1990
BTL10	B110KPF	Leyland Tiger TRCTL11/3RH	Berkhof Everest 370	C53F	1984	Ex Speedlink, 1991
BTL28	C128PPE	Leyland Tiger TRCTL11/3RH	Berkhof Everest 370	C49F	1985	Ex Speedlink, 1992

The eight County Leyland Lynx were taken into stock to work LRT tendered service 66, commencing in August 1990. LX257 (H257GEV), wearing Town Link fleetnames, is seen at the bus stop outside London Buses' North Street garage in Romford. *G R Mills*

DP301-313

DP301-313		Dennis Dart 9SDL3002*		Plaxton Pointer		B35F	1991	309 rebodied 1993.

*302-7 are 9SDL3011

301	J301WHJ	304	J304WHJ	307	J307WHJ	310	J310WHJ	312	J312WHJ
302	J302WHJ	305	J305WHJ	308	J308WHJ	311	J311WHJ	313	J313WHJ
303	J303WHJ	306	J306WHJ	309	J309WHJ				

DW314	J314XVX	Dennis Dart 9SDL3011	Wright Handy-bus	B35F	1992
DW315	J315XVX	Dennis Dart 9SDL3011	Wright Handy-bus	B35F	1992
DW316	J316XVX	Dennis Dart 9SDL3011	Wright Handy-bus	B35F	1992
DW317	J317XVX	Dennis Dart 9SDL3011	Wright Handy-bus	B35F	1992

DP318-323

DP318-323		Dennis Dart 9SDL3011		Plaxton Pointer		B35F	1992

318	K318CVX	320	K320CVX	321	K321CVX	322	K322CVX	323	K323CVX
319	K319CVX								

DWL401	J401XVX	Dennis Dart 9.8SDL3012	Wright Handy-bus	B40F	1992
DWL402	J402XVX	Dennis Dart 9.8SDL3012	Wright Handy-bus	B40F	1992
DWL403	J403XVX	Dennis Dart 9.8SDL3012	Wright Handy-bus	B40F	1992
DWL404	J404XVX	Dennis Dart 9.8SDL3012	Wright Handy-bus	B40F	1992

DPL405-414

DPL405-414		Dennis Dart 9.8SDL3018		Plaxton Pointer		B40F	1993

405	K405FHJ	407	K407FHJ	409	K409FHJ	411	K411FHJ	413	K413FHJ
406	K406FHJ	408	K408FHJ	410	K410FHJ	412	K412FHJ	414	K414FHJ

LD552	OMA504V	Leyland Leopard PSU3E/4R	Duple Dominant II Express	C49F	1980	Ex Davian, Enfield, 1991
LD554	FYX814W	Leyland Leopard PSU3E/4R	Duple Dominant II Express	C49F	1980	Ex Davian, Enfield, 1991
LD557	FYX817W	Leyland Leopard PSU3E/4R	Duple Dominant II Express	C46F	1980	Ex Davian, Enfield, 1991
LD558	FYX818W	Leyland Leopard PSU3E/4R	Duple Dominant II Express	C46F	1980	Ex Davian, Enfield, 1991
LN604	PNW604W	Leyland National 2 NL116L11/1R		B52F	1980	Ex Harrogate & District, 1990
LN606	PNW606W	Leyland National 2 NL116L11/1R		B52F	1980	Ex Harrogate & District, 1990
LP549	PPM889R	Leyland Leopard PSU3E/4R	Plaxton Supreme III Exp	C49F	1977	Ex Golden Boy, Roydon, 1992
LP550	KUB550V	Leyland Leopard PSU3E/4R	Plaxton Supreme IV Exp	C49F	1979	Ex West Yorkshire, 1989
LP551	KUB551V	Leyland Leopard PSU3E/4R	Plaxton Supreme IV Exp	C49F	1980	Ex West Yorkshire, 1989
LP555	WJM814T	Leyland Leopard PSU3E/4R	Plaxton Supreme IV Exp	C46F	1979	Ex Golden Boy, Roydon, 1992
LP556	WJM816T	Leyland Leopard PSU3E/4R	Plaxton Supreme IV Exp	C49F	1979	Ex Golden Boy, Roydon, 1992

LR1-23

LR1-23		Leyland Olympian ONTL11/1R		Roe		H43/29F	1982

1	TPD101X	4	TPD104X	9	TPD109X	11	TPD111X	17	TPD117X
2	TPD102X	5	TPD105X	10	TPD110X	15	TPD115X	23	TPD123X
3	TPD103X	7	TPD107X						

LX251-258

LX251-258		Leyland Lynx LX2R11C15Z4S		Leyland		B49F	1990

251	H251GEV	253	H253GEV	255	H255GEV	257	H257GEV	258	H258GEV
252	H252GEV	254	H254GEV	256	H256GEV				

MB45	D45OKH	Iveco Daily 49.10	Robin Hood City Nippy	DP19F	1987	Ex East Yorkshire, 1989
MB46	D46OKH	Iveco Daily 49.10	Robin Hood City Nippy	DP19F	1987	Ex East Yorkshire, 1989

MB47-51

MB47-51		Iveco Daily 49.10		Robin Hood City Nippy		DP19F	1988	Ex Sovereign, 1989

47	E347SWY	48	E348SWY	49	E349SWY	50	E350SWY	51	E351SWY

MB52-57

MB52-57		Iveco Daily 49.10		Robin Hood City Nippy		DP19F	1988	Ex Premier Travel, 1989

52	E352NEG	53	E353NEG	54	E354NEG	56	E356NEG	57	E357NEG

MB115	F115JGS	Iveco Daily 49.10	Robin Hood City Nippy	B25F	1988	Ex Sampsons, Hoddesdon, 1988
MB154	F154DKV	Iveco Daily 49.10	Reeve Burgess Beaver	B25F	1988	Ex Iveco demonstrator, 1989
MB700	E700EHJ	Iveco Daily 49.10	Dormobile Routemaker	DP25F	1988	Ex Sampson, Hoddesdon, 1989
MB701	E701EHJ	Iveco Daily 49.10	Dormobile Routemaker	B25F	1988	Ex Sampson, Hoddesdon, 1989
MB706	E296VOM	Iveco Daily 49.10	Carlyle Dailybus II	B23F	1988	Ex Southend, 1992

MB707-712

MB707-712		Iveco 59.12		Dormobile Routemaker		B25F	1993

707	K707FNO	709	K709FNO	710	K710FNO	711	K711FNO	712	K712FNO
708	K708FNO								

MB745	E445TYG	Iveco Daily 49.10	Robin Hood City Nippy	B23F	1988	Ex Keighley & District, 1992
MB749	E449TYG	Iveco Daily 49.10	Robin Hood City Nippy	B23F	1988	Ex Keighley & District, 1992
MB751	E451TYG	Iveco Daily 49.10	Robin Hood City Nippy	B23F	1988	Ex Keighley & District, 1992
MB752	E452TYG	Iveco Daily 49.10	Robin Hood City Nippy	DP25F	1988	Ex Harrogate & District, 1993
MB755	E455TYG	Iveco Daily 49.10	Robin Hood City Nippy	B23F	1988	Ex Harrogate & District, 1993
MB795	F795JKX	Iveco Daily 49.10	Reeve Burgess Beaver	B21F	1988	Ex Sovereign, 1992
MB796	F796JKX	Iveco Daily 49.10	Reeve Burgess Beaver	B21F	1988	Ex Sovereign, 1992
MBT801	L801KNO	Peugeot-Talbot Pullman	Talbot	B18FL	1993	
MBT802	L802KNO	Peugeot-Talbot Pullman	Talbot	B18FL	1993	
MBT803	L803KNO	Peugeot-Talbot Pullman	Talbot	B18FL	1993	
MBT804	L804KNO	Peugeot-Talbot Pullman	Talbot	B18FL	1993	

MB806-820

Volkswagen LT55 — Optare City Pacer — DP25F — 1987-88 — Ex Welwyn-Hatfield Line, 1991

806	E996UYG	807	E997UYG	808	E998UYG	809	E999UYG	820	E520PWR

MB918-938

Mercedes-Benz 709D — Reeve Burgess Beaver — B23F — 1989-92

918	G918UPP	926	G926WGS	930	G930WGS	933	J933WHJ	936	J936WHJ
919	G919UPP	927	G927WGS	931	G931WGS	934	J934WHJ	937	J937WHJ
924	G924WGS	928	G928WGS	932	G932WGS	935	J935WHJ	938	J938WHJ
925	G925WGS	929	G929WGS						

MC540	D40MAG	Iveco Daily 49.10	Robin Hood City Nippy	C19F	1987	Ex West Yorkshire, 1989

MD601-612

Mercedes-Benz 811D — Reeve Burgess Beaver — B28F — 1991

601	J601WHJ	604	J604WHJ	607	J607WHJ	609	J609WHJ	611	J611WHJ
602	J602WHJ	605	J605WHJ	608	J608WHJ	610	J610WHJ	612	J612WHJ
603	J603WHJ	606	J606WHJ						

Originally supplied to Jubilee, Stevenage in 1988, whose operations passed to Sovereign the following year, were the trio of Leyland Tiger with Duple 300 bodywork. Rationalisation moved the type onto the County operations. TDB62 (F62SMC), one of the nomadic three, is seen in Waltham Cross. *G R Mills*

MD613	L613LVX	Mercedes-Benz 811D	Dormobile Routemaker	B31F	1993	
MD614	L614LVX	Mercedes-Benz 811D	Dormobile Routemaker	B31F	1993	
SN213	LPB213P	Leyland National 10351/1R		B41F	1976	
SN215	LPB215P	Leyland National 10351/1R		B41F	1976	
SN227	LPB227P	Leyland National 10351/1R		B41F	1976	
SN251	NPK251R	Leyland National 10351A/1R		B41F	1976	Ex Sovereign, 1989
SN277	SPC277R	Leyland National 10351A/1R		B41F	1977	Ex Sovereign, 1989
SN306	UPB306S	Leyland National 10351A/1R		B41F	1977	Ex Sovereign, 1989
SN312	UPB312S	Leyland National 10351A/1R		B41F	1977	Ex Sovereign, 1989
SN319	UPB319S	Leyland National 10351A/1R		B41F	1977	Ex Sovereign, 1989
SN338	UPB338S	Leyland National 10351A/1R		B41F	1977	Ex Sovereign, 1989
STL10	C210PPE	Leyland Tiger TRCTL11/3RH	Plaxton Paramount 3500 II	C49FT	1985	Ex London & Country, 1992
TDB61	F61SMC	Leyland Tiger TRBTL11/2RP	Duple 300	B55F	1988	Ex Sovereign, 1989
TDB62	F62SMC	Leyland Tiger TRBTL11/2RP	Duple 300	B55F	1988	Ex Sovereign, 1989
TDB63	F63SMC	Leyland Tiger TRBTL11/2RP	Duple 300	B55F	1988	Ex Sovereign, 1989
TDL37	A137RMJ	Leyland Tiger TRCTL11/3RH	Duple Caribbean	C55F	1984	Ex Premier Travel, 1989
TDL53	C253SPC	Leyland Tiger TRCTL11/3RH	Duple 320	C53F	1986	Ex London & Country, 1993
TDL54	C254SPC	Leyland Tiger TRCTL11/3RH	Duple 320	C53F	1986	Ex London & Country, 1993
TDL55	C255SPC	Leyland Tiger TRCTL11/3RH	Duple 320	C53F	1986	Ex London & Country, 1993
TDL60	C260SPC	Leyland Tiger TRCTL11/3RH	Duple 320	C53F	1986	Ex London & Country, 1993
TDL63	C263SPC	Leyland Tiger TRCTL11/3RH	Duple 320	C49F	1986	Ex London & Country, 1993
TDL65	C265SPC	Leyland Tiger TRCTL11/3RH	Duple 320	C53F	1986	
TL10	TPC110X	Leyland Tiger TRCTL11/2R	Eastern Coach Works B51	C49F	1982	Ex Luton & District, 1991
TL13	TPC113X	Leyland Tiger TRCTL11/2R	Eastern Coach Works B51	C49F	1982	Ex Coppins & Wall, 1993
TL15	UJN634Y	Leyland Tiger TRCTL11/2R	Eastern Coach Works B51	C49F	1982	Ex Luton & District, 1991
TL17	KIW6511	Leyland Tiger TRCTL11/2R	Eastern Coach Works B51	C49F	1982	
TL20	UJN429Y	Leyland Tiger TRCTL11/2R	Eastern Coach Works B51	C49F	1982	
TL27	KIW8513	Leyland Tiger TRCTL11/2R	Eastern Coach Works B51	C49F	1982	
TL29	FBZ2514	Leyland Tiger TRCTL11/2R	Eastern Coach Works B51	C49F	1982	Ex Luton & District, 1991
TL30	WPH130Y	Leyland Tiger TRCTL11/2R	Eastern Coach Works B51	C49F	1982	Ex Luton & District, 1991
TL31	WPH131Y	Leyland Tiger TRCTL11/2R	Eastern Coach Works B51	C53F	1982	Ex Chartercoach, Gt Oakley, 1989
TL33	WPH133Y	Leyland Tiger TRCTL11/2R	Eastern Coach Works B51	C53F	1982	Ex Chartercoach, Gt Oakley, 1989
TP61	B261KPF	Leyland Tiger TRCTL11/2R	Plaxton Paramount 3200 II	C49F	1985	Ex Sovereign, 1990
TP70	OIB3520	Leyland Tiger TRCTL11/2R	Plaxton Paramount 3200 II	C49F	1985	
TP71	OIB3521	Leyland Tiger TRCTL11/2R	Plaxton Paramount 3200 II	C49F	1985	
TP72	OIB3522	Leyland Tiger TRCTL11/2R	Plaxton Paramount 3200 II	C49F	1985	
TP75	OIB3523	Leyland Tiger TRCTL11/2R	Plaxton Paramount 3200 II	C49F	1985	
TPL510	OIB3510	Leyland Tiger TRCTL11/3RH	Plaxton Paramount 3200	C53F	1983	Ex Keighley & District, 1992
TPL518	E118KFV	Leyland Tiger TRCTL11/3ARZ	Plaxton Paramount 3500	C51FT	1988	Ex A Moore, Jefferies Weldon, 1993
VPB64	E564BNK	Volvo B10M-56	Plaxton Derwent II	B54F	1988	Ex Sampson, Hoddesdon, 1989
VPB65	E565BNK	Volvo B10M-56	Plaxton Derwent II	B54F	1988	Ex Sampson, Hoddesdon, 1989
VPL530	530MUY	Volvo B58-61	Plaxton Supreme III	C57F	1976	Ex Sampson, Hoddesdon, 1989
VDL537	EBZ6531	Volvo B58-61	Duple Dominant II	C53F	1982	Ex Davian, Enfield, 1991

Special Liveries:

Davian : BP504/7
Green Line: TL20,33, TDL53-5/60/3/5, TP61/70-2/5, TPL510.
Sampsons: AN110, BCL501, BTL6/10/28, LD554/7/8, MC540, STL10, TDL37, TPL518, VDL537, VPL530,
Overall advertisment: DW316, LR2-5/15, SN227/319/586, VPB64/5, MB51/4,154,701/6/95,809/20,918/32, TL10/7/31
Other vehicles carry one of four logos: Lea Valley (Edmunton, Hoddesdon and Ware); Sampsons (coaches only);
Thameside (Grays) and Townlink (Harlow, Debden and Wyatts Green).

Previous Registrations:

530MUY	NVW556P	KIW8513	WPH127Y	OIB3522	B272KPF
EBZ6531	HSF487X	OIB3510	EWW994Y	OIB3523	B275KPF
FBZ2514	WPH129Y	OIB3520	B270KPF	UJN429Y	WPH120Y
KIW6511	WPH117Y	OIB3521	B271KPF	UJN634Y	WPH115Y,OIB3510

Many of the services from Walthamstow are now operated under LRT contracts. Minibus service M15 requires Lea Valleys MD class, and MD612, from Edmonton, is seen in Walthamstow bus station. *Colin Lloyd*

The Dennis Dart is available in three lengths: 8.5, 9 and 9.8 metres. Four of the longest type were supplied to the Lea Valley operation in 1992, fitted with the Wright Handy-bus design of body. DLW404 (J404XVX) is seen on its regular haunt in Hertford. *Colin Lloyd*

A registration originating from Ireland, OIB3523, disguises the age of TP75, originally B275KPF. One of a number of Leyland Tigers with Plaxton Paramount bodywork it is regularly allocated to the 724 express service to Heathrow and is seen loading at Watford Junction bound for Harlow. *Colin Lloyd*

DISTRICT BUS

D W Tomlin, 170 Beauchamps Drive, Wickford, Essex, SS11 8NJ

21	E962SVP	Freight Rover Sherpa 405	Carlyle Citybus 2	B18F	1988	
22	E509TOV	Freight Rover Sherpa 405	Carlyle Citybus 2	B18F	1988	
23	E105SOG	Freight Rover Sherpa 405	Carlyle Citybus 2	B18F	1988	
24	F892XOE	Freight Rover Sherpa 405	Carlyle Citybus 2	B18F	1989	
26	F995XOV	Iveco Daily 49.10	Carlyle Dailybus	B23F	1990	Ex Strathclyde, 1990
27	F996XOV	Iveco Daily 49.10	Carlyle Dailybus	B23F	1990	Ex Strathclyde, 1990
28	G148GOL	Iveco Daily 49.10	Carlyle Dailybus 2	B23F	1991	
29	G145GOL	Iveco Daily 49.10	Carlyle Dailybus 2	B23F	1991	
30	D873LWR	Freight Rover Sherpa 374	Dormobile	B20F	1987	Ex Cunningham, Stanford, 1992

Livery: Primrose, red, blue and white.

District Bus has grown from an initial fleet of four vehicles in 1988 to a total of nine, all within a five year span. To cope with an increasing work load F995XOV, one of a pair of Carlyle-bodied Ivecos formerly with Strathclyde, is seen in St Edwards Way, Romford and was added to a fleet of, otherwise, new stock. *G R Mills*

EASTERN COUNTIES

Eastern Counties Omnibus Co Ltd, 79 Thorpe Road, Norwich, NR1 1UA

Depots: Bury St Edmunds; Great Yarmouth; Ipswich; King's Lynn; Lowestoft and Norwich.

DD1-5
Leyland Olympian ONLXB/1RZ   Northern Counties   H40/35F   1989

1	F101AVG	2	F102AVG	3	F103AVG	4	F104AVG	5	F105AVG

S6-10
Dennis Javelin 11SDL1933   Duple 300   DP48F   1989

6	G706JAH	7	G707JAH	8	G708JAH	9	G709JAH	10	G710JAH

S11-20
Dennis Javelin 11SDL1924   Plaxton Derwent II   DP51F   1990

11	H611RAH	13	H613RAH	15	H615RAH	17	H617RAH	19	H619RAH
12	H612RAH	14	H614RAH	16	H616RAH	18	H618RAH	20	H620RAH

DD21-25
Leyland Olympian ON2R50G13Z4   Leyland   H47/31F   1991

21	J621BVG	22	J622BVG	23	J623BVG	24	J624BVG	25	J625BVG

MB26-35
Mercedes-Benz 709D   Dormobile Routemaker   B20F*   1992   *31 is B19F

26	K26HCL	28	K28HCL	30	J530FCL	32	K732JAH	34	K734JAH
27	K27HCL	29	K29HCL	31	K731JAH	33	K733JAH	35	K735JAH

S36-40
Dennis Lance 11SDA3103   Northern Counties Palatine   B49F   1993

36	K736JAH	37	K737JAH	38	K738JAH	39	K739JAH	40	K740JAH

S41	J741JAH	Dennis Dart 9SDL3011	Plaxton Pointer	B33F	1992
S42	J742JAH	Dennis Dart 9SDL3011	Plaxton Pointer	B33F	1992
S43	J743JAH	Dennis Dart 9SDL3011	Plaxton Pointer	B33F	1992
S44	J744JAH	Dennis Dart 9SDL3011	Plaxton Pointer	B33F	1992

Rural Suffolk has some charming villages, none more so than Kersey. Eastern Counties S14 (H614RAH), a Dennis Javelin with Plaxton Derwent bodywork adds interest to this superb setting. *G R Mills*

Five all-Leyland Olympians were added to the Easteren Counties fleet in 1991, each featuring the revised front grill and roof-high repeater lights. DD24 (J624BVG) is seen in Castle Place, Norwich, early in 1992.
G R Mills

The first Olympians for Eastern Counties came after the company left NBC control, five being delivered in 1989. DD1 (F101AVG) shows the style of the new designed of body by Northern Counties, later to be retrospectively named Palatine I.
Colin Lloyd

Latest arrivals for the Eastern Counties minibus fleet are ten Mercedes-Benz 709s with Dormobile Routemaker bodywork.
G R Mills

VR129-160 Bristol VRT/SL2/6LX Eastern Coach Works H43/31F 1974-75

129	RAH129M	138	SNG439M	143	GNG709N	151	JNG49N	158	JNG56N
130	RAH130M	139	SNG439M	147	GNG713N	153	JNG51N	159	JNG57N
134	RAH134M	141	TAH554N	148	GNG714N	154	JNG52N	160	JNG58N
136	SNG436M	142	GNG708N	149	GNG715N	156	JNG54N		

VR161	JNU137N	Bristol VRT/SL3/6LXB	Eastern Coach Works	H43/31F	1975	Ex Western National, 1992
VR162	MCL938P	Bristol VRT/SL3/6LXB	Eastern Coach Works	H43/31F	1976	
VR163	OUP683P	Bristol VRT/SL3/6LXB	Eastern Coach Works	H43/31F	1976	Ex Western National, 1992

VR164-171 Bristol VRT/SL3/6LXB Eastern Coach Works H43/31F 1976

164	MCL940P	168	MEX770P	169	MCL944P	170	MEX765P	171	MEX768P
165	MCL941P								

VR172	NAH135P	Bristol VRT/SL3/501	Eastern Coach Works	H43/31F	1976	
VR176	NAH139P	Bristol VRT/SL3/6LXB	Eastern Coach Works	H43/31F	1976	
VR178	NAH141P	Bristol VRT/SL3/6LXB	Eastern Coach Works	H43/31F	1976	
VR181	OPW181P	Bristol VRT/SL3/6LXB	Eastern Coach Works	H43/31F	1976	
VR183	WDM345R	Bristol VRT/SL3/501	Eastern Coach Works	H43/31F	1977	Ex PMT, 1991
VR184	ODL657R	Bristol VRT/SL3/6LXB	Eastern Coach Works	H43/31F	1977	Ex Southern Vectis, 1991
VR185	ODL658R	Bristol VRT/SL3/6LXB	Eastern Coach Works	H43/31F	1977	Ex Southern Vectis, 1991
VR186	ODL659R	Bristol VRT/SL3/6LXB	Eastern Coach Works	H43/31F	1977	Ex Southern Vectis, 1991

VR187-211 Bristol VRT/SL3/6LXB Eastern Coach Works H43/31F 1976-77

187	PVF359R	192	TEX402R	197	TEX407R	203	XNG203S	206	XNG206S
188	PVF360R	193	TEX403R	198	TEX408R	204	XNG204S	207	XNG207S
189	RPW189R	194	TEX404R	199	WPW199S	205	XNG205S	211	YNG211S
191	TEX401R	196	TEX406R						

VR215	BRF691T	Bristol VRT/SL3/501	Eastern Coach Works	H43/31F	1977	Ex PMT, 1993

VR216-236 Bristol VRT/SL3/6LXB Eastern Coach Works H43/31F 1977-78

216	BCL216T	219	BVG219T	222	BVG222T	225	BVG225T	230	DEX230T
217	BCL217T	220	BVG220T	223	BVG223T	226	DEX226T	236	DNG236T
218	BVG218T	221	BVG221T	224	BVG224T	229	DEX229T		

VR237	GRA844V	Bristol VRT/SL3/6LXB	Eastern Coach Works	H43/31F	1979	Ex Trent, 1991

VR238-244 Bristol VRT/SL3/6LXB Eastern Coach Works H43/31F 1978-79

238	HAH238V	240	HAH240V	242	JAH242V	243	JAH243V	244	JAH244V
239	HAH239V	241	JAH241V						

VR245-250 Bristol VRT/SL3/6LXB Eastern Coach Works H43/31F 1979 Ex Trent, 1991

245	GRA841V	247	GRA843V	248	GRA845V	249	GRA847V	250	GRA846V
246	GRA842V								

VR251-282 Bristol VRT/SL3/6LXB Eastern Coach Works H43/31F 1979-80

251	PCL251W	256	PCL256W	262	RAH262W	270	RAH270W	275	TAH275W
252	PCL252W	257	PCL257W	263	RAH263W	271	TAH271W	276	TAH276W
253	PCL253W	258	RAH258W	266	RAH266W	272	TAH272W	277	VAH277X
254	PCL254W	259	RAH259W	267	RAH267W	273	TAH273W	281	VAH281X
255	PCL255W	261	RAH261W	269	RAH269W	274	TAH274W	282	VAH282X

VR283-302 Bristol VRT/SL3/6LXB Eastern Coach Works H43/31F* 1981 *284-7 are DPH41/25F

283	VEX283X	286	VEX286X	288	VEX288X	292	VEX292X	297	VEX297X
284	VEX284X	287	VEX287X	290	VEX290X	294	VEX294X	302	VEX302X
285	VEX285X								

VR303-310 Bristol VRT/SL3/6LXB Eastern Coach Works H43/31F* 1981 Ex Trent, 1991

303	PRC848X	305	PRC851X	307	PRC853X	309	PRC855X	310	PRC857X
304	PRC850X	306	PRC852X	308	PRC854X				

HVR331	KKE731N	Bristol VRT/SL3/6LXB	Eastern Coach Works	H43/34F	1975	Ex Hastings & District, 1985
HVR332	KKE732N	Bristol VRT/SL3/6LXB	Eastern Coach Works	H43/34F	1975	Ex Hastings & District, 1985

HVR333	KKE733N	Bristol VRT/SL3/6LXB	Eastern Coach Works	H43/34F	1975	Ex Hastings & District, 1985
HVR334	KKE734N	Bristol VRT/SL3/6LXB	Eastern Coach Works	H43/34F	1975	Ex Hastings & District, 1985
OT351	OCK995K	Bristol VRT/SL2/6LX	Eastern Coach Works	O43/31F	1971	Ex Ribble, 1985
OT352	NCK980J	Bristol VRT/SL2/6LX	Eastern Coach Works	O43/31F	1972	Ex Ribble, 1985
OT353	JNG50N	Bristol VRT/SL2/6LX	Eastern Coach Works	O43/31F	1975	
VR378	OCK988K	Bristol VRT/SL2/6LX	Eastern Coach Works	H39/31F	1972	Ex Ribble, 1985
VR384	OCK994K	Bristol VRT/SL2/6LX	Eastern Coach Works	H39/31F	1972	Ex Ribble, 1985
VR385	OCK985K	Bristol VRT/SL2/6LX	Eastern Coach Works	H39/31F	1972	Ex Ribble, 1985
VR410	CJO470R	Bristol VRT/SL3/6LX	Eastern Coach Works	H43/31F	1977	Ex City of Oxford, 1984
VR411	CJO471R	Bristol VRT/SL3/6LX	Eastern Coach Works	H43/31F	1977	Ex City of Oxford, 1984
VR412	CJO472R	Bristol VRT/SL3/6LX	Eastern Coach Works	H43/31F	1977	Ex City of Oxford, 1984
VR501	GAG48N	Bristol VRT/SL2/6G	Eastern Coach Works	H39/31F	1974	Ex Rosemary, Terrington St Clement, 1993
VR502	YHN654M	Bristol VRT/SL2/6G	Eastern Coach Works	H43/31F	1974	Ex Rosemary, Terrington St Clement, 1993
DD503	CKC302L	Daimler Fleetline CRG6LXB	MCW	H43/32F	1973	Ex Rosemary, Terrington St Clement, 1993
DD504	THX573S	Leyland Fleetline FE30ALRSp	Park Royal	H44/27D	1978	Ex Rosemary, Terrington St Clement, 1993
DD505	OJD195R	Daimler Fleetline FE30AGR	MCW	H45/32F	1977	Ex Rosemary, Terrington St Clement, 1993
DD506	THX531S	Leyland Fleetline FE30ALRSp	Park Royal	H44/27D	1977	Ex Rosemary, Terrington St Clement, 1993
DD507	WWH26L	Daimler Fleetline CRG6LX	Park Royal	H43/32F	1973	Ex Rosemary, Terrington St Clement, 1993
DD508	CKC312L	Daimler Fleetline CRG6LXB	MCW	H43/32F	1973	Ex Rosemary, Terrington St Clement, 1993
S521	6149KP	AEC Reliance 6U3ZR	Plaxton Elite III	C53F	1974	Ex Rosemary, Terrington St Clement, 1993
S522	VPH31S	AEC Reliance 6U2R	Plaxton Supreme III Exp	C53F	1978	Ex Rosemary, Terrington St Clement, 1993
S523	6920MX	Leyland Leopard PSU3B/4R	Plaxton Elite III Exp	C51F	1974	Ex Rosemary, Terrington St Clement, 1993
S524	RYL720R	Bedford YMT	Duple Dominant II	C53F	1977	Ex Rosemary, Terrington St Clement, 1993
S525	EHE234V	Bedford YMT	Duple Dominant II	C53F	1980	Ex Rosemary, Terrington St Clement, 1993
S526	JTY926P	Bedford YRT	Plaxton Supreme III	C53F	1976	Ex Rosemary, Terrington St Clement, 1993

LN567-599

Leyland National 11351A/1R — B52F — 1977-78 — 563 is B49F

567	PVF367R	585	TVF620R	588	WAH588S	592	WAH592S	598	WVF598S
568	PVF368R	586	WAH586S	589	WAH589S	593	WAH593S	599	WVF599S
569	PVF369R	587	WAH587S	590	WAH590S	594	WAH594S		

For many years the use of Leyland Nationals with Eastern Counties excluded the Bury St Edmunds operation. LN594 is seen heading away from Bury on service 85 to Ipswich. *Colin Lloyd*

LN601-617   Leyland National 2 NL116L11/1R   B49F   1980

601	KVG601V	604	KVG604V	608	KVG608V	613	PEX613W	616 PEX616W
602	KVG602V	606	KVG606V	609	KVG609V	614	PEX614W	617 PEX617W
603	KVG603V	607	KVG607V	610	PEX610W	615	PEX615W	

LN624-628   Leyland National 2 NL116AL11/1R   B49F   1981

624	UVF624X	625	UVF625X	626	UVF626X	627	UVF627X	628 UVF628X

SD633-661   Freight Rover Sherpa 365   Dormobile   B16F   1986

633	C633BEX	638	C638BEX	644	C644BEX	652	C652BEX	660 C660BEX
636	C636BEX	640	C640BEX	647	C647BEX	658	C658BEX	661 C661BEX
637	C637BEX	642	C642BEX	648	C648BEX			

SD669	D669HAH	Freight Rover Sherpa 374	Dormobile	B18F	1986
SD670	D670HAH	Freight Rover Sherpa 374	Dormobile	B18F	1986
MH701	E701TNG	Mercedes-Benz 609D	Robin Hood	B20F	1988
MH702	E702TNG	Mercedes-Benz 609D	Robin Hood	B20F	1988

MA711-728   Mercedes-Benz L608D   Alexander AM   B20F   1986

711	C711BEX	715	C715BEX	719	C719BEX	723	C723BEX	726 C726BEX
712	C712BEX	716	C716BEX	720	C720BEX	724	C724BEX	727 C727BEX
713	C713BEX	717	C717BEX	721	C721BEX	725	C725BEX	728 C728BEX
714	C714BEX	718	C718BEX	722	C722BEX			

MA741-757   Mercedes-Benz L608D   Reeve Burgess   B20F   1986

741	C741BEX	745	C745BEX	749	C749BEX	752	C752BEX	755 C755BEX
742	C742BEX	746	C746BEX	750	C750BEX	753	C753BEX	756 C756BEX
743	C743BEX	747	C747BEX	751	C751BEX	754	C754BEX	757 C757BEX
744	C744BEX	748	C748BEX					

MB758	D758LEX	Mercedes-Benz 609D	Reeve Burgess	B20F	1987
MB759	D759LEX	Mercedes-Benz 609D	Reeve Burgess	B20F	1987

LN762-782   Leyland National 11351A/1R   B52F   1978-79   762/74-82 are B49F

LN762	XNG762S	LN766	XNG766S	LN769	XNG769S	LN775	CCL775T	LG781 DPW781T
LN763	XNG763S	LN767	XNG767S	LN770	XNG770S	LN776	CCL776T	LN782 DPW782T
LN765	XNG765S	LN768	XNG768S	LN774	CCL774T	LN778	CCL778T	

LL792-809   Leyland Leopard PSU3E/4R   Willowbrook 003   C49F   1979-80   Ex Ambassador Travel, 1987

792	OEX792W	794	OEX794W	796	OEX796W	808	JCL808V	809 JCL809V
793	OEX793W							

TD850	D779NUD	Ford Transit VE6	Dormobile	B16F	1987 Ex East Kent, 1988

TH851-856   Ford Transit VE6   Robin Hood   B16F   1987

851	E851PEX	853	E853PEX	854	E854PEX	855	E855PEX	856 E856PEX
852	E852PEX							

TH891-920   Ford Transit 190D   Robin Hood   B16F   1988

891	C891BEX	897	C897BEX	902	C902BEX	907	C907BEX	913 C913BEX
892	C892BEX	898	C898BEX	903	C903BEX	908	C908BEX	914 C914BEX
893	C893BEX	899	C899BEX	904	C904BEX	909	C909BEX	916 C916BEX
894	C894BEX	900	C900BEX	905	C905BEX	910	C910BEX	917 C917BEX
895	C895BEX	901	C901BEX	906	C906BEX	912	C912BEX	919 C919BEX
896	C896BEX							

MB950-961   Ford Transit 190D   Carlyle   B16F   1985

950	C950YAH	953	C953YAH	956	C956YAH	958	C958YAH	960 C960YAH
951	C951YAH	954	C954YAH	957	C957YAH	959	C959YAH	961 C961YAH
952	C952YAH	955	C955YAH					

MB962-984 Ford Transit 190D Dormobile B16F 1985

962	C962YAH	967	C967YAH	972	C972YAH	976	C976YAH	981	C981YAH
963	C963YAH	969	C969YAH	973	C973YAH	977	C977YAH	982	C982YAH
964	C964YAH	970	C970YAH	974	C974YAH	979	C979YAH	983	C983YAH
965	C965YAH	971	C971YAH	975	C975YAH	980	C980YAH	984	C984YAH
966	C966YAH								

MB985	C725FKE	Ford Transit VE6	Dormobile	B16F	1986	Ex East Kent, 1989
MB986	C726FKE	Ford Transit VE6	Dormobile	B16F	1986	Ex East Kent, 1989
MB987	C727FKE	Ford Transit VE6	Dormobile	B16F	1986	Ex East Kent, 1989

Livery: Red, yellow and orange (buses); cream, red and orange (dual purpose).

Previous Registrations:

6149KP	TJH677M	6920MX	RUP388M

On order: 15 Mercedes-Benz 709D with Guy bodies

Eastern Counties 'veteran' double decker is OT352 (NCK980J) a Bristol VRT2 new to Ribble in 1971. Converted to open top at Norwich early in 1986, the bus has worn two different liveries prior to its current advertising scheme as seen in Gorleston High Street. *G R Mills*

Additional school contracts and updating of the double-deck fleet has resulted in Eastern Counties acquiring numerous second hand Bristol VRT3s, principally direct from Trent, while others are much travelled. VR163 (OUP683P) seen in the sylvan setting of Spring Road, Ipswich was originally new to United but was acquired from Western National. *G R Mills*

EASTERN NATIONAL

Eastern National Ltd, 48-49 New Writtle Street, Chelmsford, Essex, CM2 0SD

Depots: South St, Bishops Stortford; Fairfield Rd, Braintree; Duke St, Chelmsford; Telford Rd, Clacton-on-Sea; Queen St, Colchester; Station Rd, Harwich and High St, Maldon

| 120 | B258CHK | | Peugeot 505 | | Peugeot | M7 | 1985 | |

200-234
Mercedes-Benz L608D — Reeve Burgess — B20F — 1985/6

200	C200HJN	206	C206HJN	211	C211HJN	216	C216HJN	221	C221HJN
202	C202HJN	207	C207HJN	212	C212JHN	217	C217HJN	222	C222HJN
203	C203HJN	208	C208HJN	213	C213HJN	218	C218HJN	223	C223HJN
204	C204HJN	209	C209HJN	214	C214HJN	219	C219HJN	224	C224HJN
205	C205HJN	210	C210HJN	215	C215HJN	220	C220HJN		

601-617
Mercedes-Benz 709D — Reeve Burgess Beaver — B23F — 1991

601	H601OVW	605	H605OVW	609	J609OVW	612	J612UTW	615	J615UTW
602	H602OVW	606	H606OVW	610	J610UTW	613	J613UTW	616	J616UTW
603	H603OVW	607	H607OVW	611	J611UTW	614	J614UTW	617	J617UTW
604	H604OVW	608	H608OVW						

618-630
Mercedes-Benz 709D — Plaxton Beaver — B23F — 1991

618	H618UTW	621	H621UTW	624	J624UTW	627	J627UTW	629	J629UTW
619	H619UTW	622	H622UTW	625	J625UTW	628	J628UTW	630	J630UTW
620	H620UTW	623	H623UTW	626	J626UTW				

631-656
Mercedes-Benz 709D — Plaxton Beaver — B23F — 1993

631	K631GVX	637	K637GVX	642	K642GVX	647	L647MEV	652	L652MEV
632	K632GVX	638	K638GVX	643	K643GVX	648	L648MEV	653	L653MEV
633	K633GVX	639	K639GVX	644	K644GVX	649	L649MEV	654	L654MEV
634	K634GVX	640	K640GVX	645	K645GVX	650	L650MEV	655	L655MEV
635	K635GVX	641	K641GVX	646	K646GVX	651	L651MEV	656	L656MEV
636	K636GVX								

700-721
Ford Transit 190D — Dormobile — B16F — 1986 — Ex Cityline, 1990-92

700	B461WTC	705	B472WTC	710	C433BHY	714	C441BHY	718	C448BHY
701	B463WTC	706	B473WTC	711	C436BHY	715	C443BHY	719	C457BHY
702	B468WTC	707	C427AHT	712	C437BHY	716	C444BHY	720	B454WTC
703	B469WTC	708	C429AHT	713	C438BHY	717	C447BHY	721	B464WTC
704	B471WTC	709	C432BHY						

Eastern National have now decided that the leading '0' displayed on the minibus fleet will gradually be removed. One of the Ford Transits from Bristol's Cityline is 709 (C432BHY), seen working a service in Bishops Stortford. *Colin Lloyd*

A dozen of Eastern National's Leyland Tigers are fitted with Alexander TE-type bodywork, being part of the 1983 NBC purchasing programme. Working route 301 through Bishops Stortford is 1125 (A694OHJ).
Colin Lloyd

Whitehall is the setting for this view of 1130 (C130HJN) as it works one of the Highwayman commuter services into the city from its Chelmsford base. This is the only example of the Plaxton Paramount 3500 body in the fleet, and can be identified as the mark II version from the front panal arrangement.
Colin Lloyd

Only fourteen Leyland Lynx remained with Eastern National once the Thamesway operation commenced. One of those remaining is 1426 (F426MJN) seen turning into Romford bus station.
Colin LLoyd

750-754

Ford Transit VE6 — Dormobile — B16F — 1986

750	D750RWC	751	D751RWC	752	D752RWC	753	D753RWC	754	D754RWC

1110-1127

Leyland Tiger TRCTL11/3R — Alexander TE — C53F — 1983

1110	HHJ371Y	1114	HHJ375Y	1119	HHJ380Y	1121	HHJ382Y	1125	A694OHJ
1111	HHJ372Y	1115	HHJ376Y	1120	HHJ381Y	1123	A692OHJ	1127	A696OHJ
1112	HHJ373Y	1117	HHJ378Y						

1128	B696WAR	Leyland Tiger TRCTL11/3R	Plaxton Paramount 3200 II	C51F	1985
1129	B697WAR	Leyland Tiger TRCTL11/3R	Plaxton Paramount 3200 II	C51F	1985
1130	C130HJN	Leyland Tiger TRCTL11/3R	Plaxton Paramount 3500 II	C53F	1986

1401-1429

Leyland Lynx LX112L10ZR/1R — Leyland Lynx — B49F — 1988

1401	E401HWC	1407	F407LTW	1414	F414MNO	1425	F425MJN	1428	F428MJN
1402	F402LTW	1408	F408LTW	1415	F415MWC	1426	F426MJN	1429	F429MJN
1403	F403LTW	1413	F413MNO	1416	F416MWC	1427	F427MJN		

1824-1834

Leyland National 11351A/1R — B49F — 1977-78

1824	VAR901S	1831	VNO733S	1832	VAR898S	1833	VAR899S	1834	VAR894S

1841-1924

Leyland National 11351A/1R — B49F — 1978-79

1841	WJN561S	1860	YEV318S	1870	YEV328S	1892	BNO682T	1916	JHJ142V
1843	WJN563S	1861	YEV319S	1872	ANO271S	1899	DAR121T	1917	JHJ143V
1844	WJN564S	1862	YEV320S	1873	ANO272S	1901	DAR123T	1921	JHJ147V
1850	YEV308S	1863	YEV321S	1874	BNO664T	1909	DAR131T	1923	JHJ149V
1851	YEV309S	1865	YEV323S	1885	BNO675T	1910	DAR132T	1924	JHJ150V
1855	YEV313S	1867	YEV325S	1890	BNO680T	1914	JHJ140V		

Eastern National, part of the Badgerline group, has chosen to modify the livery and to incorporate the badger motif. The first vehicle to be repainted was Harwich-based 4019 (C419HJN) seen here returning to its home town from Colchester. The bright colours include red fleetnames, and blue wheels and doors. *G R Mills*

1940	KEP829X	Leyland National 2 NL116L11/1R		B49F	1980	Ex SWT, 1990	
2383	WNO479	Bristol KSW5G	Eastern Coach Works	O33/28R	1953		
2384	WNO480	Bristol KSW5G	Eastern Coach Works	O33/28R	1953		
3064	UVX1S	Bristol VRT/SL3/501	Eastern Coach Works	H39/31F	1977		

3068-3076
Bristol VRT/SL3/6LXB   Eastern Coach Works   H39/31F   1980

3068	KOO786V	3070	KOO788V	3071	KOO789V	3072	KOO790V	3076	KOO794V
3069	KOO787V								

3077-3094
Bristol VRT/SL3/6LXB   Eastern Coach Works   H39/31F   1980-81

3077	STW21W	3079	STW23W	3084	STW28W	3092	STW36W	3094	STW38W
3078	STW22W	3083	STW27W	3091	STW35W	3093	STW37W		

3095-3128
Bristol VRT/SL3/6LXB   Eastern Coach Works   H43/31F   1981

3095	UAR585W	3106	UAR596W	3111	XHK216X	3114	XHK219X	3128	XHK233X
3103	UAR593W	3109	UAR599W	3112	XHK217X	3127	XHK232X		

3218	OVH924V	Bristol VRT/SL3/501	Eastern Coach Works	H43/31F	1980	Ex Milton Keynes City Bus, 1987
3219	VTH941T	Bristol VRT/SL3/501	Eastern Coach Works	H43/31F	1978	Ex Brewers, 1990
3220	WTH949T	Bristol VRT/SL3/501	Eastern Coach Works	H43/31F	1978	Ex Brewers, 1990
3221	WTH958T	Bristol VRT/SL3/501	Eastern Coach Works	H43/31F	1978	Ex Brewers, 1990
3222	BEP963V	Bristol VRT/SL3/501	Eastern Coach Works	H43/31F	1979	Ex Brewers, 1990
3500	WNO546L	Bristol VRT/SL2/6LX	Eastern Coach Works	O39/31F	1973	
3501	NPU974M	Bristol VRT/SL2/6LX	Eastern Coach Works	O39/31F	1973	

4007-4021
Leyland Olympian ONLXB/1R   Eastern Coach Works   DPH42/30F   1986

4007	C407HJN	4012	C412HJN	4015	C415HJN	4018	C418HJN	4020	C420HJN
4008	C408HJN	4013	C413HJN	4016	C416HJN	4019	C419HJN	4021	C421HJN
4011	C411HJN	4014	C414HJN	4017	C417HJN				

4501	B689BPU	Leyland Olympian ONTL11/2RHSp	Eastern Coach Works	CH45/28F	1985
4501	B691BPU	Leyland Olympian ONTL11/2RHSp	Eastern Coach Works	CH45/28F	1985
4510	D510PPU	Leyland Olympian ONTL11/2RHSp	Eastern Coach Works	CH45/28F	1986
4511	D511PPU	Leyland Olympian ONTL11/2RHSp	Eastern Coach Works	CH45/24F	1986
4512	D512PPU	Leyland Olympian ONTL11/2RHSp	Eastern Coach Works	CH45/24F	1986

Livery: Green and yellow
Overall adverts: 0201/5/21/4/7/31, 1742/87, 1830/7/64-6/8/9/73/81/99, 1913/7/8/23/4, 3084/127, 4005/11.

In the mid 1980s, Eastern Coach Works produced an inter-urban coach version of their bodywork designed for the Leyland Olympian. These used a special version of that chassis, and were most common on commuter routes into London. Now five of these remain, and 4512 (D512PPU) is seen here representing the type. *Colin Lloyd*

EMBLINGS

J W Embling & Son, Bridge Garage, Guyhirn, Cambridgeshire, PE13 4ED

Reg	Chassis	Body	Layout	Year	Notes
EJR791	Leyland Royal Tiger PSU1/15	Plaxton Panorama I(1966)	C43F	1952	Ex OK, Bishop Auckland, 1992
MEB626	Trojan	Trojan	M13	1961	
OFL113J	Daimler Fleetline CRG6LX	Alexander AL	H48/32D	1971	Ex Partridge, Hadleigh, 1984
UUF110J	Bristol VRT/SL2/6G	Eastern Coach Works	H39/31F	1971	Ex Brighton & Hove, 1987
UUF112J	Bristol VRT/SL2/6G	Eastern Coach Works	H39/31F	1971	Ex Brighton & Hove, 1987
UUF115J	Bristol VRT/SL2/6G	Eastern Coach Works	H39/31F	1971	Ex Brighton & Hove, 1987
JOA600L	Bedford YRT	Duple Dominant	C53F	1973	Ex Pullman, Norwich, 1981
WXI9252	Leyland Leopard PSU3B/4R	Duple Dominant II	C53F	1973	Ex Fowler, Holbeach Drove, 1991
VNK472M	Bedford YRT	Duple Dominant I	C53F	1974	Ex Pullman, Norwich, 1981
PRP54M	Ford R1014	Plaxton Elite III	C45F	1974	Ex Canham, Whittlesey, 1984
3196DD	Bristol VRT/SL2/6G	Eastern Coach Works	H43/34F	1975	Ex Rover, Horsley, 1990
HPR105N	Ford R1114	Plaxton Elite III	C49F	1975	Ex AC, Bournemouth, 1977
HTU154N	Bristol VRT/SL2/6G	Eastern Coach Works	H43/31F	1975	Ex Crosville, 1988
MDC565P	Bedford YRT	Plaxton Supreme III	C53F	1976	Ex Easey, March, 1988
DFS789S	Ford R1114	Duple Dominant II	C53F	1977	Ex Horseshoe, Kempston, 1989
SVA7S	Ford R1114	Plaxton Supreme III	C53F	1978	
VVA7T	Ford R1114	Plaxton Supreme IV	C53F	1978	Ex Smith, Tysoe, 1979
CAV312V	Ford Transit	S & N	M12	1979	
CEW205V	Ford R1114	Plaxton Supreme IV Exp	C53F	1979	
WXI9253	DAF MB200DKTL600	Plaxton Supreme IV	C57F	1980	Ex Knights, Harrow Weald, 1992
RGV684W	Bedford YMT	Duple Dominant II	C53F	1980	Ex Haines, Frampton, 1991
B392BJO	DAF SB2300DHS585	Berkhof Esprite 340	C49FT	1985	Ex Grayline, Bicester, 1992
D300XFL	Freight Rover Sherpa 365	Optare	C16F	1986	
D616FVF	Ford Transit VE6	Deansgate	M12	1985	Ex Yoosoof, Batley, 1992
F434RRY	Toyota Coaster HB31R	Caetano Optimo	C18F	1989	Ex Frazer, Castle Donington, 1991
F148NVE	Bova FHD12.290	Bova Futura	C53F	1989	
G697VAV	Bova FHD12.290	Bova Futura	C49FT	1990	
H271CEW	Scania K113CRB	Van Hool Alizée	C49FT	1990	
H854DAV	Scania K113CRB	Van Hool Alizée H	C49FT	1990	

Livery: White, red and blue

Previous Registrations:

3196DD	GUD750N, YWD687, KAD397N	OFL113J	PRG132J, 3196DD
B392BJO	B676BTW, MJI1676	VVA7T	DWK420T
EJR791	From new	WXI9252	JKE107L, 805AFC, LFL304L
MEB626	From new	WXI9253	PNM666W

The March to Wisbech service has been provided for by a galaxy of blue liveried vehicles for some four decades, worked by three operators. OFL113J, a Daimler Fleetline with Alexander AL-type bodywork, disguises its Dundee origins having carried two other registration marks.
G R Mills

ENTERPRISE

Enterprise Safety Coaches Ltd, Black Horse Lane, Chatteris,
Cambridgeshire, PE16 6RB

BFS18L	Leyland Atlantean AN68/1R	Alexander AL	H45/30D	1973	Ex Lothian, 1989
BFS19L	Leyland Atlantean AN68/1R	Alexander AL	H45/30D	1973	Ex Lothian, 1989
BFS21L	Leyland Atlantean AN68/1R	Alexander AL	H45/30D	1973	Ex Lothian, 1989
RAX624R	Bedford YMT	Plaxton Supreme III	C53F	1977	Ex Dew, Somersham, 1983
SHL882S	Bedford YMT	Plaxton Supreme III	C53F	1978	Ex Angel, Tottenham, 1984
THX225S	Leyland National 10351A/2R		B48F	1978	Ex London Buses, 1991
THX513S	Leyland Fleetline FE30ALRSp	Park Royal	H44/27D	1977	Ex London Buses, 1992
THX625S	Leyland Fleetline FE30ALRSp	Park Royal	H44/27D	1978	Ex London Buses, 1992
RNY313Y	Leyland Tiger TRCTL11/2R	Plaxton Paramount 3200 E	C49F	1982	Ex Hill's, Tredegar, 1991
C333HHB	DAF SBR2305DHS570	Jonckheere Jubilee P99	CH55/16CT	1986	Ex Thomas, Clydach Vale, 1989
E816UKW	Freight Rover Sherpa 350	Whittaker	M16	1987	
G954GRP	LAG Panoramic G355Z	LAG	C49FT	1990	Ex Northern Star, Poulton, 1992
G957GRP	LAG Panoramic G355Z	LAG	C49FT	1990	Ex Scotts Tours, London, 1992
G818YJF	Bova FHD12.290	Bova Futura	C53FT	1990	
G828YJF	Bova FHD12.290	Bova Futura	C53FT	1990	
H2LWJ	LAG Panoramic G355Z	LAG	C49FT	1991	Ex Crown, Cramlington, 1993
J2EST	Hestair Duple SDA1512	Duple 425	C55F	1991	

Livery: Olive green and grey

Previous registrations:
H2LWJ   H749UCU

Certain Enterprise journeys into Peterborough require a higher capacity vehicle than a Leyland National. This is provided for by any of the trio of former Lothian Leyland Atlanteans. Typical is BFS18L, in grey and green, and seen in Queensgate shopping centre in Cambridge bound for the bus lay-over area to park up before the return trip to Ramsey. *G R Mills*

FELIX

Felix Taxi Co, 8 Windmill Hill, Long Melford, Suffolk, CO10 9AD

DBU889	Bedford OB	Duple Vista	C27F	1947	Ex Dangerfield, Stroud, 1988
A197RUR	Mercedes-Benz L608D	Plaxton Mini Supreme	C25F	1984	Ex Croxford, Farnham, 1988
C818FMC	Mercedes-Benz L608D	Reeve Burgess	C19F	1986	
C914FMP	Mercedes-Benz L307D	Reeve Burgess	M12	1986	Ex CharterCoach, Gt Oakley, 1989
E856GFV	Mercedes-Benz 609D	Elme	C16F	1987	
F679FFJ	Peugeot-Talbot Freeway	Talbot	B16FL	1988	Ex Sochulbus, Ashford, 1992
F301RMH	Mercedes-Benz 709D	Reeve Burgess Beaver	B25F	1988	
G530GSC	Dennis Javelin 8.5SDA1915	Duple 320	C35F	1989	Ex Glass, Haddington, 1991
J220HDS	Mercedes-Benz 811D	Dormobile Routemaker	B33F	1992	
K392BVS	Mercedes-Benz 711D	Reeve Burgess Beaver	C25F	1993	

Livery: White, red and black.

This view in picturesque Cavendish shows two of Felix's vehicles. A197RUR, a Mercedes-Benz with a Plaxton Mini Supreme bodywork, new to The Londoners, and DBU889 an example of the Bedford OB/Duple Vista combination typifying a type that once abounded in rural Suffolk. *G R Mills*

FLYING BANANA

Halesworth Transit Ltd, 1 Stone Road, Cobholm, Great Yarmouth, Norfolk, NR31 0AQ

YHA359J	Ford R192	Plaxton Derwent	DP27F	1971	Ex Lamcote, Radcliffe, 1991
B201GNL	Ford Transit 190D	Alexander AM	DP16F	1985	Ex Go-Ahead Northern, 1991
B204GNL	Ford Transit 190D	Alexander AM	DP16F	1985	Ex Go-Ahead Northern, 1991
B420NJF	Ford Transit 190D	Rootes	B16F	1985	Ex Midland Fox, 1991
C430BHY	Ford Transit 190D	Dormobile	B16F	1986	Ex City Line, 1989
C431BHY	Ford Transit 190D	Dormobile	B16F	1986	Ex City Line, 1989
C535TJF	Ford Transit 190D	Rootes	B16F	1986	Ex Midland Fox, 1991
D226GLJ	Freight Rover Sherpa 365	Dormobile	B16F	1987	Ex Crosville, 1991
D179LTA	Renault-Dodge S56	Reeve Burgess	B23F	1987	Ex Plymouth, 1993
D70TLV	Freight Rover Sherpa 374	Carlyle	B16F	1987	Ex Isaac, Morriston, 1992
E237VOM	Freight Rover Sherpa 374	Carlyle Citybus II	B20F	1988	Ex Strathclyde, 1990
K340HNG	Leyland DAF 405	Minibus Options	B20F	1992	

Livery: Yellow and green.

Flying Banana is the unusual title of one of Britain's brightest bus companies. It is based in Great Yarmouth and operates a set of mini/midibuses on four services within the borough. D179LTA, one of the latest intake, is a former Plymouth Citybus Renault-Dodge S56 with Reeve Burgess bodywork. It is seen in Cobholm. *G R Mills*

The Eastern Bus Handbook

FORDS COACHES

A A W Ford, The Garage, Fambridge Road, Althorne, Essex, CM3 6BZ

PRG124J	Daimler Fleetline CRG6LX	Alexander L	H48/35F	1971	Ex Moffat & Williamson, 1984
PRG127J	Daimler Fleetline CRG6LX	Alexander L	H48/35F	1971	Ex Moffat & Williamson, 1984
PRG134J	Daimler Fleetline CRG6LX	Alexander L	H48/32D	1971	Ex Partridge, Hadleigh, 1984
820KPO	Bedford YRT	Plaxton Elite III	C53F	1975	Ex Porter, Great Totham, 1988
ONR79R	Bedford YRQ	Plaxton Elite III	C45F	1976	Ex Wells, Maldon, 1984
WGR66R	Bedford YRQ	Plaxton Supreme III	C45F	1977	Ex Weardale, Frosterley, 1981
RRP857R	Bristol VRT/SL3/6LXB	Eastern Coach Works	H43/31F	1976	Ex Thamesway, 1991
AUD460R	Bristol VRT/SL3/6LXB	Eastern Coach Works	H43/31F	1977	Ex Carter, Colchester, 1990
TDT32S	Bedford YMT	Duple Dominant II	C53F	1977	Ex Morris, Borehamwood, 1978
XNV802S	Bristol VRT/SL3/6LXB	Eastern Coach Works	H43/31F	1978	Ex Thamesway, 1991
LJI477	Bedford YRT	Willowbrook Warrior(1986)	B55F	1978	Ex Cave, Solihull, 1992
CKX392T	Bedford YMT	Duple Dominant II	C53F	1979	Ex Morris, Borehamwood, 1980
EYH693V	Bedford YMT	Plaxton Supreme IV	C53F	1980	Ex Barnes, Clacton-on-Sea, 1987
CHK831X	Bedford YNT	Plaxton Supreme IV	C53F	1982	
GEX790Y	Bova EL26/581	Bova Europa	C53F	1983	Ex Bird's, Hunstanton, 1985
JEV245Y	Van Hool T824	Van Hool Astromega	C57/27F	1983	Ex Southend, 1990
A128NAR	Volvo B10M-61	Van Hool Alizée	C48FT	1983	
238JUO	Leyland Royal Tiger B50	Van Hool Alizée	C48FT	1984	Ex Rosemary, Terrington, 1993
C658KVW	Bedford Venturer YNV	Van Hool Alizée	C53F	1986	
C995ERO	Bedford YNT	Plaxton Paramount 3200 II	C53F	1986	Ex Dinsey, Luton, 1988
C141KFL	DAF SB2300DHS585	Jonckheere Jubilee P599	C53FT	1985	Ex Fenn, Maldon, 1989
D66ONS	Bedford Venturer YNV	Duple 320	C57F	1986	Ex Squirrell, Hitcham, 1990
G854VAY	Dennis Javelin 12SDA1907	Caetano Algarve	C53FT	1989	Ex APT, Rayleigh, 1992
H830YGA	Mercedes-Benz 609D	Scott	C21F	1990	Ex Gem Liner, Stockton, 1992

Livery: Green and red (contract fleet); white, red and orange (coach fleet).

Previous Registrations:

238JUO	A839NNK		LJI477	XNM830S
820KPO	LAY474P		ONR79R	KUT589P

Acquired by Fords of Althorne to operate excursions more economically, the impressive Van Hool Astromega has also been utilised on a variety of other tasks. JEV245Y is seen in St Edwards Way, Romford bound for Pontins holiday camp at Hemsby with a large party of holiday makers.
G R Mills

GALLOWAY

Galloway European Coachlines Ltd, Denters Hill, Stowmarket Road,
Mendlesham, Suffolk, IP14 5RR

R = Rex Motor Services, Thorndon.

R	GXC717L	Bedford VAS5	Plaxton Panorama IV	C29F	1973	Ex Soames, Otley, 1980
R	XMA194M	Ford R1114	Plaxton Elite III	C53F	1974	Ex Bickers, Coddenham, 1980
	NDX309P	Bedford YRT	Plaxton Elite III Express	C53F	1976	Ex Cropley, Fosdike, 1988
	RCH501R	Bedford YMT	Plaxton Supreme III Exp	C53F	1976	Ex Eastern Counties, 1989
	RCH502R	Bedford YMT	Plaxton Supreme III Exp	C53F	1976	Ex Bantam, Ipswich, 1988
	GOI1294	Bedford YMT	Plaxton Supreme III	C53F	1978	Ex Bebb, Llantwit Fardre, 1982
R	XPV657S	Ford R1114	Plaxton Supreme III Exp	C53F	1978	Ex Simonds, Botesdale, 1989
R	FVG666T	Ford R1114	Plaxton Supreme IV	C53F	1979	Ex Norfolk, Gt Yarmouth, 1985
	DHE699V	Bedford YMT	Plaxton Supreme IV	C53F	1978	Ex Wells, Thorndon, 1990
R	2513PP	Ford R1114	Plaxton Supreme IV	C53F	1979	Ex Bennett, Newbury, 1988
	DFD953B	DAF MB200DKTL600	Plaxton Supreme IV	C51F	1979	Ex Fenn, March, 1991
	BBM53A	Bedford YMT	Plaxton Supreme IV	C53F	1980	Ex Sampson, Cheshunt, 1990
	1440PP	DAF MB200DKTL600	Plaxton Supreme IV	C57F	1980	Ex Majestic, Shareshill, 1985
	TPA666X	Bedford YNT	Plaxton Supreme IV	C53F	1981	Ex Beckett, Little Horwood, 1988
	5611PP	Bova EL26/581	Bova Europa	C49FT	1983	Ex Wallace Arnold, 1988
	5048PP	Bova FLD12.250	Bova Futura	C53F	1984	Ex Stevensons, 1989
R	EGS223Y	Ford Transit 150	Tricentrol	M8	1982	Ex Springham, Orpington, 1987
R	FPW200Y	Ford Transit 150	Dolphin	M8	1983	Ex Dolphin, Norwich, 1990

Working on National Express service is Galloway 4092PP, a Plaxton Paramount 3200 body fitted to a rear-engined DAF SB chassis. *Colin Lloyd*

R	A504HUT	Bedford YNT	Duple Laser	C53F	1984	Ex Bexleyheath Transport, 1989
	4092PP	DAF SB2305DHTD585	Plaxton Paramount 3200	C53F	1985	Ex Smith, Alcester, 1989
	C46DUR	Bedford YNT	Plaxton Paramount 3200 II	C53F	1985	Ex Dinsey, Luton, 1988
	2086PP	Bova FLD12.250	Bova Futura	C53F	1986	Ex Supreme, Coventry, 1988
R	E226WKW	Freight Rover Sherpa 374	Whittaker	M16	1987	
R	E233WKW	Mercedes-Benz 609D	Whittaker	C24F	1988	
R	F863FWB	Mercedes-Benz 609D	Whittaker	C24F	1989	
	1482PP	DAF SB2305DHTD585	Plaxton Paramount 3200 III	C53F	1989	
	F886SRT	DAF SB2305DHTD585	Plaxton Paramount 3200 III	C53F	1989	
	5516PP	DAF SB3000DKV601	Van Hool Alizée	C53F	1989	Ex Hughes-DAF, 1991
	1754PP	Bova FHD12.290	Bova Futura	C49FT	1989	
R	G434ART	Mercedes-Benz 609D	Whittaker	C24F	1990	
	K110TCP	DAF SB3000DKV601	Van Hool Alizée	C49FT	1993	
	K120TCP	DAF SB3000DKV601	Van Hool Alizée	C49FT	1993	

Livery: Cream, yellow and orange
National Express: F886SRT.

Previous Registrations:

1440PP	NRO229V, 7476PP	5048PP	125EJU
1482PP	F764RRT	5516PP	F254RJX
1754PP	G494WDX	BBM53A	KBH850V
2086PP	C126AHP	DFD953B	YEB103T
2513PP	PNB785W	GOI1294	YUE593S
4092PP	B885AJX		

A504HUT is seen in full Galloway livery but retaining the Rex Motor Services fleet name and represents a business acquired from Wells, Thorndon in 1990. It is still operated as a separate entity. This vehicle is the only Duple Laser-bodied Bedford in the combined fleets. *G R Mills*

GOLDEN BOY

Jetsie Ltd, 13 Burford Street, Hoddesdon, Hertfordshire, EN11 8HP

401	YOI2642	Leyland Leopard PSU3E/4R	Plaxton Supreme III	C53F	1978	Ex H & M Coaches, 1991
402	YOI7757	Volvo B10M-61	Van Hool Alizée	C53F	1986	Ex Shearings, 1992
403	YOI5475	Leyland Leopard PSU5C/4R	Plaxton Supreme IV	C50F	1980	Ex Mulligan, Harlow, 1992
405	YOI7725	Leyland Tiger TRCTL11/2R	Plaxton Supreme V Exp	C53F	1982	Ex Capital, Cwmbran, 1992
406	DHE698V	Bedford YMT	Plaxton Supreme IV	C53F	1980	Ex Elgar & Fox, Inkpen, 1986
408	EGS173T	Bedford YMT	Plaxton Supreme IV	C53F	1979	Ex Transauto, High Wycombe, 1986
409	YOI7353	Volvo B10M-61	Van Hool Alizée	C53F	1985	Ex Shearings, 1991
410	WJM810T	Leyland Leopard PSU3E/4R	Plaxton Supreme IV Exp	C46F	1979	Ex Alder Valley South, 1987
412	WJM812T	Leyland Leopard PSU3E/4R	Plaxton Supreme IV Exp	C46F	1979	Ex Alder Valley South, 1987
413	YOI2805	Leyland Tiger TRCTL11/3R	Plaxton Paramount 3200 E	C57F	1983	Ex Merlyn's, Skewen, 1990
416	YOI7079	Mercedes-Benz L307D	Reeve Burgess	M12	1983	Ex Graves, Hertford, 1991
417	YOI7373	Leyland Tiger TRCTL11/3R	Plaxton Viewmaster IV	C53F	1982	
418	F580RML	Van Hool T815	Van Hool Alizée	C53F	1989	
419	YOI5997	Leyland Leopard PSU3E/4R	Plaxton Elite III	C49F	1977	Ex Bonners, 1992
421	YOI7374	Leyland Leopard PSU3E/4R	Duple Dominant II	C53F	1980	Ex Sampson, Hoddesdon, 1988
424	YOI7575	Leyland Tiger TRCTL11/3R	Plaxton Supreme IV	C40FT	1983	Ex Green, Brierley Hill, 1987
435	YOI7744	Leyland Leopard PSU3E/4R	Plaxton Supreme IV Exp	C53F	1979	Ex Houston & Bryant, London, 1992
436	YOI2517	AEC Reliance 6UZR	Duple Dominant II Exp	C53F	1974	Ex Bonner, Ongar, 1992
458	C358LVV	Iveco 79F14	Caetano Viana	C19F	1986	Ex Linkline, London, 1986
407	D459POO	Renault Extra	Renault	M12	198	Ex Macs,

Previous Registrations:

YOI2517	XPK51T	YOI7079	KAR986Y	YOI7575	A80NHK
YOI2642	RYG537R	YOI7145	C358LVV	YOI7725	NDW138X
YOI2805	DBJ369Y	YOI7353	B473UNB	YOI7744	HGA748T
YOI5475	KBH840V	YOI7373	DNK581Y	YOI7757	C333DND
YOI5997	GNM225N	YOI7374	MNK428V		

Named vehicles: 401 *Miss Cara*, 402 *Miss Geraldine*, 403 *Miss Maria*, 405 *Miss Elaine*, 406 *Miss Geraldine*, 408 *Miss Jane*, 409 *Miss Shelagh*, 410 *Miss Gemma*, 412 *Miss Kelly*, 413 *Miss Bernadette*, 417 *Miss Mary*, 418 *Miss Angela*, 421 *Miss Patricia*, 424 *Miss Annie*, 435 *Miss Leanne*, 436 *Miss Karen*, 458 *Miss Jacqueline*.

Livery: Gold, burgundy and black

Golden Boy have moved away from stage operation recently, but still provide a service to the public with coaching activities. Seen in Harlow bus station is YOI5475, a Leyland Leopard with Plaxton Supreme IV bodywork.
Colin Lloyd

GRAHAM'S

G M Ellis, 19 Church Road, Kelvedon, Essex, CO5 9JH

Depot: Station Road, Kelvedon

ACP832V	Ford R1114	Plaxton Supreme IV	C53F	1980	Ex Holden Bay, Bury, 1984
MFK786V	Volvo B58-61	Duple Dominant II	C57F	1980	Ex Lattimore, Markyate, 1991
TJN981W	Bedford YMQS	Wadham Stringer Vanguard	DP33F	1981	Ex Hedingham & District, 1992
XKX640X	Ford R1114	Plaxton Supreme IV	C53F	1981	Ex Blue Diamond, Harlow, 1985
HBH419Y	Mercedes-Benz L307D	Reeve Burgess	M12	1983	
E786MEU	Ford Transit VE6	Steedrive	M13	1988	
F651OHD	DAF SB2305DHS585	Duple 340	C53FT	1989	Ex Browne, East Grinstead, 1992
F652OHD	DAF SB2305DHS585	Duple 340	C53FT	1989	Ex Browne, East Grinstead, 1992
J830OPD	Toyota Hiace	Toyota	M11	1992	

Originally new to Eastern National, TJN981W was one of ten Bedford YMQs with Wadham Stringer bodywork and the only one to pass to Hedingham Omnibuses. Fully repainted by Lodge Coaches of High Easter for the current owners the vehicle, seen outside Kelvedon Church, regularly works on a Malbus service from Gt Braxted to Maldon. *G R Mills*

GREAT YARMOUTH TRANSPORT

Great Yarmouth Transport Ltd, Caister Road, Great Yarmouth,
Norfolk, NR30 4DF

1	4750WY	Volvo B10M-61	Plaxton Paramount 3200	C51F	1983	Ex Wallace Arnold, 1988
2	6220WY	Volvo B10M-61	Plaxton Paramount 3200	C51F	1983	Ex Wallace Arnold, 1988
3	C517DND	Volvo B10M-61	Plaxton Paramount 3200 II	C53F	1986	Ex Shearings, 1993

24-36

Bristol VRT/SL3/6LXB   Eastern Coach Works   H43/31F*   1977-81   *35-36 are H43/34F

| 24 | PVG24W | 26 | PVG26W | 28 | CVF28T | 30 | CVF30T | 35 | RVF35R |
| 25 | PVG25W | 27 | PVG27W | 29 | CVF29T | 31 | CVF31T | 36 | RVF36R |

40	E40OAH	Volvo Citybus B10M-50	East Lancashire	DPH45/33F	1987	
41	E41OAH	Volvo Citybus B10M-50	East Lancashire	DPH45/33F	1987	
42	E42OAH	MCW MetroRider MF151/9	MCW	DP25F	1987	
43	E43OAH	MCW MetroRider MF151/9	MCW	DP25F	1987	
44	E44OAH	MCW MetroRider MF151/9	MCW	DP25F	1987	
45	E45OAH	MCW MetroRider MF151/9	MCW	DP25F	1987	
46	E46RVG	MCW MetroRider MF159/1	MCW	B33F	1988	
47	E47RVG	MCW MetroRider MF159/1	MCW	B33F	1988	
48	E48RVG	MCW MetroRider MF159/1	MCW	B33F	1988	
49	E49RVG	MCW MetroRider MF159/1	MCW	B33F	1988	
50	F50ACL	Volvo Citybus B10M-50	Alexander RH	H47/35F	1989	
51	F51ACL	Volvo Citybus B10M-50	Alexander RH	H47/35F	1989	
52	G52GEX	Mercedes-Benz 811D	Reeve Burgess Beaver	DP33F	1989	
53	G53GEX	Mercedes-Benz 811D	Reeve Burgess Beaver	DP33F	1989	
54	G54GEX	Mercedes-Benz 811D	Reeve Burgess Beaver	B33F	1989	
55	G55GEX	Mercedes-Benz 811D	Reeve Burgess Beaver	B33F	1989	
56	G456KNG	Dennis Dart 9SDL3002	Duple Dartline	B39F	1990	
57	G457KNG	Dennis Dart 9SDL3002	Duple Dartline	B39F	1990	
58	G458KNG	Dennis Dart 9SDL3002	Duple Dartline	B39F	1990	
59	E452SON	MCW Metrobus DR102/63	MCW	H45/30F	1987	Ex London Buses, 1991
60	E453SON	MCW Metrobus DR102/63	MCW	H45/30F	1987	Ex London Buses, 1991
61	E455SON	MCW Metrobus DR102/63	MCW	H45/30F	1987	Ex London Buses, 1991
62	K62KEX	Dennis Dart 9.8SDL3025	East Lancashire	DP43F	1993	
63	K63KEX	Dennis Dart 9.8SDL3025	East Lancashire	DP43F	1993	

79-90

AEC Swift 3MP2R   Eastern Coach Works   B43D   1973

| 79 | WEX679M | 81 | WEX681M | 83 | WEX683M | 86 | WEX686M | 88 | WEX688M |
| 80 | WEX680M | 82 | WEX682M | 85 | WEX685M | 87 | WEX687M | | |

Livery: Blue and cream

Previous Registrations:

| 4750WY | FUA385Y | | 6220WY | FUA386Y |

Great Yarmouth has joined the growing ranks of Dennis Dart operators. No.58 (G458KNG), one of the initial trio with Carlyle bodies, was caught in Southtown Road, a riverside industrial area of the town. *G R Mills*

For over six decades all Great Yarmouth double deck intake had been new vehicles. However, 60 (E453SON) is one of the trio of former London Buses Metrobuses, rendered surplus at Harrow, which have broken this long tradition. It is seen passing through Priory Plain. *G R Mills*

The first examples of East Lancashire bodywork to be supplied to Great Yarmouth are a pair of Volvos with high-back seating. No.41 (E41OAH) is seen, caught up in traffic, while passing through Gorleston High Street. *G R Mills*

The only batch of AEC Swifts still with their original owner are the 1973 Eastern Coach Works-bodied examples with Great Yarmouth where the dozen remained intact for some twenty years. No.86 (WEX686M), is seen crossing New Haven Bridge on route to Gorleston. *G R Mills*

HARRIS BUS

Frank Harris (Coaches) Ltd, & Harris Bus Company Ltd, Manor Road, West Thurrock, Essex, RM16 1EH

BUF425C	Leyland Titan PD3/4	Northern Counties	FCO39/30F	1965	Ex Southdown, 1988
NFB112R	Bristol VRT/SL3/6LXB	Eastern Coach Works	H43/27D	1977	Ex Crown, Bristol, 1990
VRP36S	Bristol VRT/SL3/6LXB	Alexander AL	H45/27D	1977	Ex Northampton, 1990
VRP37S	Bristol VRT/SL3/6LXB	Alexander AL	H45/27D	1977	Ex Northampton, 1990
VRP39S	Bristol VRT/SL3/6LXB	Alexander AL	H45/27D	1977	Ex Northampton, 1990
PBD40R	Bristol VRT/SL3/6LXB	Alexander AL	H45/27D	1977	Ex Northampton, 1990
PBD41R	Bristol VRT/SL3/6LXB	Alexander AL	H45/27D	1977	Ex Northampton, 1990
PBD43R	Bristol VRT/SL3/6LXB	Alexander AL	H45/27D	1977	Ex Northampton, 1990
VVV65S	Bristol VRT/SL3/6LXB	Alexander AL	H45/27D	1977	Ex Northampton, 1992
WRJ447X	Volvo-Ailsa B55-10 MkIII	Northern Counties	H43/35F	1982	Ex Lancaster, 1993
WRJ448X	Volvo-Ailsa B55-10 MkIII	Northern Counties	H43/35F	1982	Ex Lancaster, 1993
6306FH	DAF SB2300DKSB585	Van Hool Alizée	C48FT	1985	
9242FH	Scania K112TRS	Plaxton Paramount 4000 II	CH54/18CT	1985	
2942FH	Bova FHD12.280	Bova Futura	C53FT	1986	
C146NHJ	Bova FHD12.280	Bova Futura	C53FT	1986	
D301PEV	Volvo B10M-46	Plaxton Bustler	B38F	1986	
D302PEV	Volvo B10M-46	Plaxton Bustler	B38F	1986	
D303PEV	Volvo B10M-46	Plaxton Bustler	B38F	1986	
D304PEV	Volvo B10M-46	Plaxton Bustler	B38F	1986	
FHV504	Bova FHD12.290	Bova Futura	C49FT	1988	

Harris Bus originally had three Scania/Alexander double deckers until one migrated to Nottingham. F314RHK one of the surviving 78-seaters represents the largest and newest such unit in the fleet. It is seen picking up from the Lakeside Shopping Centre bus station. *G R Mills*

E305EVW	MCW MetroRider MF150/89	MCW	B25F	1988
E306EVW	MCW MetroRider MF150/89	MCW	B25F	1988
E308HPU	Leyland Swift LBM6	Wadham Stringer Vanguard II	B37F	1988
E309HPU	Leyland Swift LBM6	Wadham Stringer Vanguard II	B37F	1988
5970FH	DAF SB3000DKV601	Van Hool Alizée	C49FT	1988
7968FH	DAF SB3000DKV601	Van Hool Alizée H	C49FT	1988
8947FH	DAF SB3000DKV601	Van Hool Alizée	C49FT	1988
F310OVW	MCW MetroRider MF150/112	MCW	B23F	1988
F849LHS	Ford Transit VE6	Dormobile	M16	1989
6330FH	DAF SBR3000DKZ570	Plaxton Paramount 4000 II	CH50/14CT	1989
F312PEV	Scania N113DRB	Alexander RH	H47/31F	1989
F314RHK	Scania N113DRB	Alexander RH	H47/31F	1989
F98RAR	DAF SB3000DKV601	Van Hool Alizée	C49FT	1989
F99RAR	DAF SB3000DKV601	Van Hool Alizée	C49FT	1989
J91WWC	Kässbohrer Setra S215HD	Kässbohrer Tornado	C49FT	1991
J92YAR	Kässbohrer Setra S215HD	Kässbohrer Tornado	C49FT	1991
J582WVX	Mercedes-Benz 709D	Alexander AM	B25F	1991
J583WVX	Mercedes-Benz 709D	Alexander AM	B25F	1991
K622WOV	Peugeot-Talbot Freeway	Talbot	B18FL	1992
K623WOV	Peugeot-Talbot Freeway	Talbot	B18FL	1992
K95GEV	DAF SB3000DKV601	Van Hool Alizée	C48FT	1993
K96GEV	DAF SB3000DKV601	Van Hool Alizée	C48FT	1993
K97GEV	DAF SB3000DKV601	Van Hool Alizée	C48FT	1993

Livery: White and blue (buses); two-tone green (coaches)

Previous Registrations:

2942FH	C90LVX	6330FH	F403PEV	9242FH	C400JOO
5970FH	F96EVW	7968FH	E95EVW	C146NHJ	C91LVX, 6330FH
6306FH	B89CNO	8947FH	F97MHJ	FHV504	E93EVW

Timekeeping for the Harris Bus Volvo saloons is rarely a problem as the available power is more than adequate for the Plaxton Bustler 38-seat bodies. D303PEV, one of four similar vehicles, is seen at the vast Lakeside Shopping Centre complex. One of the former Northampton Bristol VRTs with Alexander bodywork which are employed on internal shuttles is in the background. *G R Mills*

HEDINGHAM OMNIBUSES

Hedingham & District Omnibuses Ltd, Wethersfield Road, Sible Hedingham,
Essex, CO9 3LB

Depots: Springfield Ind Est, Burnham-on-Crouch, Essex; Telford Road Ind Est, Clacton-on-Sea, Essex; Church Lane, Little Tey, Essex; 215 High Street, Kelvedon, Essex; Perry Farm, Nayland, Suffolk; Railway Station Yard, Walton-on-Naze, Essex.

L81	YNO481L	Bedford YRT	Marshall Camair	B53F	1973	
L84	RGV284N	Leyland Leopard PSU3B/4R	Willowbrook	B55F	1974	
L85	GPV685N	Bedford YRQ	Willowbrook 001	B47F	1975	
L86	KHJ786P	Bedford YRQ	Willowbrook 001	B47F	1975	
L87	PHK387R	Bedford YRQ	Duple Dominant	B47F	1976	
L88	REV188R	Bedford YLQ	Duple Dominant	B47F	1976	
L89	CEV89T	Bedford YLQ	Duple Dominant	B47F	1978	
L94	GVW894T	Bedford YMT	Plaxton Supreme IV Exp	C53F	1979	
L95	JAR495V	Bedford YLQ	Duple Dominant	B47F	1979	
L96	NFX446P	Bedford YMT	Plaxton Supreme III	C53F	1976	Ex National Travel SW, 1979
L98	SPU898W	Bedford YMQ	Duple Dominant	B47F	1980	
L100	UNO100W	Bedford YMT	Plaxton Supreme IV Exp	C53F	1981	
L103	BAR103X	Leyland Leopard PSU3E/4R	Plaxton Bustler	B55F	1982	
L105	BEV105X	Leyland Leopard PSU3E/4R	Plaxton Supreme IV Exp	C53F	1982	
L111	UVX4S	Bristol LH6L	Eastern Coach Works	B43F	1977	Ex Eastern National, 1982
L112	UVX5S	Bristol LH6L	Eastern Coach Works	B43F	1977	Ex Eastern National, 1982
L113	UVX6S	Bristol LH6L	Eastern Coach Works	B43F	1977	Ex Eastern National, 1982
L114	UVX7S	Bristol LH6L	Eastern Coach Works	B43F	1977	Ex Eastern National, 1982
L115	FEV115Y	Leyland Leopard PSU3E/4R	Plaxton Supreme IV	C53F	1982	
L116	HAR116Y	Bedford YNT	Plaxton Paramount 3200 E	C53F	1983	
L121	DBH452X	Leyland Leopard PSU5C/4R	Plaxton Supreme IV	C57F	1981	Ex Flight's, Birmingham, 1983
L122	A122PAR	Leyland Tiger TRCTL11/2R	Plaxton Paramount 3200 E	C53F	1983	
L124	B124BOO	Leyland Tiger TRCTL11/2R	Plaxton Paramount 3200	C53F	1985	
L125	BNO700T	Bedford YMT	Duple Dominant II Express	C53F	1979	Ex Eastern National, 1984
L126	BNO703T	Bedford YMT	Duple Dominant II Express	C53F	1979	Ex Eastern National, 1984
L133	BHK710X	Bedford YNT	Plaxton Supreme IV Exp	C53F	1982	Ex Jennings, Ashen, 1984
L135	KGS489Y	Leyland Tiger TRCTL11/3R	Plaxton Paramount 3500	C53F	1983	Ex Travellers, Hounslow, 1985
L136	D136XVW	Bedford YMP	Plaxton Derwent II	B47F	1987	
L137	D137XVW	Bedford YMP	Plaxton Derwent II	B47F	1987	
L138	B273AMG	Leyland Tiger TRCTL11/3R	Plaxton Paramount 3200	C57F	1984	Ex Goldenport, London, 1987
L139	FCY287W	Bedford YMQ	Duple Dominant	B43F	1981	Ex South Wales, 1987
L140	FCY288W	Bedford YMQ	Duple Dominant	B43F	1981	Ex South Wales, 1987
L141	FCY289W	Bedford YMQ	Duple Dominant	B43F	1981	Ex South Wales, 1987
L146	FCY285W	Bedford YMQ	Duple Dominant	B43F	1981	Ex South Wales, 1987
L147	NCD553M	Bristol VRT/SL2/6LX	Eastern Coach Works	H43/31F	1973	Ex Southdown, 1988
L148	WPH135Y	Leyland Tiger TRCTL11/2R	East Lancs EL2000 (1993)	B55F	1982	Ex Kentish Bus, 1988
L149	E79HVX	Iveco 49.10	Carlyle Dailybus	B25F	1988	
L150	F150LTW	Leyland Lynx LX112L10ZR1	Leyland Lynx	B51F	1988	
L151	F151NPU	Leyland Swift LBM6T/2R	Wadham Stringer Vanguard II	B39F	1988	
L152	D576VBV	Freight Rover Sherpa 374	Dormobile	B16F	1987	Ex Ribble, 1988
L153	D345WPE	Ford Transit 190	Carlyle	B16F	1987	Ex Alder Valley, 1988
L154	F154RHK	Mercedes-Benz 811D	Reeve Burgess Beaver	B33F	1989	
L155	D232HMT	Leyland Tiger TRCTL11/3RZ	Van Hool Alizée H	C53F	1986	Ex Travellers, Hounslow, 1988
L156	NPU979M	Bristol VRT/SL2/6LX	Eastern Coach Works	H39/31F	1974	Ex Eastern National, 1989
L158	VOD590S	Bristol VRT/SL3/6LXB	Eastern Coach Works	H43/31F	1978	Ex South Midland, 1989
L159	TBW451P	Bristol VRT/SL3/6LXB	Eastern Coach Works	H43/31F	1978	Ex South Midland, 1989
L160	H160HJN	Leyland Olympian ONCL10/1RZA	Alexander RL	H47/32F	1990	
L161	SNJ591R	Bristol VRT/SL3/6LX	Eastern Coach Works	H43/31F	1977	Ex Brighton & Hove, 1990
L162	MOD569P	Bristol VRT/SL3/6LX	Eastern Coach Works	H43/32F	1975	Ex United, 1990
L163	MGR672P	Bristol VRT/SL3/6LX	Eastern Coach Works	H43/31F	1975	Ex United, 1990
L164	SUP685R	Bristol VRT/SL3/6LX	Eastern Coach Works	H43/31F	1976	Ex United, 1990
L165	LRA801P	Bristol VRT/SL3/501(6LX)	Eastern Coach Works	H43/34F	1975	Ex Trent, 1990
L166	MRB802P	Bristol VRT/SL3/6LX	Eastern Coach Works	H43/34F	1976	Ex Trent, 1990
L167	JWT757V	Bristol VRT/SL3/6LXB	Eastern Coach Works	H43/31F	1979	Ex Keighley & District, 1990
L168	PWY43W	Bristol VRT/SL3/6LXB	Eastern Coach Works	H43/31F	1981	Ex Keighley & District, 1990
L169	JKV414V	Bedford YMT	Plaxton Supreme IV	C53F	1979	Ex Kemp, Clacton, 1991
L170	WOO903W	Bedford YMT	Plaxton Supreme IV	C53F	1981	Ex Kemp, Clacton, 1991
L173	HHJ772Y	Bova EL26/581	Bova Europa	C53F	1983	Ex Kemp, Clacton, 1991
L174	BRY701Y	Bova EL26/581	Bova Europa	C53F	1983	Ex Kemp, Clacton, 1991
L175	A331VHB	Leyland Tiger TRCTL11/3R	Jonckheere Jubilee P50	C49FT	1983	Ex Kemp, Clacton, 1991

L178	DWU294T	Bristol VRT/SL3/6LX	Eastern Coach Works	H43/31F	1979	Ex Keighley & District, 1991
L180	UBJ847R	AEC Reliance 6U3ZR	Plaxton Supreme III	C55F	1977	Ex Norfolk, Nayland, 1991
L181	GPV212T	AEC Reliance 6U3ZR	Plaxton Supreme III Exp	C53F	1978	Ex Norfolk, Nayland, 1991
L182	BBJ568S	Seddon Pennine VII	Plaxton Supreme III Exp	DP57F	1978	Ex Norfolk, Nayland, 1991
L183	CFM345S	Leyland National 11351A/1R (Gardner)		B49F	1978	Ex Norfolk, Nayland, 1991
L184	CFM347S	Leyland National 11351A/1R (Gardner)		B49F	1978	Ex Norfolk, Nayland, 1991
L185	LMA413T	Leyland National 11351A/1R (Gardner)		B49F	1979	Ex Norfolk, Nayland, 1991
L186	CBV305S	Leyland Atlantean AN68A/2R	East Lancashire	H50/36F	1977	Ex Norfolk, Nayland, 1991
L187	CBV306S	Leyland Atlantean AN68A/2R	East Lancashire	H50/36F	1977	Ex Norfolk, Nayland, 1991
L188	CBV307S	Leyland Atlantean AN68A/2R	East Lancashire	H50/36F	1977	Ex Norfolk, Nayland, 1991
L189	CBV308S	Leyland Atlantean AN68A/2R	East Lancashire	H50/36F	1977	Ex Norfolk, Nayland, 1991
L190	CBV309S	Leyland Atlantean AN68A/2R	East Lancashire	H50/36F	1977	Ex Norfolk, Nayland, 1991
L192	A709KRT	Van Hool T815H	Van Hool Acron	C49FT	1984	Ex Norfolk, Nayland, 1991
L193	D600MVR	Leyland Tiger TRCTL11/3RZ	Plaxton Paramount 3200 III	C53F	1986	Ex Shearings, 1991
L194	JWV271W	Bristol VRT/SL3/680	Eastern Coach Works	H43/31F	1981	Ex Brighton & Hove, 1991
L195	D584MVR	Leyland Tiger TRCTL11/3RZ	Plaxton Paramount 3200 III	C53F	1986	Ex Shearings, 1992
L196	H48NDU	Leyland Lynx LX2R11C15Z4R	Leyland Lynx 2	B51F	1990	Ex Volvo demonstrator, 1992
L197	GGM108W	Bristol VRT/SL3/6LX	Eastern Coach Works	H43/31F	1980	Ex City of Oxford, 1992
L198	K198EVW	Dennis Dart 9.8SDL3017	Alexander Dash	B43F	1992	
L199	HJB464W	Bristol VRT/SL3/6LX	Eastern Coach Works	H43/31F	1980	Ex City of Oxford, 1992
L200	J295TWK	Leyland Lynx LX2R11C14Z4S	Leyland Lynx 2	B51F	1991	Ex Volvo demonstrator, 1992
L201	F781GNA	Leyland Tiger TRCTL11/3RZ	Plaxton Paramount 3200 III	C53F	1989	Ex Shearings, 1993
L202	BRC836T	Bristol VRT/SL3/6LXB	Eastern Coach Works	H43/31F	1979	Ex Trent, 1993
L203	BRC839T	Bristol VRT/SL3/6LXB	Eastern Coach Works	H43/31F	1979	Ex Trent, 1993

Livery: Cream and red; green and cream (Norfolks).

Previous Registrations:

A709KRT	A104TVW, 90NOR	GPV212T	BPV300T, 229LRB
BBJ568S	DFS805S, 759KFC	UBJ847R	OKY65R, 301XRA

The Hedingham Omnibuses fleet includes two Leyland Lynx 2s that were previously demonstrators. One of these, L196 (H48NDU), is seen in Colchester High Street having worked an Essex County Council tendered Sunday service from Saffron Walden through Haverhill and Sudbury. *G R Mills*

All four of the Eastern National Bristol LH with Eastern Coach Works passed to Hedingham Omnibuses when only five years old. One of these, L113 (UVX6S), is now based at Little Tey to work a schools contract regularly from Mount Bures to Stanway. The vehicle is seen opposite Chappel Primary School working this service. *G R Mills*

Sixteen Bristol VRTs with Eastern Coach Works bodies are in the Hedingham fleet but only one, L178 (DWU294T) is painted in green and wears Norfolks fleetnames. This vehicle normally works from Nayland, but when photographed was on short term loan to Little Tey depot. *G R Mills*

The acquisition of the very long-established Norfolks of Nayland in April 1991 introduced five high-capacity, East Lancashire-bodied Leyland Atlanteans into the Hedingham fleet. L188 (CBV307S) one of the four formerly with Blackpool, is now repainted into red and cream livery and was seen about to leave Colchester. *G R Mills*

IPSWICH BUSES

Ipswich Buses Ltd, Constantine Road, Ipswich, Suffolk, IP1 2DL

1	HDX904N	Leyland Atlantean AN68/1R	Roe			H43/29D	1975
3	HDX906N	Leyland Atlantean AN68/1R	Roe			H43/29D	1975
6	MRT6P	Leyland Atlantean AN68/1R	Roe			H43/29D	1976
7	MRT7P	Leyland Atlantean AN68/1R	Roe			H43/29D	1976
9	MRT9P	Leyland Atlantean AN68/1R	Roe			O43/26D	1976

11-35

Leyland Atlantean AN68A/1R Roe H43/29D* 1976-77 *11 is H43/26D

11	RDX11R	16	RDX16R	21	SDX21R	26	SDX26R	31	SDX31R
12	RDX12R	17	RDX17R	22	SDX22R	27	SDX27R	32	SDX32R
13	RDX13R	18	RDX18R	23	SDX23R	28	SDX28R	33	SDX33R
14	RDX14R	19	RDX19R	24	SDX24R	29	SDX29R	34	SDX34R
15	RDX15R	20	RDX20R	25	SDX25R	30	SDX30R	35	SDX35R

63	ADX63B	AEC Regent V 2D2RA	Massey	H37/28R	1964
81	F81ODX	Dennis Dominator DDA907	East Lancashire	H45/26D	1988
82	B82NDX	Dennis Dominator DDA907	East Lancashire	H43/27D	1985

100-105

Dennis Falcon HC SDA406 East Lancashire B44D 1983

100	YDX100Y	101	YDX101Y	103	YDX103Y	104	YDX104Y	105	YDX105Y

106	C106SDX	Dennis Falcon HC SDA416	East Lancashire	B44D	1985

107-113

Dennis Falcon HC SDA416 Northern Counties B45D 1985-86

107	C107SDX	109	C109SDX	111	C111SDX	112	C112SDX	113	C113SDX
108	C108SDX	110	C110SDX						

114-124

Dennis Falcon HC SDA419* East Lancashire B44D 1988-89 *118-24 are SDA420

114	E114KDX	117	E117KDX	119	G119VDX	121	G121VDX	123	G123VDX
115	E115KDX	118	G118VDX	120	G120VDX	122	G122VDX	124	G124VDX
116	E116KDX								

140	TWJ340Y	Dennis Falcon HC SDA410	East Lancashire	B52F	1983	Ex Chesterfield, 1990
141	TWJ341Y	Dennis Falcon HC SDA410	East Lancashire	B52F	1983	Ex Chesterfield, 1990
142	TWJ342Y	Dennis Falcon HC SDA410	East Lancashire	B52F	1983	Ex Chesterfield, 1990
143	TWJ343Y	Dennis Falcon HC SDA410	East Lancashire	B52F	1983	Ex Chesterfield, 1990

The only four Bristol B21 models supplied new to an English operator were bodied in 1985 by Alexander for Ipswich. No.145 (B115LDX), named *Great Eastern*, shows the dual entrance configuration to the full in this view at Colchester bus station. *G R Mills*

144	B114LDX	Bristol B21	Alexander N	B49D	1985	
145	B115LDX	Bristol B21	Alexander N	B49D	1985	
146	B116LDX	Bristol B21	Alexander N	B47D	1985	
147	B117LDX	Bristol B21	Alexander N	B47D	1985	
148	WOI607	Bristol B21	Alexander N	B44D	1985	Ex Belfast Citybus, 1991
149	WOI3001	Bristol B21	Alexander N	B53F	1980	Ex Ulsterbus, 1991
150	XRT931X	Bristol B21	Alexander N	B53F	1981	Ex Ulsterbus, 1991
151	WOI3002	Bristol B21	Alexander N	B53F	1982	Ex Ulsterbus, 1991
152	XRT932X	Bristol B21	Alexander N	B53F	1982	Ex Ulsterbus, 1991
153	XRT947X	Bristol B21	Alexander N	B53F	1982	Ex Ulsterbus, 1991
160	J160LPV	Dennis Lance 11SDA3101	East Lancashire	B45D	1992	
161	L161	Dennis Lance SDA4..	East Lancashire	B F	On Order	
162	L162	Dennis Lance SDA4..	East Lancashire	B F	On Order	
163	L163	Dennis Lance SDA4..	East Lancashire	B F	On Order	
170	TBB283S	Bedford YMT	Plaxton Supreme III	C53F	1978	Ex ??
180	H180HPV	DAF SB220LC550	Optare Delta	B45D	1991	
181	L181	DAF SB220LC550	Optare Delta	B45D	On Order	
182	L182	DAF SB220LC550	Optare Delta	B45D	On Order	
207	E207GPV	Renault-Dodge S56	Northern Counties	B20F	1988	
208	E208GPV	Renault-Dodge S56	Northern Counties	B20F	1988	
218	J218NRT	Optare MetroRider	Optare	DP31F	1992	
219	K219PPV	Optare MetroRider	Optare	DP31F	1992	
220	F220PPV	MCW MetroRider MF155	MCW	DP31F	1989	

221-228

	Optare MetroRider	Optare	B23F	1990-91	

221	G221VDX	223	G223VDX	225	H225EDX	227	H227EDX	228	J228JDX
222	G222VDX	224	G224VDX	226	H226EDX				

Livery: Green and cream

Previous Registrations:

XRT931X	WOI3005		
		XRT932X	WOI3003
		XRT947X	WOI3004

Named vehicles:

1 Cambria; 3 Cedric; 6 Dannebrog; 7 Dauntless; 9 Eastern Belle; 11 Evening Star; 12 Gladys; 13 Glenway; 14 Ironsides; 15 Kimberley; 16 Majestic; 17 Medina; 18 Memory; 19 Mimosa; 20 Northdown; 21 Orion; 22 Perseus; 23 Phoenician; 24 Pride of Ipswich; 25 Reminder; 26 Reporter; 27 Saxon; 28 Spinaway C; 29 Sunbeam; 30 Thalatta; 31 Tollesbury; 32 Triton; 33 Vanguard; 34 Veronica; 35 Xylonite; 63 Cliff Quay 1949-1985; 81 British Oak; 82 Margaret Catchpole; 101 Agincourt; 102 Alaric; 103 Albion; 104 Alma; 105 Anglia; 106 Ardwina; 107 Beric; 108 Centaur; 109 Cygnet; 110 Ena; 111 Kindly Light; 112 Leading Light; 113 Mystery; 114 Avocet; 115 Eldred Wattains; 116 Excelsior; 117 Felix; 118 Lady Daphne; 119 Lady Jean; 120 Marjorie; 121 Nautilus; 122 Orinoco; 123 Pudge; 124 Venture; 140 Amonite; 141 Emily; 142 Ethel Ada; 143 Haste Away; 144 Great Western; 145 Great Eastern; 146 Godspeed; 147 Bristolian; 148 Maid of Connaught; 149 Hibernia; 150 Shamrock; 151 Esmeralda; 152 Kathleen; 153 Muriel; 160 Barbara Jean; 180 New Spirit of Ipswich; 207 Ganymede; 208 Io; 218 Apollo; 219 Thisbe; 220 Hyperion; 221 Dione; 222 Mimas; 223 Rhea; 224 Tethys; 225 Eros; 226 Pallas; 227 Vesta; 228 Icarus

The latest addition to the Ipswich fleet is an aditional Optare Metrorider. Similar to one delivered earlier in the year. Numbered 219 (K219PPV) it has gained the now familiar names associated with the Ipswich fleet. In this case Thisbe.

G R Mills

Ipswich have two examples of East Lancashire-bodied Dennis Dominators in the fleet, each dual-door, yet each with contrasting designs from this supplier. *Above* is the newer, 1988 example, while *below* is that built in 1985. The treatment of the entrance, seen here, resembles the idea of the Walsall and SHMD Fleetlines built by Northern Counties many years earlier. *Ivor Norman*

A unique vehicle in the Ipswich fleet is 160 (J160LPV) the solitary Dennis Lance which joined 29 Falcons from the same manufacturer already in service. *Barbara Jean*, as the bus is named, is seen working in the town centre during 1992. *Ivor Norman*

The first Optare Delta in the Ipswich fleet, 180 (H180HPV), has been favourabley received by staff and passengers alike. Named *New Spirit of Ipswich* it is seen unloading passengers in Tower Ramparts before making a return trip to the large Chantry Estate. *G R Mills*

J B S

John Brown Services, 75 Putnoe Street, Bedford, MK41 8JB

The depot is at Lodge Farm, Blunham.

RVF37R	Bristol VRT/SL3/6LXB	Eastern Coach Works	H43/31F	1977	Ex Great Yarmouth, 1991
URF666S	Bristol VRT/SL3/501	Eastern Coach Works	H43/31F	1978	Ex PMT, 1992
URF670S	Bristol VRT/SL3/501	Eastern Coach Works	H43/31F	1978	Ex PMT, 1992
VHB672S	Bristol VRT/SL3/6LXB	Eastern Coach Works	H43/31F	1978	Ex National Welsh, 1992
8552PE	Volvo B58-61	Plaxton Supreme IV	C53F	1980	Ex Marshall, Leighton Buzzard, 1992
PIJ2984	Mercedes-Benz L608D	Reeve Burgess	DP25F	1982	Ex Lewis, Cwmaman, 1993
TXI2440	DAF MB200DKTL600	Caetano Algarve	C53F	1983	Ex Simpson, Rosehearty, 1992

Livery :   Blue

Previous Registrations:

8552PE	UNP784V		PIJ2984	KGS725Y		TXI2440	UTN951Y

JACKSONS

M J Jackson, Bicknacre House, Leighams Road, Bicknacre,
Essex, CM3 4NF

1	UTR705	Leyland Leopard PSU5C/4R	Duple Dominant IV	C50F	1982	Ex Boon, Boreham, 1987
2	MJI3376	Bova EL26/581	Bova Europa	C50F	1982	Ex Harris, Grays, 1990
3	2786RU	Bedford YNT	Plaxton Supreme V	C40FT	1982	Ex County, Brentwood, 1990
4	MJI2374	Aüwaerter Neoplan N122/3	Aüwaerter Skyliner	CH47/11CT	1986	Ex Thorn, Rayleigh, 1992
5	BDZ5198	DAF SB2300DHS585	Plaxton Paramount 3200 II	C49FT	1982	Ex Angel, Edmonton, 1991
6	223ASV	Bova EL26/581	Bova Europa	C52F	1982	Ex Taylor, Derby, 1992
7	F303RMH	Mercedes-Benz L307D	Reeve Burgess	M12	1988	
8	F67NLH	Mercedes-Benz L407D	Coachcraft	M15	1988	
9	F626SAY	Toyota Coaster HB31R	Caetano Optimo	C21F	1989	Ex Brentwood Coaches, 1991
10	D202NON	Freight Rover Sherpa 365	Carlyle	B18F	1986	Ex Ribble, 1992

Livery: Cream, purple and yellow

Previous Registrations:

223ASV	SMY622X	MJI2374	28903PK
2786RU	YPR747Y	MJI3376	8947FH,AOO101X
BDZ5198	C335UFP	UTR705	SHD330X

A measure of the considerable increase in the Jacksons business can be gauged by the latest intake into the fleet. This contrasts sharply with the 11-seaters that pioneered the firms entry into the psv world thirty years ago. No.4 (MJI2374), a comparative giant, is a 78-seat Neoplan seen in Hylands Park, Chelmsford. *G R Mills*

LAMBERTS

Lamberts Coaches (Beccles) Ltd, Unit 7, Ellough Ind Est, Beccles,
Suffolk, NR34 7TD

FIL2297	Bedford YMT	Plaxton Supreme III	C53F	1977	Ex Easey, March, 1987
VNT7S	Bedford YMT	Duple Dominant II	C53F	1977	Ex Nadder Valley, Tisbury, 1991
CHK571T	Bedford YMT	Duple Dominant II	C53F	1978	Ex Crusader, Clacton, 1982
XCT474T	Bedford YMT	Duple Dominant II	C53F	1978	Ex Grayscroft, Mablethorpe, 1991
YPB824T	Bedford YMT	Duple Dominant II	C53F	1978	Ex Farnham, Wrecclesham, 1980
BFL503V	Bedford YMT	Plaxton Supreme IV	C53F	1979	Ex Matthews, Shouldham, 1980
FIL2296	Bedford YMT	Plaxton Supreme IV	C53F	1980	Ex Tate, Potten End, 1986
LJR284X	Bedford YMT	Duple Dominant	C53F	1981	Ex Dunthorne, Wells, 1992
TVN330X	Bedford YNT	Plaxton Supreme VI	C53F	1982	Ex Cropper, Leeds, 1992
SIB4671	Aüwaerter Neoplan N122/3	Aüwaerter Skyliner	CH57/20CT	1982	Ex Trathens, Plymouth, 1992
FIL2294	DAF SB2300DHS585	Berkhof Esprite 350	C53F	1983	Ex Crusader, Clacton, 1987
MIW3853	DAF MB200DKTL600	Duple Caribbean	C53FT	1984	Ex Whippet, Fenstanton, 1991

Livery: White and two-tone blue

Previous Registrations:

FIL2294	JVW159Y	SIB4671	OES628Y
FIL2296	MWU186V	MIW3853	A806REW
FIL2297	TVS238R, 8753ET, SEL121R		

Lamberts Bedfords perform a variety of duties including stage services, school contracts and private hire work.
LJR284X, seen returning to Beccles on service 523, has a Duple Dominant III body originally supplied to A Line Coches
of Felling, Tyne and Wear. *G R Mills*

LUCKYBUS

Lucketts of Watford, 15 King Street, Watford, Hertfordshire, WD1 8BY

	GKE504L	Leyland National 1151/1R/0102		B49F	1973	Ex Busbus, Hemel Hempstead, 1992
	KJD541P	Leyland National 10351A/2R		B36D	1976	Ex London Buses, 1992
	BYW368V	Leyland National 10351A/2R		B36D	1979	Ex London Buses, 1991
B930	B930KWM	Quest 80B	Locomotors	B23F	1985	Ex Ward, Watford, 1990
D203	D203RGH	Volkswagen LT55	Optare City Pacer	DP25F	1987	Ex Ward, Watford, 1990
D525	C525EWR	Volkswagen LT55	Optare City Pacer	B25F	1986	Ex Ward, Watford, 1990
D989	D989JYG	Volkswagen LT55	Optare City Pacer	DP20F	1986	Ex Ward, Watford, 1990

Livery: Grey, blue and red

Lucketts of Watford operates a small fleet of midi-buses in a distinctive grey, blue and red livery under the Luckybus name. D989JYG, one of a trio of Optare City Pacers, is seen at Watford Junction bound for Hemel Hempstead. *Colin Lloyd*

The Eastern Bus Handbook

LUTON & DISTRICT

Luton & District Transport Ltd, Castle Street, Luton, Bedfordshire, LU1 3AJ

Depots are located at: Aylesbury, Dunstable, Hemel Hempstead, High Wycombe, Hitchin, Luton, Stevenage, Watford.

AN165	XPG165T		Leyland Atlantean AN68A/1R	Park Royal		H43/30F	1978	Ex London Country NW, 1991
AN195	XPG195T		Leyland Atlantean AN68A/1R	Roe		H43/30F	1979	Ex London Country NW, 1991

AN233-243			Leyland Atlantean AN68B/1R	Roe		H43/30F	1980	Ex London Country NW, 1991
233	JPE233V	**236**	JPE236V	**239**	KPJ239W	**242**	KPJ242W	**243** KPJ243W
234	JPE234V	**237**	JPE237V	**241**	KPJ241W			

BTL47	C147SPB		Leyland Tiger TRCTL11/3R	Berkhof Everest 370		C53F	1986	Ex London Country NW, 1991
BTL48	C148SPB		Leyland Tiger TRCTL11/3R	Berkhof Everest 370		C53F	1986	Ex London Country NW, 1991
BTL49	C149SPB		Leyland Tiger TRCTL11/3R	Berkhof Everest 370		C53F	1986	Ex London Country NW, 1991

DC1-8			Dennis Dart 9.8SDL3004	Carlyle Dartline		B40F*	1990	Ex London Country NW, 1991 *DC8 is DP36F
1	H922LOX	**3**	H925LOX	**5**	H242MUK	**7**	H244MUK	**8** H245MUK
2	H923LOX	**4**	H926LOX	**6**	H243MUK			

LD1	NJF204W		Bedford YMQ	Plaxton Supreme IV		C45F	1980	Ex London Country NW, 1991
LNB69	NPD169L		Leyland National 1151/1R/0402			DP21DL	1973	Ex London Country NW, 1991

LR49-55			Leyland Olympian ONTL11/1R	Roe		H43/29F	1984	Ex London Country NW, 1991
49	A149FPG	**52**	A152FPG	**53**	A153FPG	**54**	A154FPG	**55** A155FPG
51	A151FPG							

LR70	B270LPH		Leyland Olympian ONTL11/1R	Eastern Coach Works		H43/29F	1985	Ex London Country NW, 1991
LR71	B271LPH		Leyland Olympian ONTL11/1R	Eastern Coach Works		H43/29F	1985	Ex London Country NW, 1991
LR72	B272LPH		Leyland Olympian ONTL11/1R	Eastern Coach Works		H43/29F	1985	Ex London Country NW, 1991
LR73	B273LPH		Leyland Olympian ONTL11/1R	Eastern Coach Works		H43/29F	1985	Ex London Country NW, 1991

Originally ordered by London County North West to work in Harrow the eight Dennis Darts with Carlyle bodies were delivered to LCNW in green and grey with Watfordwide names, as shown by DC2 (H923LOX) at Watford Junction.
Colin Lloyd

LR81-95

Leyland Olympian ONCL10/1RZ Leyland | | | | | | H47/31F | 1989-90 Ex London Country NW, 1991 | |

81	G281UMJ	**84**	G284UMJ	**87**	G287UMJ	**90**	G290UMJ	**93**	G293UMJ
82	G282UMJ	**85**	G285UMJ	**88**	G288UMJ	**91**	G291UMJ	**94**	G294UMJ
83	G283UMJ	**86**	G286UMJ	**89**	G289UMJ	**92**	G292UMJ	**95**	G295UMJ

LR96-102

Leyland Olympian ON2R50C13Z4 Leyland   H47/29F   1991   Ex London Country NW, 1991

96	H196GRO	**98**	H198GRO	**100**	H201GRO	**101**	H202GRO	**102**	H203GRO
97	H197GRO	**99**	H199GRO						

LRL29	G129YEV	Leyland Olympian ONCL10/2RZ Northern Counties	H49/34F	1989	Ex London Country NW, 1991
LRL30	G130YEV	Leyland Olympian ONCL10/2RZ Northern Counties	H49/34F	1989	Ex London Country NW, 1991
LRL31	G131YWC	Leyland Olympian ONCL10/2RZ Northern Counties	H49/34F	1989	Ex Ensign, Purfleet, 1991
LRL32	G132YWC	Leyland Olympian ONCL10/2RZ Northern Counties	H49/34F	1989	Ex London Country NW, 1991

Luton and District continues to use the former London County North West livery and fleet numbering system as shown by LR55 (A155FPG) wearing Watfordwide fleetnames working an LRT tendered service into Watford Junction. Visible is a discrete operator's name below the drivers windscreen.
G R Mills

Four Leyland Olympian with Northern Counties bodywork were initially supplied to Ensignbus as stock vehicles. Thses were ousted within two years by similar vehicles built to Capital Citybus specification. One of the four is now LRL29 (G129YEV), seen in Parliament Square while working a private hire through London.
Colin Lloyd

MBI52-63

	Iveco Daily 49.10	Robin Hood City Nippy	B21F	1987	Ex London Country NW, 1991

52	D495RNM	55	D498RNM	58	D21RPP	60	D472RVS	62	D25RPP
53	D496RNM	56	D499RNM	59	D473RVS	61	D26RPP	63	D23RPP
54	D497RNM	57	D500RNM						

MCW1-32

	MCW MetroRider MF150/81*	MCW	B23F	1988	Ex London Country NW, 1991

*MCW19-30 are MF150/83; MCW31/2 are MF150/72

1	E971DNK	7	E977DNK	15	E985DNK	21	E991DNK	27	E997DNK
2	E972DNK	8	E978DNK	16	E986DNK	22	E992DNK	28	E998DNK
3	E973DNK	9	E979DNK	17	E987DNK	23	E993DNK	29	E999DNK
4	E974DNK	10	E980DNK	18	E988DNK	24	E994DNK	30	E731DNM
5	E975DNK	11	E981DNK	19	E989DNK	25	E995DNK	31	E478CNM
6	E976DNK	14	E984DNK	20	E990DNK	26	E996DNK	32	E479CNM

NTL2	SMY630X	Leyland Tiger TRCTL11/3R	Plaxton Supreme V	C53F	1982	Ex London Country NW, 1991
NTL5	SMY633X	Leyland Tiger TRCTL11/3R	Plaxton Supreme V	C53F	1982	Ex London Country NW, 1991

SN233-370

	Leyland National 10351A/1R	B41F	1976-78	Ex London Country NW, 1991

233w	NPK233R	305	UPB305S	336	UPB336S	346	UPB346S	360	YPF760T
237	NPK237R	311	UPB311S	342	UPB342S	347	UPB347S	368	YPF768T
300	UPB300S	328	UPB328S	343	UPB343S	350	UPB350S	370	YPF770T

SN396-458

	Leyland National 10351B/1R	B41F	1978-79	Ex London Country NW, 1991

396	YPL396T	410	YPL410T	426	YPL426T	441	YPL441T	453	YPL453T
397	YPL397T	415	YPL415T	430	YPL430T	446	YPL446T	454	YPL454T
398	YPL398T	417	YPL417T	434	YPL434T	447	YPL447T	455	YPL455T
404	YPL404T	418	YPL418T	436	YPL436T	448	YPL448T	456	YPL456T
405	YPL405T	421	YPL421T	437	YPL437T	449	YPL449T	457	YPL457T
408	YPL408T	424	YPL424T	438	YPL438T	451	YPL451T	458	YPL458T
409	YPL409T								

SN460-523

	Leyland National 10351B/1R	B41F*	1979	Ex London Country NW, 1991

*514/5 are DP41F

460	BPL460T	465	BPL465T	470	BPL470T	501	DPH501T	515	EPD515V
461	BPL461T	466	BPL466T	471	BPL471T	505	EPD505V	516	EPD516V
462	BPL462T	467	BPL467T	472	BPL472T	506	EPD506V	517	EPD517V
463	BPL463T	468	BPL468T	473	BPL473T	512	EPD512V	521	EPD521V
464	BPL464T	469	BPL469T	500	DPH500T	514	EPD514V	523	EPD523V

TDL57	C257SPC	Leyland Tiger TRCTL11/3R	Duple 320	C53F	1986	Ex London Country NW, 1991
TP13	A113EPA	Leyland Tiger TRCTL11/2R	Plaxton Paramount 3200	C53F	1983	Ex London Country NW, 1991
TP15	A115EPA	Leyland Tiger TRCTL11/2R	Plaxton Paramount 3200	C53F	1983	Ex London Country NW, 1991
TP21	A121EPA	Leyland Tiger TRCTL11/2R	Plaxton Paramount 3200	C53F	1983	Ex London Country NW, 1991
TP36	A136EPA	Leyland Tiger TRCTL11/2R	Plaxton Paramount 3200	C53F	1984	Ex London Country NW, 1991
TPL50	A150EPA	Leyland Tiger TRCTL11/2R	Plaxton Paramount 3200	C51F	1984	Ex London Country SW, 1989

TPL51-57

	Leyland Tiger TRCTL11/3R	Plaxton Paramount 3200	C57F	1984	Ex London Country NW, 1991

51	A151EPA	52	A152EPA	53	A153EPA	55	A155EPA	57	A157EPA

TPL84	B284KPF	Leyland Tiger TRCTL11/3R	Plaxton Paramount 3200 II	C53F	1985	Ex London Country NW, 1991
TPL92	B292KPF	Leyland Tiger TRCTL11/3R	Plaxton Paramount 3200 II	C51F	1985	Ex London Country NW, 1991
TPL93	B293KPF	Leyland Tiger TRCTL11/3R	Plaxton Paramount 3200 II	C51F	1985	Ex London Country NW, 1991
TPL98	E323OMG	Leyland Tiger TRCTL11/3R	Plaxton Paramount 3200 III	C53F	1988	Ex London Country NW, 1991
VR718	LFE23P	Bristol VRT/SL3/6LXB	Eastern Coach Works	H43/34F	1975	Ex Lincoln, 1992
VR719	RFE29R	Bristol VRT/SL3/6LXB	Eastern Coach Works	H43/34F	1976	Ex Lincoln, 1992
VR720	EFE33T	Bristol VRT/SL3/6LXB	East Lancashire	H45/32F	1979	Ex Lincoln, 1992
VR721	EFE34T	Bristol VRT/SL3/6LXB	East Lancashire	H45/32F	1979	Ex Lincoln, 1992
VR722	OSR201R	Bristol VRT/LL3/6LXB	Alexander AL	H49/36F	1977	Ex Lincoln, 1992
VR723	LFE24P	Bristol VRT/SL3/6LXB	Eastern Coach Works	H43/34F	1975	Ex Lincoln, 1992
VR724	RFE26R	Bristol VRT/SL3/6LXB	Eastern Coach Works	H43/34F	1976	Ex Lincoln, 1992
VR725	OSR189R	Bristol VRT/LL3/6LXB	Alexander AL	H49/36F	1977	Ex Lincoln, 1992
VR726	OSR200R	Bristol VRT/LL3/6LXB	Alexander AL	H49/36F	1977	Ex Lincoln, 1992
VR727	OSR202R	Bristol VRT/LL3/6LXB	Alexander AL	H49/36F	1977	Ex Lincoln, 1992
VR728	OSR198R	Bristol VRT/LL3/6LXB	Alexander AL	H49/36F	1977	Ex Lincoln, 1992

The first substantial midibus delivery to London Country North West was of thirty MCW Metroriders in 1988. These were obtained to work on a scheme at Hemel Hempstead. Several, like MCW11 (E981DNK), have subsequently moved away like this example with Watfordwide fleetnames at Watford Junction. *Colin Lloyd*

The Leyland National is still the principal single decker in the Luton & District fleet. A typical former London Country (North West) example is SNB404 (YPL404T), seen outside The Marlowes shopping centre in Hemel Hempstead. *G R Mills*

Lincoln had Bristol VRTs with three different body makes and samples of each have passed to Luton & District. VR721 (EFE34T) has an East Lancashire body and is seen in Watford. *David Savage*

Also from Lincoln City came five Bristol VRTs with Alexander bodywork, new to the Tayside fleet. VR726 (OSR200R) seen at Watford Junction is part of the fleet currently allocated to Garston. *G R Mills*

At one time the largest Leyland Tiger fleet in the country was that operated by London Country on its Green Line services. Sinvce then the original company has been divided and followed by further reorganisations. TP36 (A136EPA) has survived in Green Line livery but in the changes has lost all identity, as shown in Buckingham Palace Road bound for London Victoria. *Colin Lloyd*

Seen here in Lee & District livery is F336SMD, a Leyland Tiger with Van Hool Alizée body, originally numbered VTL1 it is now 200. Since being photographed it has had a change of livery, fleet number and index mark. *G R Mills*

1-5   Renault-Dodge S56   Reeve Burgess   B25F   1986   Ex London Country NW, 1989

1	D861NVS	2	D862NVS	3	D863NVS	4	D864NVS	5	D865NVS

6-14   Mercedes-Benz 709D   Reeve Burgess Beaver   B25F   1988-90   6-11 ex Kentish Bus, 1991
    12-14 ex Argyll Bus & Coach, 1992

6	F121TRU	8	F123TRU	10	F125TRU	12	J917HGD	14	F598CET
7	F122TRU	9	F124TRU	11	F128TRU	13	H848AUS		

15	E485CNM	MCW MetroRider MF150/72	MCW	B23F	1987	Ex Sovereign, 1990
16	E486CNM	MCW MetroRider MF150/74	MCW	B23F	1987	Ex Sovereign, 1990
17	E484CNM	MCW MetroRider MF150/72	MCW	B23F	1987	Ex Sovereign, 1990

21-35   Ford Transit 190D   Carlyle   B16F   1985-86   21-7 ex United Counties, 1986

21	C21NVV	24	C24NVV	27	B27HRP	32	C196KBH	34	C198KBH
22	C22NVV	25	C25NVV	28	C192KBH	33	C197KBH	35	C199KBH
23	C23NVV	26	C26NVV	31	C195KBH				

36-42   Iveco Daily 49.10   Robin Hood City Nippy   B19F   1986

36	D753MUR	38	D755MUR	40	D757MUR	41	D758MUR	42	D759MUR
37	D754MUR	39	D756MUR						

43	E454TYG	Iveco Daily 49.10	Robin Hood City Nippy	B23F	1988	Ex Harrogate & District, 1992

44-55   Iveco Daily 49.10   Robin Hood City Nippy   B19F   1986

44	D761MUR	47	D764MUR	49	D766MUR	51	D768MUR	53	D770MUR
45	D762MUR	48	D765MUR	50	D767MUR	52	D769MUR	55	D772MUR
46	D763MUR								

60-78   Iveco Daily 49.10   Dormobile   B25F*   1988   *77/8 are DP25F

60	E338DRO	64	E337DRO	68	E333DRO	72	E343DRO	76	E347DRO
61	E339DRO	65	E336DRO	69	E335DRO	73	E344DRO	77	E348DRO
62	E340DRO	66	E331DRO	70	E341DRO	74	E345DRO	78	E349DRO
63	E334DRO	67	E332DRO	71	E342DRO	75	E346DRO		

79-87   Peugeot-Talbot Pullman   Talbot   B20F   1987   Ex Stagecoach, 1992

79	D79RVM	81	D81RVM	83	D78RVM	85	E737UNA	87	E509UNE
80	D80RVM	82	D82RVM	84	E717UNA	86	D86RVM		

88-96   Freight Rover Sherpa 374   Carlyle   B18F*   1987   *95/6 are DP18F

88	D403SGS	90w	D405SGS	92	D407SGS	94	D409SGS	96	D411SGS
89	D404SGS	91	D406SGS	93	D408SGS	95	D410SGS		

97	E727UNA	Peugeot-Talbot Pullman	Talbot	B20F	1987	Ex Stagecoach, 1992

98-105   Iveco Daily 49.10   Robin Hood   B21F   1986   Ex London Buses, 1993

98	C508DYM	100	C506DYM	102	C502DYM	104	C504DYM	105	TC515DYM
99	C509DYM	101	D519FYL	103	C503DYM				

109-113   •   Leyland Tiger TRCTL11/3RZ   Plaxton Paramount 3200 III   C53F   1988

109	E881YKY	110	E882YKY	111	E661AWJ	112	E662AWJ	113	E663AWJ

115	B282KPF	Leyland Tiger TRCTL11/3R	Plaxton Paramount 3200 II	C53F	1985	Ex Sovereign, 1990
116	B269KPF	Leyland Tiger TRCTL11/2R	Plaxton Paramount 3200 II	C49F	1985	Ex Sovereign, 1990

117-122   Leyland Tiger TRCTL11/3RH   Duple 320   C53F   1986   Ex Sovereign, 1990

117	C247SPC	118	C248SPC	119	C249SPC	120	C250SPC	122	C252SPC

128	A101EPA	Leyland Tiger TRCTL11/2R	Plaxton Paramount 3200	C53F	1983	Ex London Country NW, 1991
129	A102EPA	Leyland Tiger TRCTL11/2R	Plaxton Paramount 3200	C53F	1983	Ex London Country NW, 1991
132	B291KPF	Leyland Tiger TRCTL11/3R	Plaxton Paramount 3200 II	C51F	1984	Ex London Country NW, 1991
133	A145EPA	Leyland Tiger TRCTL11/3R	Plaxton Paramount 3200	C51F	1984	Ex London Country NW, 1991
143	A143EPA	Leyland Tiger TRCTL11/3R	Plaxton Paramount 3200	C51F	1984	Ex London Country NW, 1991
147	A147EPA	Leyland Tiger TRCTL11/3R	Plaxton Paramount 3200	C51F	1984	Ex London Country NW, 1991

200	SIB8528	Leyland Tiger TRCL10/3ARZA	Van Hool Alizée	C49FT	1989	Ex London Country NW, 1991
201	SIB8529	Leyland Tiger TRCL10/3ARZA	Plaxton Paramount 3200 III	C53F	1988	Ex London Country NW, 1991
202	SIB7480	Leyland Tiger TRCL10/3ARZA	Plaxton Paramount 3200 III	C53F	1988	Ex London Country NW, 1991
203	SIB7481	Leyland Tiger TRCL10/3ARZA	Plaxton Paramount 3500 III	C51FT	1988	Ex London Country NW, 1991
204	SIB4846	Leyland Tiger TRCL10/3ARZA	Plaxton Paramount 3200 III	C53F	1988	Ex London Country NW, 1991
205	SIB7689	Leyland Tiger TRCTL11/3RH	Duple 320	C53F	1986	Ex London Country NW, 1991
206	UMS394	Bova FHD12.280	Bova Futura	C49FT	1983	Ex London Country NW, 1991
207	SIB8583	Leyland Tiger TRCTL11/3R	Plaxton Paramount 3200	C51F	1983	Ex London Country NW, 1991
208	SIB9492	Leyland Tiger TRCTL11/3R	Plaxton Paramount 3200	C51F	1983	Ex London Country NW, 1991
209	HSV781	Bova EL26/581	Bova Europa	C53F	1983	Ex London Country NW, 1991
225	LFE25P	Bristol VRT/SL3/6LXB	Eastern Coach Works	H43/34F	1975	Ex Lincoln, 1992
227	RFE27R	Bristol VRT/SL3/6LXB	Eastern Coach Works	H43/34F	1976	Ex Lincoln, 1992
228	RFE28R	Bristol VRT/SL3/6LXB	Eastern Coach Works	H43/34F	1976	Ex Lincoln, 1992
230	RFE30R	Bristol VRT/SL3/6LXB	Eastern Coach Works	H43/34F	1976	Ex Lincoln, 1992
231	EFE31T	Bristol VRT/SL3/6LXB	East Lancashire	H45/32F	1979	Ex Lincoln, 1992
300	F300MNK	Leyland Swift LBM6T/2RA	Wadham Stringer Vanguard II	B35F	1989	
301	F301MNK	Leyland Swift LBM6T/2RA	Wadham Stringer Vanguard II	B35F	1989	
302	F302MNK	Leyland Swift LBM6T/2RA	Wadham Stringer Vanguard II	B35F	1989	
303	F303MNK	Leyland Swift LBM6T/2RA	Wadham Stringer Vanguard II	B35F	1989	
304	G97VMM	Leyland Swift LBM6T/2RS	Wadham Stringer Vanguard II	B35F	1989	Ex London Country NW, 1990

The four Leyland Swifts that were supplied new to Luton & District were initially based at Hitchin. 300 (F300MNK) is seen with a tempory blank patch on the side panels where it formerly had Hitchin Bus lettering. *Colin Lloyd*

400-404

Leyland Lynx LX112L10ZR1R — Leyland Lynx — B51F — 1989

400	F400PUR	**401**	F401PUR	**402**	F402PUR	**403**	F403PUR	**404**	F404PUR

405	D603ACW	Leyland Lynx LX112L10ZR1R	Leyland Lynx	B51F	1987	Ex Sovereign, 1990
406	E970NMK	Leyland Lynx LX112TL11ZR1S	Leyland Lynx	B49F	1987	Ex Sovereign, 1990
407	H407ERO	Leyland Lynx LX2R11C15Z4S	Leyland Lynx	DP29F	1990	
408	H408ERO	Leyland Lynx LX2R11C15Z4S	Leyland Lynx	DP29F	1990	
409	H409ERO	Leyland Lynx LX2R11C15Z4S	Leyland Lynx	DP29F	1990	
410	H410ERO	Leyland Lynx LX2R11C15Z4S	Leyland Lynx	DP29F	1990	

416-441

Leyland National 10351A/1R — B41F — 1975-77 Ex Sovereign, 1990

416	UPB316S	**421**	UPB321S	**424**	UPB324S	**437**	UPB337S	**441**	UPB341S
419	SPC269R	**423**	UPB323S						

454	NBD454M	Leyland National 1151/1R/0401		B49F	1973	Ex United Counties, 1986
LN461	ORP461M	Leyland National 1151/1R/0401		B49F	1973	Ex Milton Keynes City Bus, 1987
464	YPF764T	Leyland National 10351A/1R		B41F	1978	Ex Sovereign, 1990
466	RYG766R	Leyland National 11351A/1R		B52F	1977	Ex Sovereign, 1990
467	ORP467M	Leyland National 1151/1R/0401		B49F	1974	Ex United Counties, 1986
LN468	ORP468M	Leyland National 1151/1R/0401		B49F	1974	Ex Milton Keynes City Bus, 1986
469w	YPF769T	Leyland National 10351A/1R		B41F	1978	Ex Sovereign, 1990
470w	ORP470M	Leyland National 1151/1R/0401		B49F	1974	Ex Milton Keynes City Bus, 1986
471	YPF771T	Leyland National 10351A/1R		B41F	1978	Ex Sovereign, 1990

480-513

Leyland National 11351/1R — B49F — 1974-75

480	RNV480N	**487**	GNV654N	**491**	GNV658N	**495**	GNV662N	**509**	KNV509P
481	RNV481N	**488**	GNV655N	**492**	GNV659N	**LN498**	GVV889N	**511**	KNV511P
485	RNV485N	**489**	GNV656N	**LN493**	GNV660N	**508**	KNV508P	**513**	KNV513P
486	GNV653N								

518-579

Leyland National 11351A/1R — B49F — 1976-79 *548/9 are DP47F
Ex United Counties, 1986; *531/54/70/2/3 ex Milton Keynes City Bus, 1987

518	OVV518R	**533**	VRP533S	**548**	BVV548T	**560**	KRP560V	**572**	MNH572V
519	OVV519R	**537**	XVV537S	**549w**	ERP549T	**563**	KRP563V	**573**	MNH573V
522	SBD522R	**538**	XVV538S	**550**	ERP550T	**565**	KRP565V	**574**	MNH574V
523	SBD523R	**539**	XVV539S	**554w**	ERP554T	**566**	KRP566V	**577**	MNH577V
524	SBD524R	**542**	BVV542T	**556**	ERP556T	**569**	MNH569V	**578**	MNH578V
531	VRP531S	**545**	BVV545T	**557**	ERP557T	**570**	MNH570V	**579**	MNH579V
532w	VRP532S	**547**	BVV547T						

581	NRP581V	Leyland National 2 NL116L11/1R	B49F	1980
588	SVV588W	Leyland National 2 NL116L11/1R	B49F	1980

612-620

Leyland Olympian ONLXB/1R — Eastern Coach Works — H45/32F — 1981-82 Ex United Counties, 1986

612	ARP612X	**614**	ARP614X	**616**	ARP616X	**618**	ARP618X	**620**	ARP620X
613	ARP613X	**615**	ARP615X	**617**	ARP617X	**619**	ARP619X		

633-644

Leyland Olympian ONCL10/1RZ — Alexander RL — H47/32F* — 1988 — *636/41 are DPH47/29F

633	F633LMJ	**636**	F636LMJ	**639**	F639LMJ	**641**	F641LMJ	**643**	F643LMJ
634	F634LMJ	**637**	F637LMJ	**640**	F640LMJ	**642**	F642LMJ	**644**	F644LMJ
635	F635LMJ	**638**	F638LMJ						

645-657

Leyland Olympian ON2R50C13Z4 — Alexander RL — H47/32F* — 1989 — *654 is DPH47/29F / 649-53 are H47/34F

645	G645UPP	**648**	G648UPP	**651**	G651UPP	**654**	G654UPP	**656**	G656UPP
646	G646UPP	**649**	G649UPP	**652**	G652UPP	**655**	G655UPP	**657**	G657UPP
647	G647UPP	**650**	G650UPP	**653**	G653UPP					

661	A141DPE	Leyland Olympian ONTL11/1R	Roe	H43/29F	1983	Ex Sovereign, 1990
662	A142DPE	Leyland Olympian ONTL11/1R	Roe	H43/29F	1983	Ex Sovereign, 1990
663	A143DPE	Leyland Olympian ONTL11/1R	Roe	H43/29F	1983	Ex Sovereign, 1990
664	B262LPH	Leyland Olympian ONTL11/1R	Eastern Coach Works	H43/29F	1985	Ex Sovereign, 1990
665	BPF135Y	Leyland Olympian ONTL11/1R	Roe	H43/29F	1983	Ex Sovereign, 1990
666	BPF136Y	Leyland Olympian ONTL11/1R	Roe	H43/29F	1983	Ex Sovereign, 1990

Originally a demonstrator for Leyland Bus, D603ACW later went to work with Jubilee, Stevenage, a business that was taken-over by Sovereign in 1989, though many of the duties and some vehicles (including a pair of Leyland Lynx) passed to Luton & District the following year. No.405, seen with its fourth owner, carries Stevenage Bus fleetnames at Hertford. *G R Mills*

Coach-seated Leyland Olympian 636 was transferred into the former London Country North West area . In order to be available for Green Line work it was repainted from original Luton & District red and cream into green. F636LMJ is seen at Watford Junction. *Colin Lloyd*

779-800

Bristol VRT/SL2/6LX Eastern Coach Works H39/31F 1972-73 779-797 ex United Counties, 1986
798-800 ex Milton Keynes City Bus, 1987

779	CBD779K	796	JRP796L	798	JRP798L	799	JRP799L	800	JRP800L
795	JRP795L	797	JRP797L						

802-833

Bristol VRT/SL2/6LX Eastern Coach Works H43/31F 1974-75 Ex United Counties, 1986

802	PRP802M	805	PRP805M	812	RRP812M	815	RRP815M	825	GNV334N
803	PRP803M	807	RNV807M	813	RRP813M	823	GNV332N	833	HRP673N
804	PRP804M								

836w	KKY836P	Bristol VRT/SL3/501	Eastern Coach Works	H39/34F	1976	Ex RoadCar, 1986
837	LBD837P	Bristol VRT/SL3/6LX	Eastern Coach Works	H43/31F	1975	Ex United Counties, 1986
841	KKY841P	Bristol VRT/SL3/501	Eastern Coach Works	H43/34F	1976	Ex RoadCar, 1986
844w	OTO153R	Bristol VRT/SL3/501	Eastern Coach Works	H43/31F	1976	Ex RoadCar, 1986

851-904

Bristol VRT/SL3/6LXB Eastern Coach Works H43/31F 1976-79 Ex United Counties, 1986

851	OVV851R	855	OVV855R	867	TNH867R	893	YVV893S	898	CBD898T
852	OVV852R	864	TNH864R	874	WBD874S	894	YVV894S	899	CBD899T
853	OVV853R	865	TNH865R	877	WBD877S	895	YVV895S	900	CBD900T
854	OVV854R	866	TNH866R	892	YVV892S	897	CBD897T	904	CBD904T

913	HBD913T	Bristol VRT/SL3/6LXB	Eastern Coach Works	H43/31F	1979	Ex Milton Keynes City Bus, 1987
914	OCY914R	Bristol VRT/SL3/501	Eastern Coach Works	H43/31F	1977	Ex South Wales, 1987
916	OCY916R	Bristol VRT/SL3/501	Eastern Coach Works	H43/31F	1977	Ex South Wales, 1987
917	RTH917S	Bristol VRT/SL3/501	Eastern Coach Works	H43/31F	1977	Ex South Wales, 1987
918	HBD918T	Bristol VRT/SL3/6LXB	Eastern Coach Works	H40/31F	1979	Ex United Counties, 1986

925-960

Bristol VRT/SL3/6LXB Eastern Coach Works H43/31F* 1980-81 Ex United Counties, 1986
*955 is H40/31F

925	ONH925V	932	SNV932W	938	SNV938W	951	VVV951W	957	VVV957W
928	ONH928V	933	SNV933W	946	URP946W	955	VVV955W	960	VVV960W
929	ONH929V	934	SNV934W	947	URP947W	956	VVV956W		

On order:
52 Volvo B6 with Northern Counties Paladin bodies for 1993 delivery

Livery: Red and cream; green and grey (London Country NW); red and grey (coaches).

Green Line:	BTL48/9, TDL57, TP13/5,21,36, TPL50-98
Jetlink:	BTL47
Luton Flyer:	407/9/10.
Overall advertisments:	14/6/32/46/60/4/8/9/72, 400/5/6/67, 509/18/24/31/50/60/3/9/79/88, 652/3/4/5, 899, 904/56, LRL29, LR71, MCW3/6/10/7/26/32, VR727, SNB237,350/98,415/7/21/34/7/46/7/9/58/60/4/5/8/70, 506/12/6,
Red Rover:	143/7
School bus:	795-812
Chiltern European:	200-209

Previous Registrations:

HSV781	FUA399Y	UMS394	A732HFP

LUTONIAN BUS

Lutonian Buses Ltd, 6 High Town Road, Luton, Bedfordshire, LU2 0DD

B85TKM	Talbot Express	Rootes	M12	1984	
B312YKN	Talbot Express	Rootes	M12	1985	
C403AKP	Talbot Express	Rootes	M12	1985	
C388CKK	Talbot Express	Rootes	M12	1985	
C854AOW	Iveco 35-8	Robin Hood	M14	1985	Ex North Mymms, 1989
D42PGJ	Iveco 35-8	Elme	C16F	1985	Ex Stevens, West Bromwich, 1992
D210GLJ	Freight Rover Sherpa 374	Dormobile	B20F	1986	Ex London Country SW, 1990
D493YLN	Iveco 35-8	Elme	C16F	1986	Ex Ruffle, Castle Hedingham, 1991
D494YLN	Iveco 35-8	Elme	C16F	1986	Ex Dixon, Stevenage, 1990
D69YRF	Freight Rover Sherpa 374	Dormobile	B16F	1986	Ex Midland Red North, 1990
F358EKL	Talbot Express	Talbot	M14	1988	
F212NST	Freight Rover Sherpa 385	Aitken	B20F	1988	Ex Lumley, Speke, 1992
G270BSC	Citroen C25D	Citroen	M12	1988	Acquired 1991
F212NST	Freight Rover Sherpa 385	Carlyle Citybus 2	B20F	1990	Ex Neal & Chippenham, 1993

Livery: Grey, blue and orange.

One of a pair of Iveco 35s that were new to Ruffle, Castle Hedingham, is seen in George Street, Luton in the livery of Lutonian Bus. D493YLN carries the Elme minibus body noted for its slim window pillars. *G R Mills*

The Eastern Bus Handbook

MILTON KEYNES CITY BUS

Milton Keynes City Bus Ltd, Snowdon Drive, Winterhill, Milton Keynes,
Buckinghamshire, MK6 1AD
Buckinghamshire Road Car Co Ltd, Snowdon Drive, Winterhill, Milton Keynes,
Buckinghamshire, MK6 1AD
E & T Johnson Coaches (Hanslope) Ltd, Snowdon Drive, Winterhill, Milton Keynes,
Buckinghamshire, MK6 1AD

1-45

Mercedes-Benz L608D   Robin Hood*   B20F*   1986
*29 rebodied with Dormobile B25F body in 1990

1	D101VRP	10	D110VRP	19	D119VRP	28	D128VRP	37	D137VRP
2	D102VRP	11	D111VRP	20	D120VRP	29	D129VRP	38	D138VRP
3	D103VRP	12	D112VRP	21	D121VRP	30	D130VRP	39	D139VRP
4	D104VRP	13	D113VRP	22	D122VRP	31	D131VRP	40	D140VRP
5	D105VRP	14	D114VRP	23	D123VRP	32	D132VRP	41	D141VRP
6	D106VRP	15	D115VRP	24	D124VRP	33	D133VRP	42	D142VRP
7	D107VRP	16	D116VRP	25	D125VRP	34	D134VRP	43	D143VRP
8	D108VRP	17	D117VRP	26	D126VRP	35	D135VRP	44	D144VRP
9	D109VRP	18	D118VRP	27	D127VRP	36	D136VRP	45	D145VRP

46-51

Mercedes-Benz L608D   Alexander AM   DP19F   1986

46	D146VRP	48	D148VRP	49	D149VRP	50	D150VRP	51	D151VRP
47	D147VRP								

55-64

Mercedes-Benz L608D   Alexander AM   B20F   1986

55	D155VRP	58	D158VRP	61	D161VRP	63	D163VRP	64	D164VRP
56	D156VRP								

A new fleet of Mercedes Benz L608Ds were purchased by the newly formed Milton Keynes City Bus in 1986 to replace the Bristol VRTs inherited from United Counties. D122VRP typifies the initial batch of 45 and is seen with a background of new city. *Colin Lloyd*

66-73   Mercedes-Benz 709D   Reeve Burgess Beaver   B19F   1988

66	E66MVV	68	E68MVV	70	E70MVV	72	E72MVV	73	E73MVV
67	E67MVV	69	E69MVV	71	E71MVV				

77	D177VRP	Mercedes-Benz L608D	Dormobile (1990)	B25F	1986
81	D181VRP	Mercedes-Benz L608D	Alexander AM	B20F	1986
83	D183VRP	Mercedes-Benz L608D	Alexander AM	B20F	1986
92	D192VRP	Mercedes-Benz L608D	Alexander AM	B20F	1986

93-99   Mercedes-Benz 709D   Dormobile Routemaker   B29F   1989-90

93	G93ERP	95	G95ERP	97	G97ERP	98	G98NBD	99	G99NBD
94	G94ERP	96	G96ERP						

100	G100NBD	Mercedes-Benz 709D	Dormobile Routemaker	B29F	1990
165	WFH165S	Leyland Leopard PSU5C/4R	Duple Dominant II	C51F	1978
201	J201JRP	Mercedes-Benz 709D	Plaxton Beaver	B27F	1991
202	J202JRP	Mercedes-Benz 709D	Plaxton Beaver	B27F	1991
203	J203JRP	Mercedes-Benz 709D	Plaxton Beaver	B27F	1991
204	J204JRP	Mercedes-Benz 709D	Plaxton Beaver	B27F	1991

Milton Keynes City Bus took an interesting step in 1990 by re-bodying one of the Alexander 20-seat Mercedes-Benz with a new Dormobile 25-seat body. This bus,177 (D177VRP) is seen in Midsummer Boulevard near the large Central shopping area. *Colin Lloyd*

In reaction to growing competition, a low-cost unit was set-up as the Buckinghamshire Road Car Company using a livery of Buckingham green and cream. Mercedes-Benz 98 (G98NBD) is shown at Midsummer Boulevard, Milton Keynes. *Colin Lloyd*

221	PVT221L	Bristol RELL6G	Eastern Coach Works	B53F	1972	Ex Pennine Blue, Denton, 1992
242	KTX242L	Bristol RESL6G	Eastern Coach Works	B47F	1972	Ex Parfitts, Rhymney Bridge, 1991
246	NKG246M	Bristol RESL6G	Eastern Coach Works	DP44F	1973	Ex Parfitts, Rhymney Bridge, 1991
278	B278KPF	Leyland Tiger TRCTL11/3RH	Plaxton Paramount 3200 II	C53F	1985	Ex Luton & District, 1991
280	ONN280M	Leyland Leopard PSU3B/4R	Plaxton Elite III Express	C53F	1974	Ex Johnsons, Hanslope, 1990
359	F359GKN	Mercedes-Benz 811D	Dormobile Routemaker	B29F	1989	Ex Dormobile demonstrator, 1989
363	OCK363K	Bristol RESL6G	Eastern Coach Works	B49F	1972	Ex Pennine Blue, Denton, 1992
369	OCK369K	Bristol RESL6G	Eastern Coach Works	B49F	1972	Ex Pennine Blue, Denton, 1992
383	EHU383K	Bristol RELL6G	Eastern Coach Works	B50F	1972	Ex Northern Bus, N Anston, 1993
452	LPU452J	Bristol RELL6G	Eastern Coach Works	B53F	1971	Ex Pennine Blue, Denton, 1992
467	HJB467W	Leyland Leopard PSU3G/4R	Plaxton Supreme VI Exp	C51F	1981	Ex Johnsons, Hanslope, 1990
470	HJB470W	Leyland Leopard PSU3G/4R	Plaxton Supreme VI Exp	C51F	1981	Ex Johnsons, Hanslope, 1990
516	EPW516K	Bristol RELL6G	Eastern Coach Works	B53F	1972	Ex Viscount, 1991
522	HPW522L	Bristol RELL6G	Eastern Coach Works	B53F	1972	Ex Viscount, 1991
614w	THH614S	Leyland Leopard PSU3E/4RT	Duple Dominant II	C49F	1977	Ex Johnsons, Hanslope, 1990
616w	THH616S	Leyland Leopard PSU3E/4RT	Duple Dominant II	C49F	1977	Ex Johnsons, Hanslope, 1990
624	OAL624M	Leyland Leopard PSU3B/4R	Plaxton Elite III Express	C53F	1974	Ex Johnsons, Hanslope, 1990
635	SMY635X	Leyland Tiger TRCTL11/3RH	Plaxton Supreme V	C50F	1982	Ex Johnsons, Hanslope, 1990
681	RAH681F	Bristol RELL6G	Eastern Coach Works	B53F	1972	Ex Cambus, 1992
776w	JLP776V	Bedford YMT	Plaxton Supreme IV	C53F	1979	Ex
3009	CBV9S	Bristol VRT/SL3/501(Gardner)	Eastern Coach Works	H43/31F	1977	Ex Ribble, 1993
3019	CBV19S	Bristol VRT/SL3/501(Gardner)	Eastern Coach Works	H43/31F	1977	Ex Ribble, 1993
3028	DBV28W	Bristol VRT/SL3/6LXB	Eastern Coach Works	H43/31F	1978	Ex Ribble, 1993
3128	RAH128M	Bristol VRT/SL2/6LX	Eastern Coach Works	H43/34F	1974	Ex PMT, 1993
3282	MDM282P	Bristol VRT/SL3/6LX	Eastern Coach Works	H43/31F	1975	Ex Happy Days, Woodseaves, 1993
3353	YTU353S	Bristol VRT/SL3/501	Eastern Coach Works	H43/31F	1977	Ex Happy Days, Woodseaves, 1993
3436	OUD436M	Bristol VRT/SL2/6LX	Eastern Coach Works	H43/34F	1974	Ex Western National, 1993
3575	GNJ575N	Bristol VRT/SL2/6LX	Eastern Coach Works	H43/34F	1975	Ex Brighton & Hove, 1988
3724	LOD724P	Bristol VRT/SL3/6LX	Eastern Coach Works	H43/34F	1975	Ex ??, 1993
3826	URB826S	Bristol VRT/SL3/501(6LXB)	Eastern Coach Works	H43/34F	1976	Ex Trent, 1992
3927	ONH927V	Bristol VRT/SL3/6LXB	Eastern Coach Works	H43/34F	1980	Ex United Counties, 1986
3942	URP942W	Bristol VRT/SL3/6LXB	Eastern Coach Works	H43/34F	1981	Ex United Counties, 1986

Livery: White and yellow; Green and cream (Buckingham); Blue and white (Johnson).

Operators:
Buckinghamshire: 6, 12, 55/6, 64, 70-3, 81/3, 97-100, 201-4, 3724.
Johnson Travel: 46, 58, 61/3, 165, 229/42/6/78, 452/67/70, 516/22, 614/6/35,
Milton Keynes City Bus: remainder

Having sold newer Bristol VRTs, inherited from United Counties on its formation, Milton Keynes City Bus have recently taken in a variety of used examples from elsewhere. No.3575 (GNJ575N) is one example that was new to Southdown in 1975 and is seen outside Milton Keynes bus station. *Colin Lloyd*

The blue livery of Johnson of Hanslope is retained by 165 (WFH165S), a Leyland Leopard with Duple Dominant I bodywork, originally new to National Travel South West in 1978. The coach is seen on stage duties in Horsemarket, Northampton. *G R Mills*

Milton Keynes City Bus still operate several Bristol RELLs. Painted in Buckinghamshire Road Car livery is 221 (PVT221L). This vehicle was new to PMT, though it arrived in Milton Keynes from Pennine Blue. *Colin Lloyd*

MORLEY'S

J.R. Morley & Sons Ltd, West End Garage, Whittlesey, Cambridgeshire, PE7 1HH

UEB782K	Bedford YRQ	Willowbrook 001	B47F	1972	
UEB783K	Bedford YRQ	Willowbrook 001	B47F	1972	
NER610M	Bedford YRT	Duple Dominant Express	C53F	1973	
JFR397N	Leyland Atlantean AN68/1R	East Lancashire	H45/31F	1975	Ex Ribble, 1989
ODU254P	Bedford YLQ	Duple Dominant	C45F	1976	Ex Wainfleet, Nuneaton, 1979
NSJ19R	Seddon Pennine VII	Alexander AY	B53F	1976	Ex Western Scottish, 1987
NSJ21R	Seddon Pennine VII	Alexander AY	B53F	1976	Ex Western Scottish, 1988
NDP38R	Bristol VRT/LL3/6LXB	Northern Counties	H47/29D	1976	Ex Reading, 1990
OJD192R	Leyland Fleetline FE30AGR	MCW	H45/32F	1977	Ex London Transport, 1984
OJD232R	Leyland Fleetline FE30AGR	MCW	H45/32F	1977	Ex Thamesdown, 1985
RSD978R	Seddon Pennine VII	Alexander AY	B53F	1977	Ex Western Scottish, 1987
SPA192R	Bedford YMT	Plaxton Supreme III Exp	C53F	1977	Ex Jason, St Mary Cray, 1989
BTX39V	Ford R1114	Plaxton Supreme IV	C53F	1979	Ex Harrod, Wormegay, 1984
UAV457X	Bedford YNT	Duple Dominant IV	C53F	1982	
HBH411Y	Bedford YNT	Duple Laser	C53F	1983	Ex Hornsby, Ashby, 1990
B220JPH	Mercedes-Benz L508D	Coachcraft	M15	1984	Ex Statham, Ibstock, 1989

Livery: Red and cream

The Seddon Pennine VII chassis became a popular vehicle for Scottish Bus Group stage carriage requirements in the mid 1970s, despite its manual gearbox and heavy steering. Morleys of Whittlesey operate three examples and NSJ19R is seen in Queensgate, Peterborough. *G R Mills*

NEAVE

H S Neave & Son Ltd, Fenside, The Street, Catfield, Norfolk, NR29 5AA

RYL728R	Bedford YMT	Duple Dominant II	C53F	1977	Ex Easton, Bradiston, 1989
DIL9188	Bedford YMT	Caetano Cascais II	C53F	1977	Ex Imperial, Chislehurst, 1991
VBH605S	Bedford YMT	Duple Dominant II	C53F	1978	Ex Smith, Blofield, 1989
XHE754T	Ford R1114	Plaxton Supreme III	C53F	1978	Ex Chambers, Stevenage, 1983
ENM10T	Bedford YMT	Plaxton Supreme III	C53F	1979	Ex Court, Coventry, 1993
APH511T	Volvo B58-61	Plaxton Supreme IV	C53F	1979	Ex Embling, Guyhirn, 1984
JKV413V	Bedford YMT	Plaxton Supreme IV	C53F	1979	Ex Wood, Kirkby-le-Soken, 1984
KNK539V	Bedford YMT	Caetano Alpha	C53F	1979	Ex Tate, Markyate, 1985
JDG322V	Bedford YMT	Duple Dominant II	C53F	1980	Ex Golden Rose, Hitchin, 1990
GEG963W	Ford R1114	Plaxton Supreme IV Exp	C53F	1980	Ex Embling, Guyhirn, 1987
UNK11W	Bedford YMT	Plaxton Supreme IV	C53F	1981	Ex Roffey, Flimwell, 1991
NRY333W	Bedford YMT	Plaxton Supreme IV	C53F	1982	Ex Parnaby, Tolworth, 1991
UHJ969Y	Bedford YNT	Plaxton Supreme V	C53F	1982	Ex Golden Boy, Roydon, 1991
A202LCL	Bedford YMP	Marshall Campaigner	B48F	1984	Ex Norfolk County Council, 1990

Livery: White, red and grey

Previous Registrations:

DIL9188	SEL742R	UHJ969Y	DNK582Y, YOI7374

Built primarily to the requirements of the armed forces and county councils, very few of the Marshall Campaigner bodies have entered pcv fleets. A202LCL, an example based on the Bedford YMP, and new to Norfolk County Council, is seen working towards its home village of Catfield. *G R Mills*

NIBS

Nelson Independent Bus Services, W H Nelson Coaches (Wickford) Ltd, Bruce Grove,
Wickford, Essex, SS11 8BZ

17	BIL9406	Leyland Leopard PSU3E/4R	Plaxton Supreme IV	C53F	1979	
18	RTH550K	Leyland Leopard PSU3A/4R	Plaxton Derwent	DP51F	1972	Ex West Wales, Ammanford, 1981
29	BIL7894	Leyland Leopard PSU3E/4R	Plaxton Supreme IV	C53F	1980	Ex Pan Atlas, London, 1983
30	BIL4539	Leyland Leopard PSU3E/4R	Plaxton Supreme III	C53F	1977	Ex Pan Atlas, London, 1983
33	GHM803N	Daimler Fleetline CRL6	MCW	H44/27D	1974	Ex London Transport, 1984
35	SMU721N	Daimler Fleetline CRL6	MCW	H44/27D	1974	Ex London Transport, 1984
36	GHM797N	Daimler Fleetline CRL6	MCW	H44/27D	1974	Ex London Transport, 1984
38	TUO255J	Bristol RELL6G	Eastern Coach Works	B53F	1971	Ex Cullinan, London, 1986
40	TUO260J	Bristol RELL6G	Eastern Coach Works	B53F	1971	Ex Southern National, 1987
41	TUO259J	Bristol RELL6G	Eastern Coach Works	B53F	1971	Ex Southern National, 1987
42	TUO261J	Bristol RELL6G	Eastern Coach Works	B53F	1971	Ex Southern National, 1987
43	TGX892M	Daimler Fleetline CRL6	Park Royal	H44/27D	1974	Ex Avro, Orsett, 1987
44	THM705M	Daimler Fleetline CRL6	MCW	H44/27D	1974	Ex Avro, Orsett, 1987
45	ATA767L	Bristol RELL6G	Eastern Coach Works	B53F	1973	Ex Southern National, 1987
201	BIL4419	Renault-Dodge S56	East Lancashire	B21F	1986	Ex Ipswich, 1990
202	BIL6538	Renault-Dodge S56	East Lancashire	B21F	1986	Ex Ipswich, 1990
203	BIL4710	Renault-Dodge S56	Northern Counties	B18F	1986	Ex GM Buses, 1991
	GCL341N	Leyland National 11351/1R		B52F	1975	Ex West, Woodford Green, 1992
	NDL652R	Bristol VRT/SL3/6LXB	Eastern Coach Works	H43/31F	1976	Ex Pegg, Rotherham, 1991
	STW25W	Bristol VRT/SL3/6LXB	Eastern Coach Works	H39/31F	1980	Ex Thamesway, 1991

Livery: Yellow (buses); White, maroon and grey (coaches)

Previous Registrations:

BIL4419	C201YDX	BIL4710	C808CBU	BIL7894	LVS431V
BIL4539	VMJ960S	BIL6538	C202YDX	BIL9406	CTM404T

**Bill Nelson has a mixed fleet of buses, coaches and midibuses. The minibus fleet consists of the Renault-Dodge S56
of which three example are used. Two with East Lancashire bodywork were new to Ipswich, while the third has come
from GM Buses and carries a Northern Counties body.** *Colin Lloyd*

Contrast in the deliveries of 1981 and 1984 is seen in these two photographs. Above is Northampton 75 (ABD75X) a Bristol VRT with East Lancashire bodywork, while below is 77 (A77RRP), another body by the same company, built on the Leyland Olympian. *K Crawley*

NORTHAMPTON TRANSPORT

Northampton Transport Ltd, The Bus Depot, St James Road, Northampton, NN5 5JD

48-70		Bristol VRT/SL3/6LXB		Alexander AL		H45/27D	1978		
48	CNH48T	50	CNH50T	53	CNH53T	55	CNH55T	70	VVV70S
49	CNH49T	52	CNH52T	54	CNH54T	57	CNH57T		

71-76		Bristol VRT/SL3/6LXB		East Lancashire		H44/28D*	1981	*75/6 are DPH43/27D	
71	ABD71X	73	ABD73X	74	ABD74X	75	ABD75X	76	ABD76X
72	ABD72X								

77-82		Leyland Olympian ONLXB/1R		East Lancashire		H47/25D	1984		
77	A77RRP	79	A79RRP	80	A80RRP	81	A81RRP	82	A82RRP
78	A78RRP								

83-88		Volvo Citybus B10M-50		Alexander RV		DPH47/35F	1989		
83	F83XBD	85	F85XBD	86	F86DVV	87	F87DVV	88	F88DVV
84	F84XBD								

89-94		Volvo Citybus B10M-55		Alexander RV		DPH47/35F	1990		
89	H289VRP	91	H291VRP	92	H292VRP	93	H293VRP	94	H294VRP
90	H290VRP								

95-100		Volvo Citybus B10M-50		Alexander RV		DPH47/35F	1991		
95	J295GNV	97	J297GNV	98	J298GNV	99	J299GNV	100	J210GNV
96	J296GNV								

101	D101XNV	Volvo Citybus B10M-50	East Lancashire	DPH45/31F	1986
102	D102XNV	Volvo Citybus B10M-50	East Lancashire	DPH45/31F	1986
106	E106JNH	Renault-Dodge S56	Alexander AM	DP23F	1988
107	E107JNH	Renault-Dodge S56	Alexander AM	DP23F	1988
108	E108JNH	Renault-Dodge S56	Alexander AM	DP23F	1988
110	E110JNH	Renault-Dodge S56	Alexander AM	DP23F	1988
111	E111NNV	Volvo Citybus B10M-50	Duple 300	DP49F	1988
112	G112ENV	Volvo Citybus B10M-55	Duple 300	DP49F	1989
113	G113ENV	Volvo Citybus B10M-55	Duple 300	DP49F	1989
114	G114ENV	Volvo Citybus B10M-55	Duple 300	DP47F	1989
115	J115MRP	Volvo Citybus B10M-55	East Lancashire	DP49F	1992

121-132		Volvo Citybus B10M-50		Alexander RV		H47/35F	1992-93		
121	K121URP	124	K124URP	127	L127	129	L129	131	L131
122	K122URP	125	K125URP	128	L128	130	L130	132	L132
123	K123URP	126	K126URP						

267	JVV267G	Daimler CVG6	Roe	H43/26R	1968

Livery: Red and cream

Named vehicles:
83 *Northampton Charter 1189*, 84 *Northampton Castle*, 85 *Richard the Lionheart*, 86 *Queen Eleanor*, 87 *Danes Camp*, 88 *Simon De Senlis*, 89 *Delapre Abbey*, 90 *Rush Mills*, 91 *Knights Templar*, 92 *Master Cobbler*, 93 *Nene Navigation*, 94 *Philip Doddridge*, 95 *Thos Chipsey*, 96 *Becketts Well*, 97 *William Carey 1761-1834*, 98 *John Clare*, 99 *Chas Bradlaugh*, 100 *All Saints Church*, 106 *Daisy*, 107 *Polly*, 108 *Sally*, 110 *June*, 121 *Sir Phillip Manfield*, 122 *Hazelrigg House*, 123 *The Guildhall*, 124 *The Welsh House*, 125 *Notre Dame*, 126 *Lt Col Mobbs DSO*.

Mark 3 Bristol VRTs with Alexander bodies were the mainstay of the Northampton double-deck fleet in the late 1970s and 1980s. The original batch of 36 has now been reduced to nine, represented by 55 (CNH55T). *G R Mills*

The current double deck choice for Northampton is the Volvo Citybus fitted with coachwork by Alexander. Typical of the combination is 97 (J297GNV) which has been named *William Carey 1761- 1834* . It is seen when new. *G R Mills*

Northampton do not operate any luxury coaches but all four of the Volvo Citybus saloons have high-back seating with the livery incorporateing more cream than the bus version.
113 (G113ENV), has a Duple 300-style body and displays this layout. It is seen as it enters the Greyfriars shopping complex. *G R Mills*

OSBORNE'S

G W Osborne & Sons, 62 New Road, Tollesbury, Essex, CM9 8QD

2	KUC228P	Daimler Fleetline CRL6	MCW	H45/32F	1975	Ex London Transport, 1983
3	OUC38R	Leyland Fleetline FE30AGR	MCW	H45/32F	1977	Ex Ensign, Purfleet, 1988
4	GSL897N	Daimler Fleetline CRG6LXB	Alexander AL	H49/38F	1975	Ex Tayside, 1985
5	PHK620V	Volvo B58-56	Caetano Alpha	C53F	1980	
6	JJU442V	Volvo B58-56	Plaxton Supreme IV	C53F	1980	Ex Limebourne, London, 1985
7	JJU443V	Volvo B58-56	Plaxton Supreme IV	C53F	1980	Ex Limebourne, London, 1985
8	GVS984V	Leyland Tiger TRCTL11/2R	Plaxton Supreme VI Exp	C53F	1983	
9	CPU125X	Leyland Tiger TRCTL11/2R	Plaxton Supreme VI Exp	C53F	1982	
10	JVW160Y	Leyland Tiger TRCTL11/3R	Berkhof Esprite 350	C53F	1983	
11	OSR191R	Bristol VRT/LL3/6LXB	Alexander AL	H45/34D	1977	Ex Tayside, 1980
12	GSL902N	Daimler Fleetline CRG6LXB	Alexander AL	H49/34D	1975	Ex Tayside, 1984
14	MNK427V	Leyland Leopard PSU3E/4R	Duple Dominant II	C53F	1981	Ex Alder Valley, 1989
16	MNK429V	Leyland Leopard PSU3E/4R	Duple Dominant II	C53F	1981	Ex Alder Valley, 1989
17	XGS767X	Leyland Tiger TRCTL11/3R	Plaxton Supreme V	C57F	1981	Ex Ebdon, Sidcup, 1984
18	GSL901N	Daimler Fleetline CRG6LXB	Alexander AL	H49/34D	1975	Ex Tayside, 1984
19	MNK430V	Leyland Leopard PSU3E/4R	Duple Dominant II	C53F	1981	Ex Alder Valley, 1989
26	GSL900N	Daimler Fleetline CRG6LXB	Alexander AL	H49/34D	1975	Ex Tayside, 1984
27	GSL899N	Daimler Fleetline CRG6LXB	Alexander AL	H49/34D	1975	Ex Tayside, 1984
31	5367RU	Leyland Royal Tiger RTC	Leyland Doyen	C43FT	1984	Ex Clyde Coast, Saltcoats, 1987
32	B444BAR	Leyland Tiger TRCTL11/3R	LAG Galaxy	C53F	1985	
35	G430VML	Van Hool T815H	Van Hool Alicron	C49FT	1990	
36	G431VML	Van Hool T815H	Van Hool Alicron	C49FT	1990	
40	RWC40W	Leyland Leopard PSU3E/4R	Plaxton Supreme IV Exp	C49F	1981	
41	RWC41W	Leyland Leopard PSU3E/4R	Plaxton Supreme IV Exp	C49F	1981	
45	KBC2V	Volvo B58-61	Plaxton Supreme IV	C57F	1979	Ex Ementon, Cranfield, 1987
53	FNM860Y	Leyland Tiger TRCTL11/3R	Plaxton Paramount 3200	C57F	1983	Ex Goldenport, London, 1985
54	LUA289V	Leyland Leopard PSU3F/4R	Plaxton Supreme IV	C53F	1980	Ex Wallace Arnold, 1986
55	C101AFX	Volvo B10M-61	Plaxton Paramount 3500 II	C49FT	1986	Ex Excelsior, Bournemouth, 1988
60	EWW213T	Leyland Leopard PSU3E/4R	Plaxton Supreme IV	C53F	1979	Ex Wallace Arnold, 1984
	G70RGG	Volvo B10M-60	Plaxton Paramount 3500 III	C49FT	1990	Ex Parks, Hamilton, 1992
	G85RGG	Volvo B10M-60	Plaxton Paramount 3500 III	C53F	1990	Ex Parks, Hamilton, 1992
	G88RGG	Volvo B10M-60	Plaxton Paramount 3500 III	C53F	1990	Ex Parks, Hamilton, 1992

Livery: Red, white and maroon (buses); white, blue and red (coaches)

Previous Registrations:
5367RU   From new

Osbornes of Tollesbury have operated numerous former London Transport stock including RF, RT and RTW types. So it was not suprising that the DMS would also find its way into this well known Essex fleet. KUC228P seen in Queen Street, Colchester is one of two examples currently owned.
G R Mills

PARTRIDGE COACHES

H A C Claireaux, Mount Pleasant, George Street, Hadleigh, Suffolk, IP7 6AE

UAT274R	Leyland Leopard PSU3/3RT	Plaxton Supreme III(1977)	C53F	1964	Ex Burdett, Mosbrough, 1984
DAU379C	AEC Renown 3B3RA	Weymann Orion	O40/30F	1965	Ex Hedingham Omnibuses, 1991
UUF332J	Leyland Leopard PSU3B/4R	Plaxton Elite III	C51F	1971	Ex Southdown, 1987
DSU105	Leyland Leopard PSU5/4R	Plaxton Elite III	C57F	1973	Ex Hedingham & District, 1984
LGV34	Leyland Leopard PSU5/4R	Plaxton Elite III	C57F	1973	Ex Hedingham & District, 1984
THM630M	Daimler Fleetline CRL6	MCW	H44/33F	1974	Ex CK, Cardiff, 1985
YWE503M	Bedford YRT	Duple Dominant	C53F	1974	Ex British Coal, Barnsley, 1985
HHB48N	Leyland Atlantean AN68/1R	East Lancashire	H45/33F	1975	Ex Waddon, Bedwas, 1992
MDW584P	Bedford YRQ	Duple Dominant	C45F	1976	Ex Chenery, Dickleburgh, 1985
MKK458P	Bedford YRT	Plaxton Supreme III	C53F	1976	Ex Coronet Bingo, Clacton, 1989
759KFC	Bedford YRT	Plaxton Supreme III	C53F	1976	Ex Colchester Coaches, 1989
KJD58P	Leyland Fleetline FE30ALR	Park Royal	H45/32F	1976	Ex Premier Travel, 1988
OJD126R	Leyland Fleetline FE30ALR	Park Royal	H45/32F	1976	Ex Ementon, Cranfield, 1989
AUD463R	Bristol VRT/SL3/6LXB	Eastern Coach Works	H43/31F	1977	Ex Maybury, Cranborne, 1992
SWW300R	Bristol VRT/SL3/6LXB	Eastern Coach Works	H43/31F	1977	Ex Capital Citybus, Dagenham, 1993
THX324S	Daimler Fleetline FE30ALRSp	MCW	H44/32F	1978	Ex London Buses, 1992
VOD592S	Bristol VRT/SL3/6LXB	Eastern Coach Works	H43/31F	1978	Ex Capital Citybus, Dagenham, 1993
DNK431T	Ford R1114	Duple Dominant II	C53F	1979	Ex Stevens, Colchester, 1992
UFT924T	Bedford VAS5	Plaxton Supreme IV	C29F	1979	Ex Jones, Oldham, 1992
229LRB	Leyland Leopard PSU5C/4R	Plaxton Supreme IV	C57F	1979	Ex Rapson, Brora, 1990
HAX94W	Bedford YMT	Duple Dominant II	C53F	1980	Ex Williams, CrossKeys, 1990
RDX539	MAN SR280H	MAN	C49FT	1982	Ex Leamland, Hassocks, 1986
A486FPV	Bedford YNT	Duple Laser	C53F	1983	
A487FPV	Bedford YNT	Duple Laser	C53F	1983	
129SDV	Leyland Tiger TRCTL11/3R	Duple Laser	C57F	1985	
JSK951	Aüwaerter Neoplan N722/3	Plaxton Paramount 4000 III	CH53/18CT	1986	Ex Maybury, Cranborne, 1992
PIJ601	Aüwaerter Neoplan N722/3	Plaxton Paramount 4000 III	CH53/18CT	1986	Ex Maybury, Cranborne, 1992
F464NRT	Leyland Tiger TRCTL11/3RZ	Duple 320	C61F	1988	
F145SPV	Leyland Tiger TRCTL11/3RZM	Plaxton Paramount 3200 III	C57F	1989	
F146SPV	Leyland Tiger TRCTL11/3RZM	Plaxton Paramount 3200 III	C57F	1989	
F147SPV	Leyland Tiger TRCTL11/3RZM	Plaxton Paramount 3200 III	C57F	1989	
F148SPV	Leyland Tiger TRCTL11/3RZM	Plaxton Paramount 3200 III	C57F	1989	
J245MFP	Dennis Javelin 12SDA1929	Plaxton Paramount 3200 III	C51FT	1991	Ex Maybury, Cranborne, 1992

Livery: White, caramel and black

Previous Registrations:

129SDV	B288OGV	LGV34	MJH275L
229LRB	VWS976T, 162EKH, VAS589T	PIJ601	WCY701, C357KEP
759KFC	MNW731P	RDX539	STT620X
DSU105	MJH276L	UAT274R	TRN754
JSK951	300CUH, C366KEP, LST873		

The only all-foreign vehicle in the Partridge fleet is a MAN SR280H integral coach dating from 1982. New to Trathens as STT620X, the coach has latterly been with Leamland of Hassocks.
Geoff Mills

PREMIER TRAVEL

Premier Travel Services Ltd, Kilmaine Close, Kings Hedges Road,
Cambridge, CB4 2PH
Millers Coaches Ltd, 18 Cambridge Road, Foxton, Cambridge, CB2 6SH
Cambridge, CB4 2PH

Millers Coaches Ltd and Premier Travel Services Ltd are both autonomous subsidiary companies of the CHL Group, under one common management. Each company trades using separate liveries and each has its own operator's licence.

276	WEB406T	AEC Reliance 6U3ZR	Plaxton Supreme IV Exp	C49F	1979
277	WEB407T	AEC Reliance 6U3ZR	Plaxton Supreme IV Exp	C49F	1979
278	WEB408T	AEC Reliance 6U3ZR	Plaxton Supreme IV Exp	C49F	1979
329	C329PEW	Leyland Tiger TRCTL11/3RZ	Plaxton Paramount 3200 II	C53F	1986
330	C330PEW	Leyland Tiger TRCTL11/3RZ	Plaxton Paramount 3200 II	C53F	1986
332	C332PEW	Leyland Tiger TRCTL11/3RZ	Plaxton Paramount 3200 II	C53F	1986

369-382

		Volvo B10M-60		Plaxton Expressliner	C49FT	1990

369	G369REG	372	G372REG	375	G375REG	378	G378REG	381	G381REG
370	G370REG	373	G373REG	376	G376REG	379	G379REG	382	G382REG
371	G371REG	374	G374REG	377	G377REG	380	G380REG

387	G742TEW	Volvo B10M-60	Plaxton Paramount 3500 III	C49FT	1990	Ex Viscount, 1990
388	F325DCL	Volvo B10M-60	Plaxton Paramount 3500 III	C49FT	1989	Ex Viscount, 1990
389	F107NRT	Volvo B10M-61	Plaxton Paramount 3500 III	C53F	1989	Ex Viscount, 1990
390	F108NRT	Volvo B10M-61	Plaxton Paramount 3500 III	C53F	1989	Ex Viscount, 1990
391	E315OEG	Volvo B10M-61	Plaxton Paramount 3500 III	C49FT	1988	Ex Viscount, 1990
392	E558UHS	Volvo B10M-61	Plaxton Paramount 3500 III	C49FT	1987	Ex Viscount, 1990
393	D802SGB	Volvo B10M-61	Plaxton Paramount 3500 III	C49FT	1988	Ex Viscount, 1990
394	D813SGB	Volvo B10M-61	Plaxton Paramount 3500 III	C49FT	1987	Ex Viscount, 1990
398	C455OFL	Leyland Tiger TRCTL11/3RH	Plaxton Paramount 3500 III	C49FT	1986	Ex Viscount, 1990
402	H402DEG	Volvo B10M-60	Plaxton Paramount 3500 III	C53F	1990	
403	H403DEG	Volvo B10M-60	Plaxton Paramount 3500 III	C53F	1990	
404	E904UNW	Volvo B10M-61	Plaxton Paramount 3500 III	C49FT	1988	Ex Wallace Arnold, 1991
405	E905UNW	Volvo B10M-61	Plaxton Paramount 3500 III	C49FT	1988	Ex Wallace Arnold, 1991
406	H406GAV	Volvo B10M-60	Plaxton Paramount 3500 III	C51F	1991	
407	H407GAV	Volvo B10M-60	Plaxton Paramount 3500 III	C51F	1991	
408	J408TEW	Volvo B10M-60	Plaxton Paramount 3500 III	C51F	1992	
409	J409TEW	Volvo B10M-60	Plaxton Paramount 3500 III	C49FT	1992	
410	F947NER	Scania K112CRB	Plaxton Paramount 3500 III	C49F	1988	Ex Miller, Foxton, 1993
411	F948NER	Scania K112CRB	Plaxton Paramount 3500 III	C49F	1988	Ex Miller, Foxton, 1993

Premier Travel Services have recently acquired a pair of the first examples of the Plaxton Premiére body on the second-hand market. No.413 (J447HDS) was formerly with Parks of Hamilton and is seen in Kilmaine Close, Cambridge newly repainted .
G R Mills

412	G860VAY	Toyota HB31R	Caetano Optimo	C21F	1989	Ex Turner, Bristol, 1993
413	J447HDS	Volvo B10M-60	Plaxton Premiére 350	C49FT	1992	Ex Parks, Hamilton, 1993
414	J448HDS	Volvo B10M-60	Plaxton Premiére 350	C49FT	1992	Ex Parks, Hamilton, 1993
415	G389PNV	Volvo B10M-60	Plaxton Expressliner	C46FT	1990	Ex United Counties, 1993
416	G390PNV	Volvo B10M-60	Plaxton Expressliner	C46FT	1990	Ex United Counties, 1993
417	G391PNV	Volvo B10M-60	Plaxton Expressliner	C46FT	1990	Ex United Counties, 1993
452	JAH552D	Bristol FLF6G	Eastern Coach Works	O38/32F	1966	Ex Viscount, 1990
	C452OFL	Leyland Tiger TRCTL11/3RH	Plaxton Paramount 3500	C49FT	1986	On extended hire
	C454OFL	Leyland Tiger TRCTL11/3RH	Plaxton Paramount 3500	C49FT	1986	On extended hire
	E320EVH	DAF MB200DKTL600	Van Hool Alizée	C53F	1988	On extended hire
	F252OFP	Volvo B10M-60	Plaxton Paramount 3500 III	C53F	1988	On extended hire
	F269RFP	Volvo B10M-60	Plaxton Paramount 3200 III	C53F	1989	On extended hire

Millers of Cambridge

	ESU913	Bedford YMT	Plaxton Supreme III	C53F	1977	
	WEB410T	AEC Reliance 6U3ZR	Plaxton Supreme IV Exp	C49F	1979	Ex Premier, 1993
	WEB411T	AEC Reliance 6U3ZR	Plaxton Supreme IV Exp	C49F	1979	Ex Premier, 1993
	BEG866T	AEC Reliance 6U3ZR	Plaxton Supreme IV Exp	C57F	1979	
	A832PPP	Leyland Tiger TRCTL11/3R	Plaxton Paramount 3200	C57F	1984	Ex Premier, 1993
	A833PPP	Leyland Tiger TRCTL11/3R	Plaxton Paramount 3200	C57F	1984	Ex Premier, 1993
	HSV194	DAF SB2305DHS585	Plaxton Paramount 3200 II	C55F	1985	
	ESU920	DAF MB200DKTL600	Plaxton Paramount 3500 II	C49FT	1986	Ex Axe Vale, Biddisham, 1993
	HSV196	Volvo B10M-61	Plaxton Paramount 3200 II	C53F	1986	Ex Premier, 1993
	HSV195	Leyland Tiger TRCTL11/3R	Plaxton Paramount 3200 II	C57F	1987	Ex Premier, 1993
	E169KNH	DAF SB2300DHS585	Caetano Algarve	C49FT	1988	
	E170KNH	DAF SB2300DHS585	Caetano Algarve	C49FT	1988	
	F949NER	Scania K112CRB	Van Hool Alizée	C51FT	1988	
	F950NER	Scania K92CRB	Van Hool Alizée	C55F	1988	
	F951NER	Scania K92CRB	Van Hool Alizée	C55F	1988	
	G855VAY	Volvo B10M-61	Duple 320	C57F	1990	On extended hire

Liveries: White, two-tone blue and grey (Premier); White, red and blue (Millers)
Eurolines: F252OFP
Grand UK: 392, E320EVH
Miller Bus: 276-8
National Express: 369-82, 393-5, 415-17
Stirling Holidays: HSV196, F269RFY
Wallace Arnold: 406-8.

Named vehicles:
329 *Chalkhill Blue;* 330 *Idonis Blue;* 332 *Holly Blue;* 387 *Monarch;* 388 *Valiant;* 389 *Imperial;* 391 *Emperor;* 392 *Regent*;*
398 *Jim Darling;* 402 *Guardsman;* 403 *Bandsman;* 404 *Marksman;* 405 *Manxman;* 406 *Scotsman;* 407 *Clansman;* 408
Huntsman; 409 *Norseman;* 410 *Broadsman;* 412 *Gulliver;* 413 *Marco Polo;* 414 *Columbus.* *Not displayed in present livery.

Previous Registrations:
BEG866T	WEB132T, HSV194	ESU920	C150EME	HSV195	C328PEW
ESU913	PEB152R	HSV194	B257NUT	HSV196	D524LCS

Many of the Premier Travel fleet have received large names to add to the fleet numbers. Monarch is the name given to 387 (G742TEW) as displayed when the vehicle called into the South Mimms service station.
Colin Lloyd

PRESTWOOD TRAVEL

P & GL Baird, Prestwood Travel, 152 Wrights Lane, Prestwood, Great Missenden,
Buckinghamshire, HP16 0LG

TJO54K	AEC Reliance 6MU4R	Marshall	B53F	1971	Ex Chiltern Queens, Woodcote
APM111T	AEC Reliance 6U2R	Plaxton Supreme IV Exp	C49F	1979	Ex London Country, 1985
APM117T	AEC Reliance 6U2R	Plaxton Supreme IV Exp	C53F	1979	Ex London Country, 1985
EPM140V	AEC Reliance 6U2R	Plaxton Supreme IV Exp	C49F	1979	Ex London Country, 1986
EPM144V	AEC Reliance 6U2R	Plaxton Supreme IV Exp	C49F	1979	Ex London Country, 1986
EPM146V	AEC Reliance 6U2R	Plaxton Supreme IV Exp	C49F	1979	Ex London Country, 1986
VPG339X	Bova EL26/581	Bova Europa	C53F	1981	Ex Tates, Margate, 19..
DOY133Y	Bova EL26/581	Bova Europa	C53F	1982	Ex Atlas, London, 1992
DOY134Y	Bova EL26/581	Bova Europa	C53F	1982	Ex Atlas, London, 1992
8726FH	Bova EL26/581	Bova Europa	C53F	1983	Ex Grays, Essex, 19..
E901LVE	Volkswagen LT55	Optare City Pacer	B25F	1987	Ex Cambus, 1993
E902LVE	Volkswagen LT55	Optare City Pacer	B25F	1987	Ex Cambus, 1993

Livery: White

Prestwood Travel provide local services in the Great Missenden area using a fleet of AECs once used on the Green
Line network. In addition, Bova coaches feature in the private hire fleet, and Europa model, DOY133Y is seen passing
Parliament Square in London. *Colin Lloyd*

R & I BUSES

R & I Buses Ltd, Llewelyns Yard, Chesney Wold, Bleak Hall,
Milton Keynes, Buckinghamshire

016	URK222X	Iveco 60F10	Harwin	C23F	1981	
023	PFR727	Karrier BFD3023	Plaxton	C14F	1981	Ex Goodwin, Sandy, 1981
043	C842KGK	Iveco 35.8	Elme	C16F	1985	Ex Limebourne, London SW1, 1987
044	C843KGK	Iveco 35.8	Elme	C16F	1985	Ex Limebourne, London SW1, 1987
057	43FJF	Iveco 35.8	Devon Conversions	M14	1988	Ex Monk, London NW10, 1989
058	33LUG	Iveco 35.8	Devon Conversions	M14	1988	Ex Monk, London NW10, 1989
059	RIB7002	Bedford YMP(S)	Plaxton Supreme V	C35F	1982	Ex Ardenvale, Knowle, 1988
060	SVO89	Toyota HB31R	Caetano Optimo	C16F	1989	Ex Monk, London NW10, 1989
061	OO1942	Toyota HB31R	Caetano Optimo	C21F	1989	Ex Monk, London NW10, 1989
064	672DYA	Toyota HB31R	Caetano Optimo	C16F	1989	Ex Monk, London NW10, 1989
065	165BXP	Toyota HB31R	Caetano Optimo	C21F	1989	Ex Monk, London NW10, 1989
067	ULL897	Mercedes-Benz 811D	Optare StarRider	B29F	1988	Ex Monk, London NW10, 1989
077	C945FMJ	Ford Transit 190D	Chassis Developments	M12	1985	Ex Monk, London NW10, 1989
081	RIB6197	Kässbohrer Setra S210HI	Kässbohrer	C26FT	1989	
082	RIB6198	Kässbohrer Setra S210HI	Kässbohrer	C28FT	1989	
083	RIB6199	Kässbohrer Setra S210HI	Kässbohrer	C28FT	1989	
084	F84GGC	Mercedes-Benz 811D	Robin Hood	DP29F	1989	
085	F85GGC	Mercedes-Benz 811D	Robin Hood	DP29F	1989	
086	F86GGC	Mercedes-Benz 811D	Robin Hood	DP29F	1989	
087	F87GGC	Mercedes-Benz 811D	Robin Hood	DP29F	1989	
088	F88GGC	Mercedes-Benz 811D	Robin Hood	DP29F	1989	
089	F89GGC	Mercedes-Benz 811D	Robin Hood	DP29F	1989	
090	F90GGC	Mercedes-Benz 811D	Robin Hood	DP29F	1989	
091	RIB8432	Iveco Daily 49.10	Robin Hood City Nippy	B12F	1989	
092	G92LGK	Toyota HB31R	Caetano Optimo	C18F	1990	
093	J361BNW	Mercedes-Benz 811D	Optare StarRider	C21F	1992	Ex Castleways, Winchcombe, 1991
094	J310KFP	Toyota HDB30R	Caetano Optimo II	C21F	1992	

201-207

			Iveco Daily 49.10		Robin Hood City Nippy	B23F*	1989	*206 is B21F	
201	RIB8431	203	RIB5083	205	RIB5085	206	RIB4316	207	F207HGN
202	RIB5082	204	RIB5084						

208	G208LGK	Iveco Daily 49.10	LHE	B23F	1990	
209	G209LGK	Iveco Daily 49.10	Robin Hood City Nippy	B19F	1989	
210	G210LGK	Iveco Daily 49.10	Robin Hood City Nippy	B19F	1989	
211	G211LGK	Iveco Daily 49.10	Robin Hood City Nippy	B19F	1989	

216-229

			Dennis Dart 9SDL3002		Carlyle Dartline	B36F	1990		
216	G216LGK	219	G219LGK	222	G122RGT	225	G125RGT	228	G128RGT
217	G217LGK	220	G220LGK	223	G123RGT	226	G126RGT	229	G129RGT
218	G218LGK	221	G121RGT	224	G124RGT	227	G127RGT		

230	RIB7017	Mercedes-Benz 811D	Optare StarRider	B27F	1987	Ex Reading, 1991
231	RIB7018	Mercedes-Benz 811D	Optare StarRider	B27F	1987	Ex Reading, 1991
232	H403HOY	Dennis Dart 9SDL3002	Carlyle Dartline	B36F	1990	Ex Carlyle demonstrator, 1992
233	J823GGF	Dennis Dart 9.8SDL3017	Plaxton Pointer	B40F	1992	

234-239

			Dennis Dart 9SDL3011		Plaxton Pointer	B36F	1993		
234	K414MGN	236	K416MGN	237	K417MGN	238	K418MGN	239	K419MGN
235	K415MGN								

To attract the Buckinghamshire public R & I have added many new Dennis Darts to its Inter MK operations. One of the latest six is 235 (K415MGN), seen well to the south of the area it is about to enter Golders Green bus station while working LRT tendered service 268. *Colin Lloyd*

R & I Buses initial operations into Milton Keynes were with Leyland Nationals which were promptly re-registered with appropriate private index marks. No.403 (RIB5083), originally new to West Yorkshire as RYG767R, is seen bound for Bletchley along one of the typical new town grid roads. *G R Mills*

301	F24HGG	Volvo B10M-60	Plaxton Paramount 3500 III	C49FT	1989	Ex Park's, Hamilton, 1993
302	F25HGG	Volvo B10M-60	Plaxton Paramount 3500 III	C49FT	1989	Ex Park's, Hamilton, 1993
303	D85DOT	Mercedes-Benz 609D	Robin Hood	DP15F	1987	Ex Victoria Shuttle, London SW1, 1991
330	G44RGG	Volvo B10M-60	Plaxton Paramount 3500 III	C49FT	1990	Ex Parks, Hamilton, 1992
331	G71RGG	Volvo B10M-60	Plaxton Paramount 3500 III	C49FT	1990	Ex Parks, Hamilton, 1992
332	G72RGG	Volvo B10M-60	Plaxton Paramount 3500 III	C53F	1990	Ex Parks, Hamilton, 1992
333	G43RGG	Volvo B10M-60	Plaxton Paramount 3500 III	C49FT	1990	Ex Parks, Hamilton, 1992
334	G74RGG	Volvo B10M-60	Plaxton Paramount 3500 III	C53F	1990	Ex Parks, Hamilton, 1992
335	F975HGE	Volvo B10M-61	Plaxton Paramount 3500 II	C49FT	1989	Ex Parks, Hamilton, 1992
336	G86RGG	Volvo B10M-60	Plaxton Paramount 3500 III	C49FT	1990	Ex Parks, Hamilton, 1992
337	G77RGG	Volvo B10M-60	Plaxton Paramount 3500 III	C49FT	1990	Ex Parks, Hamilton, 1992
338	G78RGG	Volvo B10M-60	Plaxton Paramount 3500 III	C49FT	1990	Ex Parks, Hamilton, 1992
401	RIB5081	Leyland National 10351A/1R		B41F	1975	Ex Alcock, Litherland, 1992
402	ULO380R	Leyland National 11351A/1R		B52F	1975	Ex Rotherham & District, 1992
403	ULO379R	Leyland National 11351A/1R		B52F	1975	Ex BTS, Borehamwood, 1992
404	BLE743S	Leyland National 11351A/1R		B49F	1975	Ex Cherry, Bootle, 1992
406	RIB5086	Leyland National 1151/1R/0402		B45F	1973	Ex John Laing, 1992
407	DBY711M	Leyland National 1151/1R/0401		B45F	1973	Ex Ribble, 1992
408	RIB7003	Leyland National 1151/1R/0401		B45F	1973	Ex Ribble, 1992
409	RIB7004	Leyland National 11351/1R		B49F	1975	Ex United, 1992
411	xxxxxxx	Leyland National 11351A/1R		DP49F	1975	Ex Morrow, Clydebank, 1992
413	D849CRY	Volkswagen LT55	Optare City Pacer	DP25F	1987	Ex Derby, 1992
414	RIB4315	Volkswagen LT55	Optare City Pacer	DP25F	1987	Ex Derby, 1992
479	TOE482N	Leyland National 11351A/1R		B48F	1975	On loan from West Midlands Travel
481	LOA369X	MCW Metrobus DR102	MCW	H45/33F	1980	On loan from West Midlands Travel
482	GOG200W	MCW Metrobus DR102	MCW	H45/33F	1980	On loan from West Midlands Travel
483	GOG155W	MCW Metrobus DR102	MCW	H45/33F	1980	On loan from West Midlands Travel
484	GOG197W	MCW Metrobus DR102	MCW	H45/33F	1980	On loan from West Midlands Travel
485	GOG170W	MCW Metrobus DR102	MCW	H45/33F	1980	On loan from West Midlands Travel
488	GOG183W	MCW Metrobus DR102	MCW	H45/33F	1980	On loan from West Midlands Travel
489	ROK476M	Leyland National 11351A/1R		B48F	1975	On loan from West Midlands Travel
491	TOE491N	Leyland National 11351A/1R		B48F	1975	On loan from West Midlands Travel
493	TOE512N	Leyland National 11351A/1R		B48F	1975	On loan from West Midlands Travel
494	TOE515N	Leyland National 11351A/1R		B48F	1975	On loan from West Midlands Travel
495	OOX801R	Leyland National 11351A/1R		B48F	1975	On loan from West Midlands Travel
496	OOX815R	Leyland National 11351A/1R		B48F	1975	On loan from West Midlands Travel
497	TOE478N	Leyland National 11351A/1R		B48F	1975	On loan from West Midlands Travel
901	RIB6195	Kässbohrer Setra S215HR	Kässbohrer Rational	C49FT	1987	Ex Naylor, London SE13, 1992

Previous Registrations:

165BXP	E165KNH	RIB5081	YPF767T	RIB7003	NTC622M
33LUG	E779VGK	RIB5082	F202HGN	RIB7004	GFJ668N
43FJF	E778VGK	RIB5083	F203HGN	RIB7017	F607SDP
672DYA	E164KNH	RIB5084	F204HGN	RIB7018	F608SDP
BLE743S	CUP660S, RIB5084	RIB5085	F205HGN	RIB8431	F201HGN
DBY711M	NTC608M, RIB7002	RIB5086	NRD140M	RIB8432	F91JGJ
H403HOY	CMN12A	RIB6195	D396BPE	SVO89	E180DBB
OO1942	E181DBB	RIB6197	F81GGC	ULL897	E200UWT
PFR727	From New	RIB6198	F82GGC	ULO379R	RYG762R, RIB5083
RIB4315	D844CRY	RIB6199	F83GGC	ULO380R	RYG762R, RIB5082
RIB4316	F206HGN	RIB7002	BAC551Y		

Named buses:
216 *Windsor Castle*; 217 *Dover Castle*; 218 *Stirling Castle*; 219 *Edinburgh Castle*; 220 *Cardiff Castle*; 221 *Caernarfon Castle*; 222 *Conwy Castle*; 223 *Belvoir Castle*; 224 *Leeds Castle*; 225 *Hever Castle*; 226 *Balmoral Castle*; 227 *Inverness Castle*; 228 *Warwick Castle*; 229 *Tower of London*; 401 *Buffalo Bill*; 402 *Annie Oakley*; 403 *Hopalong Cassidy*; 404 *Billy the Kid*; 406 *Jessie James*; 407 *Wyatt Earp*; 408 *The Lone Ranger*; 409 *Doc Holliday*; 411 *the Sundance Kid*; 414 *Minnie*; 901 *Ron Naylor*; .

Livery: Grey blue and red.

RED ROSE

T W Khan, Hartwell Sidings, Oxford Road, Aylesbury, Buckinghamshire

Reg	Chassis	Body	Seating	Year	Notes
Q956UOE	Bedford YRT	Willowbrook Warrior(1987)	B53F	1976	Ex Sussex Bus, Ford, 1992
D814BVT	Ford Transit 196	Ford	M14	1987	non-psv to 1991
D501MJA	Iveco Daily 49.10	Robin Hood City Nippy	B19F	1987	Ex GM Buses, 1992
E456VUM	Mercedes-Benz 811D	Optare StarRider	B31F	1988	Ex Crystals, Dartford, 1991
F427AWD	Iveco Daily 49.10	Carlyle Dailybus 2	DP25F	1989	Acquired 1993
H389SYG	Mercedes-Benz 811D	Optare StarRider E	B26F	1990	Ex Optare demonstrator, 1991
K540OGA	Mercedes-Benz 814D	Dormobile Routemaker	B29F	1992	

Livery: Red, cream and black

Previous Registrations:
Q956UOE   NFP735P

Waiting in Watford are two of the Red Rose minibuses. Leading the pair is F427AWD, an Iveco 49.10 with Carlyle Dailybus 2 design of body. The vehicle behind is H389SYG, one of only four StarRider Es. This model from Optare retained the basic Mercedes-Benz front. *Colin Lloyd*

REG'S COACHES

Reg's Coaches Ltd, Spencer Street, Hertford, Hertfordshire, SG13 7AW

GFV182S	Leyland Leopard PSU3E/4R	Plaxton Supreme III	C51F	1978	Ex Robinson, Gt Harwood, 1985
GFV184S	Leyland Leopard PSU3E/4R	Plaxton Supreme III	C51F	1978	Ex Robinson, Gt Harwood, 1985
PHG186T	Leyland Leopard PSU5C/4R	Plaxton Supreme IV	C57F	1979	Ex Robinson, Gt Harwood, 1985
YYL771T	Leyland Leopard PSU5C/4R	Duple Dominant II	C50F	1979	Ex Grey Green, 1985
NMJ268V	Bedford YMT	Duple Dominant II	C53F	1979	
NMJ269V	Bedford YMT	Duple Dominant II	C53F	1979	
CYH770V	Leyland Leopard PSU3E/4R	Duple Dominant II	C53F	1979	Ex Grey Green, 1986
YBV191V	Bedford YLQ	Duple Dominant II	C35F	1980	Ex Robinson, Gt Harwood, 1983
LVS418V	Leyland Leopard PSU5C/4R	Duple Dominant II	C57F	1980	Ex Robinson, Gt Harwood, 1986
HHG192W	Leyland Leopard PSU5C/4R	Duple Dominant II	C57F	1981	Ex Robinson, Gt Harwood, 1986
HHG193W	Leyland Leopard PSU5C/4R	Duple Dominant II	C57F	1981	Ex Robinson, Gt Harwood, 1988
HHG194W	Leyland Leopard PSU5C/4R	Duple Dominant II	C57F	1981	Ex Robinson, Gt Harwood, 1988
D593MVR	Leyland Tiger TRCTL11/3RZ	Plaxton Paramount 3200 III	C53F	1987	Ex Shearings, 1993
E502JWP	Dennis Javelin 12SDA1908	Plaxton Paramount 3200 III	C57F	1988	Ex Whittle, Kidderminster, 1990
E544JWP	Dennis Javelin 12SDA1908	Plaxton Paramount 3200 III	C57F	1988	Ex Whittle, Kidderminster, 1990
G541JBV	Dennis Dart 9SDL3002	Duple Dartline	B39F	1989	Ex Duple demonstrator, 1990
G350GCK	Dennis Dart 9SDL3002	Duple Dartline	B39F	1989	Ex Carlyle demonstrator, 1992
G624WPB	Dennis Dart 9SDL3002	Duple Dartline	B39F	1990	
J216XKY	Mercedes-Benz 709D	Alexander AM	B25F	1991	
J217XKY	Mercedes-Benz 709D	Alexander AM	B25F	1991	

Livery: White, green and black (buses); Green, black and red (coaches)

Named vehicles: YYL771T *Reg's Caribbean Cruiser*; CYH770V *Reg's Sovereign Cruiser*; LVS418V *Reg's Panoramic Cruiser*; HHG193V *Reg's Pathfinder*; D593MVR *Reg's Highwayman*; E544JWP *Reg's Moonraker*; F502JWP *Reg's Starliner*.

Three Leyland Nationals previously with London Country were replaced in the Reg's fleet by Dennis Darts fitted with Duple bodies of the type later to be assembled by Carlyle. G350GCK, originally registered by Duple, is seen in the centre of Hertford with Reg's distinctive green and black bands on an otherwise white vehicle. *G R Mills*

ROVER BUS SERVICE

J R Dell, Rover Bus Service, Delmar, Lycrone Road, Lye Green, Chesham,
Buckinghamshire, HP5 3LF

SFU718	Bedford YRT	Plaxton Supreme III	C53F	1976	Ex Morley, West Row, 1985
VUR118W	Ford R1114	Duple Dominant	B53F	1980	Ex Lee-Roy, Brentwood, 1984
VKX539	Leyland Tiger TRCTL11/3R	Plaxton Paramount 3500	C55F	1984	Ex Cavalier, Hounslow, 1985
PSU377	Leyland Tiger TRCTL11/3R	Plaxton Paramount 3500	C55F	1984	Ex Armchair, Brentford, 1987
IIB278	Leyland Tiger TRCTL11/3R	Plaxton Paramount 3500 II	C53F	1985	Ex Leyland demonstator, 1986
B265AMG	Mercedes-Benz L608D	Reeve Burgess	C19F	1984	
KIW3769	Leyland Tiger TRCTL11/3RZ	Plaxton Paramount 3200	C57F	1985	Ex Shearings, 1991
760BUS	Bedford YMT	Plaxton Derwent II	B53F	1986	
HIL3470	Volvo B10M-61	Duple 320	C53F	1986	Ex Capital, West Drayton, 1991
E240NSE	Mercedes-Benz 609D	Reeve Burgess	C16F	1988	Ex Mayne, Buckie, 1991
OJR338	Volvo B10M-61	Plaxton Paramount 3500 III	C53F	1988	Ex Shearings, 1992
F309RMH	Leyland Tiger TRBTL11/2H	Duple 300	B55F	1988	
662JJO	Volvo B10M-60	Plaxton Paramount 3500 III	C53F	1989	Ex Horseshoe, Tottenham, 1992
F491WPR	Dennis Javelin 11SDL1905	Duple 320	C53F	1989	Ex Horsham, Warnham, 1993
G900TJA	Mercedes-Benz 811D	Mellor	C32F	1990	Ex Cocahes, St Athan, 1992

Previous Registrations:

662JJO	F886SMU	KIW3769	B512UNB	SFU718	LHW508P
760BUS	D620PWA	OJR338	E659UNE	VKX539	A148RMJ
HIL3470	C949TLF	PSU377	A151RMJ	VUR118W	PNM663W, 662JJO
IIB278	B263AMG				

Livery: Cream and blue

Rover Bus Service has made much use of the availabilty of personalised number plates. In the current fashion 760BUS
a Bedford with Plaxton Derwent body was once D620PWA. *G R Mills*

RULES

Rule's Coaches Ltd, 1 Ellis Street, Boxford, Suffolk, CO6 5HH

273AUF	Leyland Leopard PSU3R/1R	Marshall	B49F	1963	Ex Galloway, Mendlesham, 1981
APA46B	AEC Reliance 2U3RA	Willowbrook	B53F	1964	Ex Beeston, Hadleigh, 1978
JGE987N	AEC Reliance 6U3ZR	Plaxton Elite Exp(1975)	C51F	1969	Ex Hutchison, Overtown, 1977
DAL771J	AEC Reliance 6U2R	Plaxton Elite Express	C53F	1970	Ex Overton, Stockton, 1981
YHA386J	Ford R192	Plaxton Derwent	B45F	1971	Ex Beeston, Hadleigh, 1978
LIB1611	Leyland Leopard PSU5A/4R	Plaxton Supreme III	C53F	1976	Ex JD, Airdrie, 1990
GNK781T	AEC Reliance 6U2R	Duple Dominant II	C53F	1978	Ex Olde London Town, Luton, 1980
FBJ713T	AEC Reliance 6U3ZR	Plaxton Supreme IV Exp	C53F	1979	
UWH314T	Ford Transit 130	Reeve Burgess	C17F	1979	Ex Davies, Bridgwater, 1990
KIB5227	Volvo B10M-61	Van Hool Alizée	C49FT	1983	Ex Caravelle, Felixstowe, 1990
D203NON	Freight Rover Sherpa 365	Carlyle	B20F	1986	Ex Bee Line Buzz, 1992

Livery: Red, maroon and white

Previous Registrations:

273AUF	From new	KIB5227	A51UMB
JGE987N	RNL440G	LIB1611	SFV202P

The post-war fleet of Rules was principally made up of the Bedford and AECs. Of the former none remain and only four AECs are still in stock. Away from tradition was the purchase of YHA386J, a Ford R192 with Plaxton Derwent body that has now been in Suffolk for thrice the time it spent with its original owner, Midland Red. It is seen in Boxford. *G R Mills*

SANDERS COACHES

Sanders Coaches, Heath Drive, Hempstead Road, Holt, Norfolk, NR25 6JU

Depots: Cadogan Rd, Cromer; Heath Dr, Holt; Clay Pit Lane, Fakenham; Cornish Way, Lyngate Ind Estate, North Walsham.

JDN506L	Bedford YRT	Plaxton Elite III	C53F	1973	Ex York Pullman, 1981
PHE728M	Bedford YRT	Plaxton Elite III	C53F	1974	Ex Gardiner, Spennymoor, 1981
JNK551N	Bedford YRT	Plaxton Elite III	C53F	1975	Ex JR Deluxe, Foulden, 1982
LJE379P	Bedford YRT	Duple Dominant	C53F	1976	Ex Norfolk Bluebird, Norwich, 1983
NBF744P	Ford R1114	Duple Dominant	C53F	1976	Ex Crescent, North Walsham, 1993
PFO664R	Bedford VAS5	Duple Dominant	C29F	1977	Ex Crescent, North Walsham, 1993
RYL717R	Bedford YMT	Duple Dominant II	C53F	1977	Ex Crescent, North Walsham, 1993
DVY755S	Bedford YMT	Plaxton Supreme III	C53F	1977	Ex Martin, Sheffield, 1985
WVF635S	Bedford YMT	Duple Dominant	C53F	1977	Ex Keymer, Aylsham, 1990
XFE649S	Bedford YMT	Plaxton Supreme III Exp	C53F	1977	Ex Harrod, Wormegay, 1988
259VYC	Bedford YMT	Duple Dominant II	C53F	1977	Ex Spratt, Wreningham, 1990
YUR950S	Ford R1114	Plaxton Supreme III	C53F	1978	Ex Crescent, North Walsham, 1993
BIL8949	Bedford YMT	Duple Dominant II	C53F	1978	Ex Bebb, Llantwit Fadre, 1983
BNO695T	Bedford YMT	Duple Dominant II Exp	C53F	1978	Ex Heyfordian, Upper Heyford, 1988
BWK9T	Bedford YMT	Plaxton Supreme III	C53F	1978	Ex Bammant, Fakenham, 1992
FPP5T	Bedford YMT	Duple Dominant II	C53F	1978	Ex Premier, Watford, 1987
SFC2T	Bedford YMT	Plaxton Supreme III	C53F	1978	Ex Blunsdon, Bladon, 1990
ERJ839T	Ford R1114	Plaxton Supreme IV	C53F	1978	Ex Crescent, North Walsham, 1993
HGG997T	Bedford YMT	Plaxton Supreme IV	C53F	1979	Ex Constable, Felixstowe, 1984
KPT800T	Bedford YMT	Plaxton Supreme IV	C53F	1979	Ex Bammant, Fakenham, 1992
MVY54T	Bedford YLQ	Plaxton Supreme IV	C45F	1979	Ex Bammant, Fakenham, 1992
YJE9T	Bedford YLQ	Duple Dominant II	C45F	1979	Ex Pullman, Norwich, 1982
DEG952V	Bedford YLQ	Plaxton Supreme IV	C45F	1979	Ex Sutton, Reapsmoor, 1990
DHE695V	Bedford YMT	Plaxton Supreme IV	C53F	1979	Ex Boyden, Castle Donington, 1991
FRR686V	Bedford YMT	Plaxton Supreme IV	C53F	1979	Ex Torr, Gedling, 1991
HDB353V	Bedford YMT	Plaxton Supreme IV	C53F	1979	Ex Boyden, Castle Donington, 1991
JDX574V	Bedford YMT	Duple Dominant II	C57F	1979	Ex Burton, Haverhill, 1989
JGU938V	Bedford YMT	Duple Dominant II	C53F	1979	Ex Goodwin, Stockport, 1988

Sanders of Holt have the largest fleet of Bedford coaches in East Anglia, with over fifty of the Y series in service. Many of these are involved in weekday workings serving North Norfolk. JTL805V, a Bedford YMT with Duple Dominant II bodywork, is seen still on stage carriage duties in Cadogan Road, Cromer bound for Overstrand. *G R Mills*

JTL805V	Bedford YMT	Duple Dominant II Exp	C53F	1979	Ex Delaine, Bourne, 1989
GFH6V	Bedford YMT	Plaxton Supreme IV	C53F	1979	Ex P & H, Ilford, 1991
GRF267V	Leyland Leopard PSU3E/4R	Duple Dominant II	C53F	1979	Ex Crescent, North Walsham, 1993
SWP666V	DAF MB200DKTL600	Plaxton Supreme IV	C49FT	1979	Ex Crescent, North Walsham, 1993
NPW644V	DAF MB200DKTL600	Plaxton Supreme IV	C57F	1980	Ex Crescent, North Walsham, 1993
CVA108V	Bedford YMT	Plaxton Supreme IV	C53F	1980	Ex Crescent, North Walsham, 1993
HUX15V	Bedford YMT	Duple Dominant II Exp	C53F	1980	Ex Rover, Bromsgrove, 1990
HUX82V	Bedford YMT	Duple Dominant II Exp	C49F	1980	Ex Bammant, Fakenham, 1992
JJF879V	Bedford YMT	Plaxton Supreme IV	C53F	1980	Ex Skinner, Saltby, 1990
BIL8430	Bedford YMT	Plaxton Supreme IV	C53F	1980	Ex Coleman, Leverington, 1986
MMJ547V	Bedford YMT	Duple Dominant II	C53F	1980	Ex Tourmaster, Dunstable, 1987
VKC832V	Bedford YMT	Plaxton Supreme IV	C53F	1980	Ex Amberline, Liverpool, 1983
VKC833V	Bedford YMT	Plaxton Supreme IV	C53F	1980	Ex Amberline, Liverpool, 1983
PVF377	Bedford YMT	Duple Dominant II	C53F	1980	Ex Matthews, Shouldham, 1987
ORA688W	Bedford YMT	Duple Dominant II	C53F	1981	Ex Felix, Stanley, 1988
RJU259W	Bedford YMT	Duple Dominant IV	C53F	1981	Ex Dereham Coachways, 1990
RRT100W	Bedford YMT	Plaxton Supreme IV Express	C53F	1981	Ex Bammant, Fakenham, 1992
LJX401W	Ford R1114	Plaxton Supreme IV	C45FT	1981	Ex Crescent, North Walsham, 1993
PJT518W	Ford R1114	Plaxton Supreme IV	C53F	1981	Ex Crescent, North Walsham, 1993
FIL7286	Bova EL26/581	Bova Europa	C53F	1981	Ex Crescent, North Walsham, 1993
ATL312X	Bedford YMT	Plaxton Supreme IV Express	C53F	1981	Ex Delaine, Bourne, 1989
MIB9067	Bedford YNT	Plaxton Supreme IV	C53F	1981	Ex Dore, Leafield, 1992
FIL8693	DAF MB200DKTL600	Plaxton Supreme V	C53F	1982	Ex Crescent, North Walsham, 1993
LTG272X	Ford R1114	Plaxton Supreme IV	C53F	1982	Ex Den Caney, Birmingham, 1993
LTG274X	Ford R1114	Plaxton Supreme IV	C53F	1982	Ex Andys, Birmingham, 1993
LTG278X	Ford R1114	Plaxton Supreme IV	C53F	1982	Ex Den Caney, Birmingham, 1993
XVG686X	Bedford YNT	Duple Dominant III	C53F	1982	Ex Crescent, North Walsham, 1993
ORP204Y	DAF MB200DKTL600	Van Hool Alizée	C51FT	1983	Ex Crescent, North Walsham, 1993
LCJ633Y	Bedford YNT	Plaxton Paramount 3200 E	C49F	1983	Ex Wide Horizon, Hinckley, 1992
EWR960Y	Mercedes-Benz L207D	Coachcraft	M12	1983	Ex Bammant, Fakenham, 1992
A22UBD	Mercedes-Benz L307D	Reeve Burgess	M12	1983	Ex Bammant, Fakenham, 1992
A258SBM	Bova FHD12.280	Bova Futura	C49FT	1984	Ex Crescent, North Walsham, 1993
A604VAV	Bova FHD12.280	Bova Futura	C49FT	1984	Ex Crescent, North Walsham, 1993
WSV503	Bedford YMP	Plaxton Paramount 3200	C31F	1984	Ex Plumpton Coaches, 1989
B258AMG	Bedford YMP	Plaxton Paramount 3200	C45F	1984	Ex Bammant, Fakenham, 1992
B283AMG	Bedford Ventura YNV	Plaxton Paramount 3200 II	C53F	1985	Ex Bammant, Fakenham, 1992
B918SPR	Bedford Ventura YNV	Plaxton Paramount 3200 II	C53F	1985	Ex Excelsior, Bournemouth, 1993
C514MWJ	Bedford Ventura YNV	Plaxton Paramount 3200 II	C53F	1985	Ex Pepper, Thurnscoe, 1992
C115AFX	Bedford Ventura YNV	Plaxton Paramount 3200 II	C53F	1986	Ex Blue Line, Dallington, 1990
C294BVF	Bedford Ventura YNV	Plaxton Paramount 3200 II	C55F	1986	
FIL8605	Bedford YMP	Plaxton Paramount 3200 II	C38F	1986	Ex Bammant, Fakenham, 1992
C958PNJ	Mercedes-Benz L307D	Devon Conversions	M12	1986	Ex Bammant, Fakenham, 1992
C444KGP	Bedford Ventura YNV	Duple 320	C55F	1986	Ex Maybury, Cranborne, 1989
D410BDP	Bedford YNT	Plaxton Paramount 3200 III	C53F	1986	Ex Owen, Yateley, 1992
D930LYC	Bedford Ventura YNV	Duple 320	C57F	1987	Ex Coombs, Weston-super-Mare, 1990
D441CEW	Mercedes-Benz 609D	Reeve Burgess	C23F	1987	Ex Grey, Ely, 1990
D624KJT	Mercedes-Benz 609D	Yeates	C19F	1987	Ex Excelsior, Bournemouth, 1990
D964MAG	Mercedes-Benz 709D	Coachcraft	C26F	1987	Ex Upham, Wickford, 1990
D342SWB	Bedford Ventura YNV	Plaxton Paramount 3200 III	C53F	1987	Ex Rainworth Travel, 1992
E917EAY	Bedford Ventura YNV	Plaxton Paramount 3200 III	C57F	1987	Ex Owen, Oswestry, 1989
E863LFL	Bedford Ventura YNV	Duple 320	C53F	1987	Ex Enterprise, Chatteris, 1990
E440MSE	Bedford Ventura YNV	Plaxton Paramount 3200 III	C57F	1987	Ex Mayne, Buckie, 1988
E861TNG	Bedford Ventura YNV	Duple 320	C57F	1988	
E511JWP	Dennis Javelin 12SDA1908	Plaxton Paramount 3200 III	C49FT	1988	Ex Whittle, Kidderminster, 1992
E769HJF	Dennis Javelin 12SDA1907	Duple 320	C53FT	1988	Ex Crump, Malvern, 1992
E787DNG	Freight Rover Sherpa 400	Crystals	M16	1989	
F269GUD	Mercedes-Benz 609D	Reeve Burgess Beaver	DP19F	1989	Ex Pearce, Berinsfield, 1992
F440DUG	Volvo B10M-60	Plaxton Paramount 3500 III	C48FT	1989	Ex Wallace Arnold, 1992
G389LDT	Mercedes-Benz 609D	Whittaker	C24F	1990	Ex Crescent, North Walsham, 1993
J138OBU	Mercedes-Benz 609D	Made-to-Measure	DP24F	1991	Ex Mason, Bo'ness, 1993

Livery: White, light blue and orange

Previous Registrations:

259VYC	NHF333S, CJS447, APW668S	FIL8693	TND408X, XRL923
BIL8430	KUM983V	MIB9067	KHB14W
BIL8949	TPJ285S	NPW644V	JJU68V, 3367PP
D410BDP	D125VRM, 748COF	PVF377	NPV307W
FIL7286	URW703X	WSV503	A953FNJ
FIL8605	C407DML		

SEAMARKS

Seamarks Coach & Travel Ltd, 387-397 Dunstable Road, Luton, Bedfordshire, LU4 8BZ

182	EPP819Y	Bova EL26/581	Bova Europa	C53F	1982	
183	2267MK	Kässbohrer Setra S215HD	Kässbohrer Tornado	C49FT	1982	
192	HRO982V	Bedford YMT	Duple Dominant II	C53F	1980	Ex Kirby, High Wycombe, 1983
197	2917MK	Kässbohrer Setra S215HR	Kässbohrer Rational	C53F	1984	
198	Q684LPP	Kässbohrer Setra S215HU	Kässbohrer	C49FT	1984	
199	9569KM	Kässbohrer Setra S215HR	Kässbohrer Rational	C53F	1984	
200	MJI7855	Kässbohrer Setra S215H	Kässbohrer	C53F	1984	
201	MJI7856	Kässbohrer Setra S215H	Kässbohrer	C53F	1984	
202	MJI7857	Kässbohrer Setra S215H	Kässbohrer	C53F	1984	
205	B817BPP	Volvo B10M-61	Plaxton Paramount 3500 II	C57F	1985	
206	MJI8660	Volvo B10M-61	Plaxton Paramount 3500 II	C57F	1985	
207	MJI8661	Volvo B10M-61	Plaxton Paramount 3500 II	C57F	1985	
208	MJI8662	Volvo B10M-61	Plaxton Paramount 3500	C57F	1985	
209	MJI8663	Volvo B10M-61	Plaxton Paramount 3500	C53F	1985	
210	25CTM	Volvo C10M	Ramseier & Jenser	C49F	1985	Ex Parks, Hamilton, 1991
211	MJI7854	Volvo B10M-61	Caetano Algarve	C53F	1985	
214	F791DWT	DAF SB220LC550	Optare Delta	B47F	1989	
215	F370BUA	DAF SB220LC550	Optare Delta	B51F	1988	Ex Optare demonstrator, 1989
219	G971TTM	DAF SB220LC550	Optare Delta	B47F	1989	
220	G278WKX	DAF SB220LC550	Optare Delta	B47F	1989	
223	H846UUA	Volvo C10M	Ramseier & Jenser	C49F	1985	Ex Parks, Hamilton, 1991
224	9683ML	Volvo C10M	Ramseier & Jenser	C49F	1985	Ex Parks, Hamilton, 1991
225	J208RVS	Optare MetroRider	Optare	B31F	1992	
226	H846UUA	MAN 11.190	Optare Vecta	B41F	1990	Ex Optare demonstrator, 1992
227	D20MKK	Scania K93CRS	East Lancashire	B62F	1987	Ex Boro'line, 1992
228	D81NWW	Volkswagen LT55	Optare City Pacer	B25F	1987	Ex Lancaster, 1992

Livery: White and green

Previous Registrations:

2267MK	from new	B817BPP	B541BMH, 9683ML	MJI8660	B542BMH
2917MK	A608RNM	MJI7854	B455AUR	MJI8661	B543BMH
6101MV	C651KDS	MJI7855	B265XNK	MJI8662	B544BMH
9569KM	A531STM	MJI7856	B266XNK	MJI8663	B545BMH
9683ML	C345GSD	MJI7857	B267XNK	Q684IPP	?

'Bus of the Year' title was awarded to the Optare Vecta in 1990, and this example was used by Optare as the demonstrator upto 1992. Using many MAN components the product that meets the new low engine emissions, the type has started to gain orders for the company. H846UUA carries Seamarks green and white livery. *Colin Lloyd*

SEMMENCE

H Semmence & Co Ltd, 34 Norwich Road, Wymondham, Norfolk, NR18 0NS

LHK719P	Bedford YRT	Plaxton Elite III Express	C53F	1975	Ex Matthews, Shouldham, 1982
NKE307P	Bedford YRT	Duple Dominant	B53F	1976	Ex Maidstone, 1982
RYL705R	Bedford YMT	Duple Dominant II	C49F	1977	Ex Grey-Green, London, 1981
RYL706R	Bedford YMT	Duple Dominant II	C49F	1977	Ex Grey-Green, London, 1982
VYU753S	Bedford YMT	Duple Dominant II	C53F	1978	Ex Grey-Green, London, 1982
VYU759S	Bedford YMT	Duple Dominant II	C53F	1978	Ex Dix, Dagenham, 1985
CMJ777T	Bedford YMT	Duple Dominant II	C57F	1978	Ex Kirby's, Bushey Heath, 1983
YYL791T	Bedford YMT	Duple Dominant II	C53F	1979	Ex Dix, Dagenham, 1984
JKV420V	Bedford YMT	Plaxton Supreme IV	C53F	1979	Ex Wood, Wickford, 1989
JKV422V	Bedford YMT	Plaxton Supreme IV	C53F	1979	Ex Clarke and Goodman, Pailton, 1986
EPC911V	Bedford YRT	Duple Dominant II	C53F	1979	Ex Warnes, Hethersett, 1987
EPH27V	Bedford YLQ	Duple Dominant	B52F	1979	Ex Tillingbourne, Cranleigh, 1985
JGV336V	Bedford YMT	Plaxton Supreme IV	C53F	1979	Ex Morley's Grey, West Row, 1985
ECT999V	Bedford YMT	Duple Dominant II	C53F	1980	Ex Wing, Sleaford, 1985
KNR310V	Bedford YMT	Duple Dominant II	C53F	1980	Ex Shelton-Osborn, Wollaston, 1985
GWO111W	Bedford YMT	Plaxton Supreme IV	C53F	1980	Ex Hunt, Alford, 1986
NUF990W	Bedford YMT	Plaxton Supreme IV	C53F	1981	Ex Watts, Gillingham, 1986
TKV18W	Bedford YNT	Plaxton Supreme IV	C53F	1981	Ex Lambert, Beccles, 1987
OTO677W	Bedford YNT	Duple Dominant III	C57F	1981	Ex Bailey, Kirby-in-Ashfield, 1988
CBE882X	Bedford YNT	Plaxton Supreme IV Exp	C53F	1981	Ex Enterprise & Silver Dawn, 1987
PTV597X	Bedford YNT	Plaxton Supreme IV Exp	C53F	1981	Ex Gagg, Bunny, 1988
WAY456X	Bedford YNT	Duple Dominant III	C57F	1982	Ex Bexleyheath Transport, 1987
CKM140Y	Bedford YMT	Wright TT	B61F	1982	Ex Boro'line, 1992
CKM141Y	Bedford YMT	Wright TT	B61F	1982	Ex Boro'line, 1992
EUB552Y	Bedford YNT	Plaxton Paramount 3200	C53F	1982	Ex Dereham Coachways, 1990
OSU314	Bedford YNT	Plaxton Paramount 3200	C53F	1982	Ex Jamieson, Cullivoe, 1989
XBJ876	Bedford YNT	Plaxton Paramount 3200	C53F	1982	Ex Palmer, Dunstable, 1989
XNR997Y	Bedford YNT	Duple Dominant III	C57F	1983	Ex Torquay Travel, 1988
PVV312	Bova EL26/581	Bova Europa	C52F	1983	Ex Tourmaster, Loughborough, 1990
PVV313	Bova EL26/581	Bova Europa	C52F	1983	Ex County, Leicester, 1989
A266BTY	Bedford YNT	Plaxton Paramount 3200	C53F	1984	Ex Rochester & Marshall, Hexham, 1992
A33UGA	Bova EL28/581	Duple Calypso	C57F	1984	Ex Crawford, Neilston, 1990
149GJF	DAF SB2305DHS585	Plaxton Paramount 3200	C53F	1984	Ex Fleet Coaches, Fleet, 1992
A583MEH	Bova FHD12.280	Bova Futura	C53F	1984	Ex Stoddards, Cheadle, 1993
B512JJR	Bedford YNT	Plaxton Paramount 3200 II	C57F	1985	Ex Kerr, Wallsend, 1991
B513JJR	Bedford YNT	Plaxton Paramount 3200 II	C57F	1985	Ex Kerr, Wallsend, 1991
C72HDT	Bedford Ventura YNV	Plaxton Paramount 3200 II	C53F	1985	Ex Fourways, Leeds, 1992
D616YCX	DAF SB2305DHS585	Duple 340	C57F	1987	Ex Pan Atlas, Acton, 1992

Livery: Cream, orange and brown

Previous Registrations:

149GJF	A272KEL	OSU314	RPS380Y	PVV313	JRO614Y
A583MEH	A866XOP, A10MPS	PVV312	JRO613Y	XBJ876	HBH422Y

The oldest service bus in the Semmence fleet is NKE307P, a Bedford YRT with Duple Dominant body that was new to Maidstone Corporation. It has recently been joined by two other Bedfords from that fleet, latterly known as Boroline.
G R Mills

SIMONDS

Simonds of Botesdale Ltd, The Garage, Botesdale, Diss, Norfolk, IP22 1BX

Depots are located at The Garage, Botesdale; Victoria Road, Diss and Harleston.

RBJ46R	Bedford YMT	Plaxton Derwent	B66F	1976	
TPV41R	Ford R1114	Plaxton Supreme III Exp	C53F	1977	Ex Bickers, Coddenham, 1983
PFL435R	Ford R1114	Plaxton Supreme III	C53F	1977	Ex Duncan, Sawtry, 1983
PFL436R	Ford R1114	Plaxton Supreme III	C53F	1977	Ex Duncan, Sawtry, 1983
UUX360S	Ford R1114	Plaxton Supreme III	C49F	1977	Ex Salopia, Whitchurch, 1983
CPV2T	Ford R1114	Plaxton Supreme III	C53F	1978	Ex Bickers, Coddenham, 1983
APH510T	Bedford YMT	Plaxton Supreme III	C53F	1978	Ex Sovereign, Eye, 1991
MBT551T	Ford R1114	Plaxton Supreme III	C53F	1978	Ex Rydal, Richmond, 1984
XVA545T	Ford R1114	Plaxton Supreme IV	C53F	1979	Ex Safford, Little Gransden, 1984
FDX230T	Bedford YMT	Duple Dominant II	B63F	1979	
XCG264V	Ford T152	Plaxton Supreme IV	C53F	1979	Ex Summerbee, Southampton, 1983
LTG276X	Ford R1114	Plaxton Supreme	C53F	1981	Ex Capitol, Cwmbran, 1984
RLJ93X	Bedford YNT	Plaxton Supreme IV	C53F	1981	Ex Amport & District, Thruxton, 1986
461UEV	Bedford YNT	Plaxton Supreme V	C53F	1981	Ex Kiddle, St Ives, 1990
WDX663X	Ford R1114	Plaxton Supreme VI Exp	C53F	1982	
XJO46	Bedford YNT	Plaxton Supreme VI Exp	C53F	1982	Ex Cornishman, Wadebridge, 1985
JGV929	Bedford YMT	Plaxton Supreme IV	C53F	1982	Ex Sovereign, Eye, 1992
166UMB	Bedford YNT	Plaxton Supreme V Exp	C53F	1982	Ex Chapel End, Nuneaton, 1986
TCF496	Bedford YNT	Plaxton Supreme V	C53F	1982	Ex Freeman, Uffington, 1988
TVG397	Bedford YNT	Plaxton Paramount 3200 E	C53F	1983	Ex Davies, Pencader, 1988
YVF158	Bedford YNT	Plaxton Paramount 3200	C53F	1983	Ex Glennie, Newmachar, 1989
538ELX	Bedford Venturer YNV	Plaxton Paramount 3200 II	DP69F	1985	
SLK886	Bedford Venturer YNV	Plaxton Paramount 3200 II	C57F	1985	Ex Snell, Newton Abbot, 1988
7236PW	Volvo B10M-61	Plaxton Paramount 3500 II	C49FT	1985	Ex Worthing Coaches, 1988
4512UR	Bedford YNT	Plaxton Paramount 3200 II	C53F	1985	Ex Capitol, Cwmbran, 1987
8333UR	Bedford YNT	Plaxton Paramount 3200 II	C53F	1985	Ex Capitol, Cwmbran, 1988
98TNO	Volvo B10M-61	Plaxton Paramount 3500 II	C51FT	1986	Ex Moon, Warnham, 1989
VRY841	Volvo B10M-61	Plaxton Paramount 3500 III	C53F	1986	Ex Berkeley, Paulton, 1992
256JPA	Volvo B10M-61	Plaxton Paramount 3200 III	C53F	1987	Ex Dodsworth, Boroughbridge, 1992
SIJ82	Volvo B10M-61	Plaxton Paramount 3200 III	C53F	1987	Ex Excelsior, Bournemouth, 1989
4940VF	Volvo B10M-61	Plaxton Paramount 3500 III	C53F	1987	Ex Berkeley, Paulton, 1992
E346HBJ	Mercedes-Benz 609D	Reeve Burgess Beaver	DP19F	1988	
A1NPT	Volvo B10M-61	Plaxton Paramount 3500 III	C53F	1988	Ex National Plant, Bilsthorpe, 1993
H667ATN	Toyota Coaster HB31R	Caetano Optimo	C21F	1989	Ex A1 Chauffeur, Dartford, 1992
9983PW	Volvo B10M-61	Van Hool Alizée	C49FT	1989	Ex Excelsior, Bournemouth, 1991

Livery: red and white

Previous Registrations:

166UMB	XVC9X, AAC866X	A1NPT	E582UHS
256JPA	D709MWX	JGV929	AVS632X
4512UR	B610DDW	SIJ82	D252HFX
461UEV	TRY6X	SLK886	C185CTA
4940VF	D807SGB	TCF496	YRU296Y
538ELX	From new	TVG397	OBX454Y, 9983PW
7236PW	C196WJT	VRY841	D402HEU
8333UR	B631DDW	XJO46	NGL276X
98TNO	C547RWV	YVF158	A807ASE
9983PW	E306OPR, XEL941, E407SEL		

SOUTHEND TRANSPORT

Southend Transport Ltd, 87 London Road, Southend-on-Sea, Essex, SS1 1PP

101-112   AEC Routemaster R2RH   Park Royal   H36/28R   1959-65 Ex London Buses, 1988

101	OYM413A	104	WLT797	107	WLT993	109	183CLT	111	ALM101B
102	VLT172	105	WLT937	108	61CLT	110	ALM34B	112	CUV124C
103	WLT577	106	XVS319						

113	ALD871B	AEC Routemaster R2RH	Park Royal	H36/28R	1964	Ex Southampton, 1989
115	WLT378	AEC Routemaster R2RH	Park Royal	H36/28R	1960	Ex Rotherham & District, 1991
116	543CLT	AEC Routemaster R2RH	Park Royal	H36/28R	1963	Ex Southampton, 1991
117	682DYE	AEC Routemaster R2RH	Park Royal	H36/28R	1963	Ex Southampton, 1991
118	ALM11B	AEC Routemaster R2RH	Park Royal	H36/28R	1964	Ex Southampton, 1991
119	LDS280A	AEC Routemaster R2RH	Park Royal	H36/28R	1960	Ex Clydeside Scottish, 1991
120	LDS284A	AEC Routemaster R2RH	Park Royal	H36/28R	1960	Ex Western Scottish, 1991
121	CUV256C	AEC Routemaster R2RH3	Park Royal	H36/29R	1965	Ex London Buses, 1990
122	VLT44	AEC Routemaster R2RH	Park Royal	H36/28R	1959	Ex preservation, 1990
123	CUV162C	AEC Routemaster R2RH	Park Royal	H32/28R	1965	Ex London Buses, 1990
208	JTD388P	Daimler Fleetline CRL6-33	Northern Counties	H49/31D	1975	
212	JTD392P	Daimler Fleetline CRL6-33	Northern Counties	H49/31D	1975	
216	JTD396P	Daimler Fleetline CRL6-33	Northern Counties	H49/31D	1975	

221-242   Leyland Fleetline FE33ALR   Northern Counties   H49/31D   1979-81 *233/5/7/8/42 are H49/33F

221	XTE221V	226	XTE226V	231	MRJ231W	235	MRJ235W	239	MRJ239W
222	XTE222V	227	XTE227V	232	MRJ232W	236	MRJ236W	240	MRJ240W
223	XTE223V	228	XTE228V	233	MRJ233W	237	MRJ237W	241	MRJ241W
224	XTE224V	229	XTE229V	234	MRJ234W	238	MRJ238W	242	MRJ242W
225	XTE225V	230	XTE230V						

Initially a dozen Routemasters were introduced into the Southend fleet to ward off competition from mini/taxi buses, only then to be attacked by the former NBC subsidiary Eastern National with which the borough once had a co-ordinated operation. No.108 (61CLT), freshly painted in blue, is seen in Chichester Road. *G R Mills*

250	Q475MEV	Daimler Fleetline CRL6-33	Northern Counties(1984)	H49/31D	1972	
251	Q476MEV	Daimler Fleetline CRL6-33	Northern Counties(1984)	H49/31D	1972	
252	Q552MEV	Daimler Fleetline CRL6-33	Northern Counties(1985)	H49/31D	1972	
253	Q553MEV	Daimler Fleetline CRL6-33	Northern Counties(1985)	H49/31D	1972	
254	Q554MEV	Daimler Fleetline CRL6-33	Northern Counties(1985)	H49/31D	1972	
256	A110FDL	Leyland Olympian ONLXB/1R	Eastern Coach Works	DPH45/32F	1984	Ex Southern Vectis, 1991
257	B185BLG	Leyland Olympian ONLXB/1R	Eastern Coach Works	H45/32F	1984	Ex Crosville Wales, 1991
258	B189BLG	Leyland Olympian ONLXB/1R	Eastern Coach Works	H45/32F	1984	Ex Crosville Wales, 1991
259	B183BLG	Leyland Olympian ONLXB/1R	Eastern Coach Works	H45/32F	1984	Ex Crosville Wales, 1990
260	B184BLG	Leyland Olympian ONLXB/1R	Eastern Coach Works	H45/32F	1984	Ex Crosville Wales, 1990
262	H262GEV	Leyland Olympian ONCL10/1RZ	Leyland	H47/32F	1989	
263	H263GEV	Leyland Olympian ONCL10/1RZ	Leyland	H47/32F	1989	
264	H264GEV	Leyland Olympian ONCL10/1RZ	Leyland	H47/32F	1989	
281	MUH281X	Leyland Olympian ONLXB/1R	Eastern Coach Works	H45/32F	1982	Ex National Welsh, 1991
282	MUH285X	Leyland Olympian ONLXB/1R	Eastern Coach Works	H45/32F	1982	Ex National Welsh, 1991
283	MUH283X	Leyland Olympian ONLXB/1R	Eastern Coach Works	H45/32F	1982	Ex National Welsh, 1991
284	MUH286X	Leyland Olympian ONLXB/1R	Eastern Coach Works	H45/32F	1982	Ex National Welsh, 1991
301	YUM401S	Bristol VRT/SL3/6LXB	Eastern Coach Works	H43/31F	1978	Ex West Riding, 1992
302	YUM515S	Bristol VRT/SL3/6LXB	Eastern Coach Works	H43/31F	1978	Ex West Riding, 1992
303	YUM516S	Bristol VRT/SL3/6LXB	Eastern Coach Works	H43/31F	1978	Ex West Riding, 1992
304	DWY146T	Bristol VRT/SL3/6LXB	Eastern Coach Works	H43/31F	1979	Ex West Riding, 1992
305	DGR477S	Bristol VRT/SL3/6LXB	Eastern Coach Works	H43/31F	1979	Ex West Riding, 1992
306	CBV17S	Bristol VRT/SL3/501(Gardner)	Eastern Coach Works	H43/31F	1977	Ex Circle Line, Gloucester, 1992
307	WTU473W	Bristol VRT/SL3/6LXB	Eastern Coach Works	H43/31F	1980	Ex Rhondda, 1992
308	SNN159S	Bristol VRT/SL3/6LXB	Eastern Coach Works	H43/31F	1978	Ex Circle Line, Gloucester, 1992
309	WTU474W	Bristol VRT/SL3/6LXB	Eastern Coach Works	H43/31F	1981	Ex Rhondda, 1992
351	YBF686S	Bristol VRT/SL3/501	Eastern Coach Works	H43/31F	1978	Ex PMT, 1992
352	FTU380T	Bristol VRT/SL3/501	Eastern Coach Works	H43/31F	1979	Ex PMT, 1992
353	GTX740W	Bristol VRT/SL3/501	Eastern Coach Works	H43/31F	1981	Ex National Welsh, 1992
381	BUH233V	Bristol VRT/SL3/6LXB	Eastern Coach Works	H43/31F	1980	Ex Rhondda, 1992
382	GTX751W	Bristol VRT/SL3/501(Gardner)	Eastern Coach Works	H43/31F	1981	Ex National Welsh, 1992

Southend have added many second-hand double deck buses to the fleet in the couple of years prior to the company being sold to British Bus plc. With agreements to retain the blue livery and name, this Leyland Olympian, with standard Eastern Coach Works body and formerly with Crosville Wales, is likely to be around for some time. *Colin Lloyd*

401	LHG440T	Bristol VRT/SL3/501(Gardner)	Eastern Coach Works	H43/31F	1978	Ex Ribble, 1992
402	LHG441T	Bristol VRT/SL3/501(Gardner)	Eastern Coach Works	H43/31F	1978	Ex Ribble, 1992
403	LHG447T	Bristol VRT/SL3/501(Gardner)	Eastern Coach Works	H43/31F	1978	Ex Ribble, 1992
404	LHG448T	Bristol VRT/SL3/501(Gardner)	Eastern Coach Works	H43/31F	1978	Ex Ribble, 1992
546	A246SVW	Leyland Tiger TRCTL11/3RP	Duple Caribbean	C57F	1984	
547	A247SVW	Leyland Tiger TRCTL11/3RP	Duple Caribbean	C57F	1984	
548	A248SVW	Leyland Tiger TRCTL11/3RP	Duple Caribbean	C57F	1984	
549	A249SVW	Leyland Tiger TRCTL11/3RP	Duple Caribbean	C57F	1984	
550	A250SVW	Leyland Tiger TRCTL11/3RP	Duple Caribbean	C57F	1984	
551	B100XTW	Leyland Tiger TRCTL11/3RP	Duple Caribbean	C57F	1984	
553	A141EPA	Leyland Tiger TRCTL11/2R	Plaxton Paramount 3200	C51F	1984	Ex Kentish Bus, 1990
554	A154EPA	Leyland Tiger TRCTL11/3R	Plaxton Paramount 3200	C57F	1984	Ex Kentish Bus, 1990
555	A144EPA	Leyland Tiger TRCTL11/2R	Plaxton Paramount 3200	C51F	1984	Ex Kentish Bus, 1990
556	A156EPA	Leyland Tiger TRCTL11/2R	Plaxton Paramount 3200	C51F	1984	Ex Kentish Bus, 1990
557	B83SWX	Leyland Tiger TRCTL11/3R	Plaxton Paramount 3200 II	C57F	1985	Ex Yorkshire Voyager, 1992
558	B84SWX	Leyland Tiger TRCTL11/3R	Plaxton Paramount 3200 II	C57F	1985	Ex Yorkshire Voyager, 1992
559	B85SWX	Leyland Tiger TRCTL11/3R	Plaxton Paramount 3200 II	C53F	1985	Ex Yorkshire Voyager, 1992
561	A103EPA	Leyland Tiger TRCTL11/2R	Plaxton Paramount 3200	C51F	1984	Ex Kentish Bus, 1990
562	A106EPA	Leyland Tiger TRCTL11/2R	Plaxton Paramount 3200	C51F	1984	Ex Kentish Bus, 1990
563	A124EPA	Leyland Tiger TRCTL11/2R	Plaxton Paramount 3200	C51F	1984	Ex Kentish Bus, 1990
564	A126EPA	Leyland Tiger TRCTL11/2R	Plaxton Paramount 3200	C51F	1984	Ex Kentish Bus, 1990
705	XEH254M	Leyland National 1051/1R/0402		B44F	1973	Ex Halton, 1991
706	TPL292S	Leyland National 10351A/1R		B41F	1977	Ex County Bus, 1989
707	TPL293S	Leyland National 10351A/1R		B41F	1977	Ex County Bus, 1989
709	JBO345N	Leyland National 10351/2R		B41F	1975	Ex Cardiff, 1991
710	JBO352N	Leyland National 10351/2R		B41F	1975	Ex Cardiff, 1991
711	JBO349N	Leyland National 10351/2R		B41F	1975	Ex Cardiff, 1991
712	JTU593T	Leyland National 10351B/1R		B41F	1978	Ex Crosville Wales, 1991
713	LPB218P	Leyland National 10351/1R		B41F	1975	Ex London Country SW, 1989
714	NPK241R	Leyland National 10351A/1R		B41F	1977	Ex London Country SW, 1989
715	HMA560T	Leyland National 10351B/1R		B41F	1978	Ex Crosville Wales, 1991
716	GGE156T	Leyland National 10351A/1R		B41F	1978	Ex Blackpool, 1991
717	GGE158T	Leyland National 10351A/1R		B41F	1978	Ex Blackpool, 1991
718	GGE161T	Leyland National 10351A/1R		B41F	1978	Ex Blackpool, 1991

Increased competition caused Southend to search the market for more double deck vehicles in 1992. Four highbridge examples of the Bristol VRT were aqcuired from Ribble, a prospect of note considering the number of low bridges in the area. *G R Mills*

720	LPB206P	Leyland National 10351/1R		B41F	1975	Ex London & Country, 1990
721	GGE165T	Leyland National 10351A/1R		B41F	1978	Ex Blackpool, 1991
722	GGE166T	Leyland National 10351A/1R		B41F	1978	Ex Blackpool, 1991
723	GGE16.T	Leyland National 10351A/1R		B41F	1978	Ex Blackpool, 1991
725	GGE172T	Leyland National 10351A/1R		B41F	1978	Ex Blackpool, 1991
726	GGE174T	Leyland National 10351A/1R		B41F	1978	Ex Blackpool, 1991
745	PJI3745	Leyland National 10351A/1R (DAF)		B41F	1978	Ex Blackpool, 1991
751	JTU586T	Leyland National 10351B/1R (Gardner)		B41F	1978	Ex Crosville Wales, 1991
781	XPD231N	Leyland National 10351/1R/SC		DP39F	1974	Ex County Bus, 1989
782	GPD295N	Leyland National 10351/1R/SC		DP39F	1974	Ex Midland Red North, 1989
783	HPF309N	Leyland National 10351/1R		DP39F	1974	Ex County Bus, 1989
784	HPF327N	Leyland National 10351/1R		DP39F	1974	Ex County Bus, 1989
785	HPF316N	Leyland National 10351/1R		DP39F	1974	Ex London & Country, 1989
786	LPB185P	Leyland National 10351/1R		DP39F	1975	Ex London & Country, 1989
787	LPB201P	Leyland National 10351/1R		DP39F	1975	Ex London & Country, 1989
904	JTD390P	Daimler Fleetline CR6L-33	Northern Counties	O49/29F	1975	
905	JTD395P	Daimler Fleetline CR6L-33	Northern Counties	O49/29F	1975	

Livery: Blue, white and red (buses); yellow and blue (coaches)

Previous Registrations:

A110FDL	A701DDL, WDL748	PJI3745	GGE170T	Q553MEV	GHJ375L
LDS280A	VLT104	Q475MEV	GHJ377L	Q554MEV	GHJ376L
LDS284A	WLT546	Q476MEV	GHJ374L	XVS319	WLT949
OYM413A	VLT12	Q552MEV	GHJ379L		

All of the Southend intake of Leyland Nationals have been the shorter version. No.725 (GGE172T), represents a large single batch that came from Blackpool, but which were new to Strathclyde. It is seen in Chichester Road, Southend, on the final approach to the central bus station.
G R Mills

Coach services are operated by a fleet of Leyland Tigers with either Duple Caribbean or Plaxton Paramount bodywork. Of the latter type is 553 (A141EPA) once to be found on Green Line duties, the bus is often still employed on commuter work to London.
Michael Fowler

SOVEREIGN

Sovereign Bus & Coach Co Ltd, Babbage Road, Stevenage, Hertfordshire, SG1 2EQ

Depots are located at Harrow, North Mymms, St Albans, Stevenage, and Welwyn.

32	BPF132Y	Leyland Olympian ONTL11/1R	Roe	H43/29F	1983		
33	BPF133Y	Leyland Olympian ONTL11/1R	Roe	H43/29F	1983		
37	BPF137Y	Leyland Olympian ONTL11/1R	Roe	H43/29F	1983		
38	A138DPE	Leyland Olympian ONTL11/1R	Roe	H43/29F	1983		
114	LUA714V	Bristol VRT/SL3/6LXB	Eastern Coach Works	H43/31F	1980	Ex Keighley & District, 1990
126	WWY126S	Bristol VRT/SL3/6LXB	Eastern Coach Works	H43/31F	1979	Ex ??, 1993
195	DWU295T	Bristol VRT/SL3/6LXB	Eastern Coach Works	H43/31F	1979	Ex Keighley & District, 1990
197	DWU297T	Bristol VRT/SL3/6LXB	Eastern Coach Works	H43/31F	1979	Ex Keighley & District, 1990
201	G201URO	Leyland Lynx LX2R11C15Z4S	Leyland	B49F	1989	
202	G202URO	Leyland Lynx LX2R11C15Z4S	Leyland	B49F	1989	
203	G203URO	Leyland Lynx LX2R11C15Z4S	Leyland	B49F	1989	
204	G204URO	Leyland Lynx LX2R11C15Z4S	Leyland	B49F	1989	
205	G205URO	Leyland Lynx LX2R11C15Z4S	Leyland	B49F	1989	
206	G206URO	Leyland Lynx LX2R11C15Z4S	Leyland	B49F	1989	
207	G207URO	Leyland Lynx LX2R11C15Z4S	Leyland	B49F	1989	
215	F205MBT	Leyland Lynx LX112TL11ZR1R	Leyland	B49F	1988	Ex Keighley & District, 1992
217	F207MBT	Leyland Lynx LX112TL11ZR1R	Leyland	B49F	1988	Ex Keighley & District, 1992
220	E420EBH	Leyland Lynx LX112TL11ZR1R	Leyland	B51F	1988	Ex County, 1990
240	E840EUT	Leyland Lynx LX112TL11ZR1R	Leyland	B51F	1987	Ex County, 1990
258	F358JVS	Leyland Lynx LX112TL11ZR1R	Leyland	B49F	1988	Ex Jubilee, Stevenage, 1989
259	F359JVS	Leyland Lynx LX112TL11ZR1R	Leyland	B49F	1988	Ex County, 1990
271	E371YRO	Leyland Lynx LX112TL11ZR1R	Leyland	B51F	1987	Ex County, 1990
358	E358NEG	Volvo B10M-61	Plaxton Paramount 3200 III	C53F	1988	Ex Cambridge Coach Services, 1992
359	E359NEG	Volvo B10M-61	Plaxton Paramount 3200 III	C53F	1988	Ex Cambridge Coach Services, 1992
360	E360NEG	Volvo B10M-61	Plaxton Paramount 3200 III	C53F	1988	Ex Cambridge Coach Services, 1992

403-424

		Mercedes-Benz 811D	Reeve Burgess Beaver	B31F	1991

403	H403FGS	408	H408FGS	413	H413FGS	418	H418FGS	422	H422FGS
404	H404FGS	409	H409FGS	415	H415FGS	419	H419FGS	423	H423FGS
406	H406FGS	410	H410FGS	417	H417FGS	421	H421FGS	424	H424FGS
407	H407FGS	411	H411FGS						

433	K3SBC	Mercedes-Benz 814D	Plaxton Beaver	B35F	1993
434	K4SBC	Mercedes-Benz 814D	Plaxton Beaver	B35F	1993
435	K5SBC	Mercedes-Benz 814D	Plaxton Beaver	B35F	1993

The last intake of new full-size buses to the Sovereign fleet was a batch of seven Leyland Lynx of which 204 (G204URO) is seen negotiating a roundabout in Welwyn Garden City. The nearside route number box is worthy of note, providing additional passenger information.
G R Mills

503	DPH503T	Leyland National 10351B/1R			B41F	1979	
504	EPD504V	Leyland National 10351B/1R			B41F	1979	
532	EPD532V	Leyland National 10351B/1R			B41F	1979	
533	EPD533V	Leyland National 10351B/1R			B41F	1979	
539	EPD539V	Leyland National 10351B/1R			B41F	1979	
544	UPB344S	Leyland National 10351A/1R			B41F	1979	
555	XPC15S	Leyland National 10351A/1R			B41F	1977	
573	YPF773T	Leyland National 10351A/1R			B41F	1977	
575	YPF775T	Leyland National 10351A/1R			B41F	1979	
587	SPC287R	Leyland National 10351A/1R			B41F	1976	
588	BPL488T	Leyland National 10351B/1R			B41F	1979	
596	BPL496T	Leyland National 10351B/1R			B41F	1979	
597	BPL497T	Leyland National 10351B/1R			B41F	1979	
599	BPL499T	Leyland National 10351B/1R			B41F	1979	
604	YYG104S	Leyland National 11351A/1R			B49F	1978	Ex Skipton Busways, 1992
606	YEV306S	Leyland National 11351A/1R			B49F	1977	Ex Thamesway, 1991
620	MLJ920P	Leyland National 11351/1R			B49F	1976	Ex Stagecoach South, 1992
641	VNO741S	Leyland National 11351A/1R			B49F	1977	Ex Thamesway, 1991
642	JUB642V	Leyland National 11351A/1R			B52F	1979	Ex Harrogate & District, 1990
658	WJN558S	Leyland National 11351A/1R			B49F	1977	Ex Thamesway, 1991
663	LJN663P	Leyland National 11351/1R			B49F	1976	Ex Thamesway, 1991
664	VKE564S	Leyland National 11351A/1R			B49F	1977	Ex Hampshire Bus, 1992
675	PCD75R	Leyland National 11351A/1R			B49F	1976	Ex Rover, Bromsgrove, 1992
681	YCD81T	Leyland National 11351A/2R			B48F	1978	Ex Stagecoach South, 1992
685	YCD85T	Leyland National 11351A/2R			B48F	1978	Ex Stagecoach South, 1992
686	JJG886P	Leyland National 11351/1R			B49F	1976	Ex Skipton Busways, 1992
689	PTT89R	Leyland National 11351A/1R			B52F	1976	Ex Stagecoach South, 1992
690	AYJ90T	Leyland National 11351A/1R			B52F	1979	Ex Stagecoach South, 1992
692	EUM892T	Leyland National 11351A/1R			B49F	1978	Ex Skipton Busways, 1992
714	E814BMJ	MCW MetroRider MF150/58	MCW		B23F	1987	Ex Jubilee, Stevenage, 1989
729	E729CNM	MCW MetroRider MF150/72	MCW		B23F	1987	Ex Jubilee, Stevenage, 1989
730	E730CNM	MCW MetroRider MF150/72	MCW		B23F	1987	Ex Jubilee, Stevenage, 1989

774-780

		MCW MetroRider MF150/72	MCW	B23F	1987	Ex Jubilee, Stevenage, 1989

774	E974DGS	776	E976DGS	778	E978DGS	779	E979DGS	780	E980DGS
775	E975DGS	777	E977DGS						

781	E481CNM	MCW MetroRider MF150/84	MCW		B23F	1987	Ex Jubilee, Stevenage, 1989
782	E482CNM	MCW MetroRider MF150/72	MCW		B23F	1987	Ex Jubilee, Stevenage, 1989
783	E483CNM	MCW MetroRider MF150/72	MCW		B23F	1987	Ex Jubilee, Stevenage, 1989
784	E480CNM	MCW MetroRider MF150/74	MCW		B23F	1987	Ex Jubilee, Stevenage, 1989
803	C303CRH	Ford Transit 190	Carlyle		B16F	1985	Ex East Yorkshire, 1991
806	C306CRH	Ford Transit 190	Carlyle		B16F	1986	Ex Rover, Bromsgrove, 1993
809	C309DRH	Ford Transit 190	Carlyle		B16F	1986	Ex East Yorkshire, 1991
811	C311DRH	Ford Transit 190	Carlyle		B16F	1986	Ex East Yorkshire, 1992
853	HIL2553	Leyland National 1151/1R			B25FL	1973	

901-917

		Mercedes-Benz 709D	Reeve Burgess Beaver	B23F*	1989	*916/7 are DP23F
						901/12-5 ex County, 1991

901	G901UPP	905	G905UPP	909	G909UPP	912	G912UPP	915	G915UPP
902	G902UPP	906	G906UPP	910	G910UPP	913	G913UPP	916	G916UPP
903	G903UPP	907	G907UPP	911	G911UPP	914	G914UPP	917	G917UPP
904	G904UPP	908	G908UPP						

920-931

		Mercedes-Benz 709D	Reeve Burgess Beaver	B23F	1991

920	H920FGS	922	H922FGS	925	H925FGS	927	H927FGS	930	H930FGS
921	H921FGS	923	H923FGS	926	H926FGS	929	H929FGS	931	H931FGS

990	K390SLB	Mercedes-Benz 709D	Plaxton Beaver	B23F	1993	
991	K391SLB	Mercedes-Benz 709D	Plaxton Beaver	B23F	1993	
992	K392SLB	Mercedes-Benz 709D	Plaxton Beaver	B23F	1993	
993	K393SLB	Mercedes-Benz 709D	Plaxton Beaver	B23F	1993	

Previous Registrations:
HIL2553   NPD164L

Recent deliveries and repaints of Sovereign vehicles in the St Albans operating area have received a red and cream livery with Blazefield Buses fleetnames, reflecting the name of the holding company. One example is 434 (K4SBC), one of three Mercedes-Benz with Reeve Burgess Beaver bodywork. These also retain their operators identity in their Select index marks.
Colin Lloyd

A separate identity and colour is maintained for the Welwyn-Hatfield line operations. No.620 (MLJ920P), a Leyland National that started life with Hants & Dorset, now works former midibus route H2. This operates into the new town of Welwyn Garden City. *G R Mills*

A Leyland National in the Soverign livery is 539 (EPD539V). It is also to be found in Welwyn Garden City and is a vehicle that has stayed within this area since new. It was photographed before the recent re-numbering system came into effect.
Keith Grimes

124

SPRATTS

Spratts Coaches (East Anglian & Continental) Ltd, The Garage,
Wreningham, Norfolk, NR16 1AZ

TYE708S	Bedford YMT	Duple Dominant II	C53F	1977	Ex Grey Green, London, 1981
BWE193T	Bedford YMT	Duple Dominant II	C53F	1979	Ex Smith, Alcester, 1983
BWE194T	Bedford YMT	Duple Dominant II	C53F	1979	Ex Smith, Alcester, 1983
KWP443T	Bedford YMT	Duple Dominant II	C57F	1979	Ex Harris, Catshill, 1981
NRY22W	Bedford YLQ	Duple Dominant II	C45F	1980	
CTM791X	Bedford YMT	Duple Dominant V	C49FL	1982	Ex King, Stanway, 1987
HIL7240	Bova EL26/281	Bova Europa	C49FT	1982	Ex Crusader, Clacton, 1984
A881EBC	Bedford VAS5	Plaxton Supreme IV	C29F	1983	Ex Albany, Norwich, 1992
HIL6327	DAF SB2300DHS585	Berkhof Esprite 340	C57F	1985	Ex Limebourne, 1988
HIL6328	DAF SB2300DHS585	Berkhof Esprite 340	C57F	1985	Ex Limebourne, 1988
HIL7394	Van Hool T815	Van Hool Alizée	C53F	1985	
HIL7477	Scania K112CRS	Van Hool Alizée	C49FT	1985	
HIL7478	Scania K92CRS	Berkhof Esprite 340	C53F	1986	Ex The Kings Ferry, Gillingham, 1987
HIL6919	Bedford YMPS	Plaxton Paramount 3200 II	C35F	1986	Ex Coachmaster, Coulsdon, 1987
HIL7391	Bedford Ventura YNV	Plaxton Paramount 3200 II	C57F	1987	
F569MCH	Mercedes-Benz 609D	?	C24F	?	Ex NPT, Bilsthorpe, 1992
HIL7479	Scania K92CRB	Van Hool Alizée	C53F	1988	Ex Shaw, Coventry, 1991
CJS447	Scania K113CRB	Van Hool Alizée	C49FT	1989	Ex Elite, Stockport, 1992

Livery: White and blue

Previous Registrations:

CJS447	G999HKW	HIL7394	B22WEX
HIL6327	B686BTW	HIL7391	D422KVF
HIL6328	B689BTW	HIL7477	C22YEX
HIL6919	C535JTG	HIL7478	C593KVW
HIL7240	AVG870X, CJS447, BAR906X	HIL7479	684DYX, E648NHP

When NRY22W was new to Spratts the fleet was principally Duple Dominant-bodied Bedford coaches. The progress of time has changed the content such that heavyweights form the front line vehicles while the remaining older lightweight coaches perform stage carriage and contract work. The YLQ, the 10-metre contemporary of the 11-metre YMT, is seen at Mulbarton, Norfolk. *G R Mills*

STEPHENSONS

Stephensons Coaches Ltd, Riverside Industrial Estate, South Street, Rochford, Essex, SS4 1BS

JHW120P	Bristol LH6L	Eastern Coach Works	DP30FL	1975	Ex Rhymney Valley DC, 1992
TBW452P	Bristol VRT/SL3/6LXB	Eastern Coach Works	DPH39/27F	1976	Ex South Midland, 1990
WWY120S	Bristol VRT/SL3/6LXB	Eastern Coach Works	H43/31F	1977	Ex Aintree Coachlines, 1992
TPE155S	Bristol VRT/SL3/6LXB	Eastern Coach Works	H43/31F	1977	Ex The Bee Line, 1992
TNJ995S	Bristol VRT/SL3/6LXB	Eastern Coach Works	CO43/27D	1977	Ex Brighton & Hove, 1992
TNJ998S	Bristol VRT/SL3/6LXB	Eastern Coach Works	CO43/27D	1977	Ex Brighton & Hove, 1992
EWR164T	Bristol VRT/SL3/6LXB	Eastern Coach Works	H43/31F	1979	Ex West Yorkshire, 1992
MSL21X	Volvo B58-56	Duple Dominant III	C55F	1981	Ex Henning, Trimdon, 1993

Livery: White and pale green; EWR164T is an overall advert.

Previous Registration:

MSL21X	JSR42X, MSV533	FAD272Y	DAD218Y, YJV806

Previously, the seafront services at Southend have been operated by Eastern National and Southend Transport. However, for the 1993 season, the Essex County Council tender was won by Stephensons. Two former Brighton & Hove Bristol VRTs with removable tops were purchased for this work. One of the pair, TNJ998S, is seen leaving Rochford on an Asda shoppers run. *G R Mills*

STUART PALMER

Stuart Palmer Travel, 18 Tottenhoe Road, Dunstable, Bedfordshire, LU6 2AG

JPL173K	Leyland Atlantean PDR1A/1	Park Royal	H43/29D	1972	Ex London Country NE, 1988
MRO185L	Bedford YRT	Plaxton Elite III	C53F	1973	Ex Cook, Westcliff, 1988
POO997M	Bedford YRT	Plaxton Elite III	C49F	1974	Ex Stewart, Bishops Tachbrook, 1987
OJD261R	Leyland Fleetline FE30ALRSp	MCW	H44/24D	1977	Ex London Buses, 1992
OJD363R	Leyland Fleetline FE30ALRSp	Park Royal	H44/24D	1976	Ex London Buses, 1993
OJD368R	Leyland Fleetline FE30ALRSp	Park Royal	H44/24D	1976	Ex London Buses, 1992
OJD425R	Leyland Fleetline FE30ALRSp	Park Royal	H44/24D	1976	Ex London Buses, 1993
THX312S	Leyland Fleetline FE30ALRSp	MCW	H44/24D	1978	Ex London Buses, 1993
THX332S	Leyland Fleetline FE30ALRSp	MCW	H44/24D	1978	Ex London Buses, 1992
THX336S	Leyland Fleetline FE30ALRSp	MCW	H44/24D	1978	Ex London Buses, 1992
THX345S	Leyland Fleetline FE30ALRSp	MCW	H44/24D	1978	Ex London Buses, 1992
THX480S	Leyland Fleetline FE30ALRSp	Park Royal	H44/24D	1977	Ex London Buses, 1993
THX481S	Leyland Fleetline FE30ALRSp	Park Royal	H44/24D	1977	Ex London Buses, 1992
THX523S	Leyland Fleetline FE30ALRSp	Park Royal	H44/24D	1977	Ex London Buses, 1993
THX525S	Leyland Fleetline FE30ALRSp	Park Royal	H44/24D	1977	Ex London Buses, 1992
THX560S	Leyland Fleetline FE30ALRSp	Park Royal	H44/27D	1978	Ex London Buses, 1992
DOA715V	Bedford YMT	Plaxton Supreme IV	C53F	1979	Ex Bowen, Birmingham
C21HUR	Bedford Ventura YNV	Plaxton Paramount 3200 II	C57F	1986	

Livery: Two-tone green (buses); white, yellow and red (coaches).

The double-deck fleet of Stuart Palmer is nearly all former London Buses DMS stock, with additional examples being added during 1993. THX525S, in green livery, is seen on service S38 in the Dunstable, an area it works in competition with Luton & District. *Colin Lloyd*

THAMESWAY

Thamesway Ltd, Office 24, Eastgate Business Centre, Basildon, Essex, SS14 1EB

Depots: Cherrydown, Basildon; North Rd, Brentwood; London Rd, Hadleigh; Morson Road, Ponders End.

| 201 | C201HJN | Mercedes-Benz L608D | Reeve Burgess | B20F | 1985 | Ex Eastern National, 1990 |
| 202 | C696ECV | Mercedes-Benz L608D | Reeve Burgess | DP19F | 1985 | Ex Western National, 1993 |

225-234

Mercedes-Benz L608D | Reeve Burgess | B20F | 1986 | Ex Eastern National, 1990

| 225 | D225PPU | 227 | D227PPU | 229 | D229PPU | 231 | D231PPU | 233 | D233PPU |
| 226 | D226PPU | 228 | D228PPU | 230 | D230PPU | 232 | D232PPU | 234 | D234PPU |

235-244

Mercedes-Benz L608D | Dormobile | B20F | 1986 | Ex Eastern National, 1990

| 235 | D235PPU | 237 | D237PPU | 239 | D239PPU | 241 | D241PPU | 243 | D243PPU |
| 236 | D236PPU | 238 | D238PPU | 240 | D240PPU | 242 | D242PPU | 244 | D244PPU |

245-260

Mercedes-Benz 709D | Reeve Burgess Beaver | B23F | 1988-89 Ex Eastern National, 1990

245	F245MVW	249	F249NJN	252	F252NJN	255	F255RHK	258	F258RHK
246	F246MVW	250	F250NJN	253	F253RHK	256	F256RHK	259	F259RHK
247	F247NJN	251	F251NJN	254	F254RHK	257	F257RHK	260	F260RHK
248	F248NJN								

301-356

Mercedes-Benz 709D | Reeve Burgess Beaver | B23F | 1991

301	H301LPU	313	H314LJN	324	H331LJN	335	H344LJN	346	H356LJN
302	H302LPU	314	H315LJN	325	H332LJN	336	H345LJN	347	H357LJN
303	H303LPU	315	H317LJN	326	H334LJN	337	H346LJN	348	H358LJN
304	H304LPU	316	H319LJN	327	H335LJN	338	H347LJN	349	H359LJN
305	H305LPU	317	H321LJN	328	H336LJN	339	H348LJN	350	H361LJN
306	H306LPU	318	H322LJN	329	H337LJN	340	H349LJN	351	H362LJN
307	H307LJN	319	H324LJN	330	H338LJN	341	H351LJN	352	H363LJN
308	H308LJN	320	H326LJN	331	H339LJN	342	H352LJN	353	H364LJN
309	H310LJN	321	H327LJN	332	H341LJN	343	H353LJN	354	H365LJN
310	H311LJN	322	H329LJN	333	H342LJN	344	H354LJN	355	H366LJN
311	H312LJN	323	H330LJN	334	H343LJN	345	H355LJN	356	H367LJN
312	H313LJN								

Over a hundred Mercedes-Benz, all fitted with Reeve Burgess bodies, are now at work in the Thamesway fleet. Typifying the intake is 258 (F258RHK) seen on a London Regional Transport service to Upshire. It was photographed passing through Waltham Cross.
Colin Lloyd

357-387

Mercedes-Benz 709D — Reeve Burgess Beaver — B23F — 1991

357	H368OHK	364	H375OHK	370	H381OHK	376	H387OHK	382	H393OHK
358	H369OHK	365	H376OHK	371	H382OHK	377	H388OHK	383	H394OHK
359	H370OHK	366	H377OHK	372	H383OHK	378	H389OHK	384	H395OHK
360	H371OHK	367	H378OHK	373	H384OHK	379	H390OHK	385	H396OHK
361	H372OHK	368	H379OHK	374	H385OHK	380	H391OHK	386	H397OHK
362	H373OHK	369	H380OHK	375	H386OHK	381	H392OHK	387	H398OHK
363	H374OHK								

388-395

Mercedes-Benz 709D — Reeve Burgess Beaver — B23F — 1991 — Ex Eastern National, 1992

388	H388MAR	390	H390MAR	392	H392MAR	394	H394MAR	395	H395MAR
389	H389MAR	391	H391MAR	393	H393MAR				

396	K396KHJ	Mercedes-Benz 709D	Plaxton Beaver	B23F	1993
397	K397KHJ	Mercedes-Benz 709D	Plaxton Beaver	B23F	1993
398	K398KHJ	Mercedes-Benz 709D	Plaxton Beaver	B23F	1993
399	K399KHJ	Mercedes-Benz 709D	Plaxton Beaver	B23F	1993

501-507

Leyland Tiger TRCTL11/3RZ — Plaxton Paramount 3200 III — C53F — 1986 — Ex Shearings, 1992

501	D588MVR	503	D592MVR	505	D597MVR	506	D598MVR	507	D601MVR
502	D590MVR	504	D596MVR						

Orange and yellow liveried coaches are used by Thamesway for its City Saver commuter services. Recent additons to the fleet dedicated to the services are seven Leyland Tigers with Plaxton Paramount 3200 bodies. These were previously in the Shearings fleet. No.502 (D590MVR) is seen in Buckingham Palace Road, London. *Colin Lloyd*

An early Ford Transit seen at Southend bus station is 716 (C508BFB), one of several transferred from the Badgerline fleet in Avon. This batch of Dormobile-bodied Transits have been dispersed to many fleets within the Badgerline group and outside. *Colin Lloyd*

Only two of the seven new style Ford Transits passed to Thamesway on the split from Eastern National. One of the pair 756 (D756RWC) is seen in Basildon bound for Rayleigh. *G R Mills*

A recent additon to the City Saver operation is 520 (J54SNY), new to Bebb of Llantwit Fardre. It is seen in a modification of the Bebbs livery as it passes Elizabeth Street in the Victoria area of London. *Colin Lloyd*

Seventeen Dennis Darts have been taken into stock to work on LRT service 214, awarded to Thamesway in 1993. Passing through Camden Town while heading for Liverpool Street is 912 (K912CVW). *Colin Lloyd*

508	MKH89A	Leyland Tiger TRCTL11/3R	Duple Caribbean	C46FT	1983	Ex SWT, 1992
509	MKH893A	Leyland Tiger TRCTL11/3R	Duple Caribbean	C46FT	1982	Ex United Welsh Coaches, 1992
510	MKH68A	Leyland Tiger TRCTL11/3R	Duple Caribbean	C48FT	1983	Ex United Welsh Coaches, 1992
511	278TNY	Leyland Leopard PSU5C/4R	Duple 320(1989)	C53F	1978	Ex United Welsh Coaches, 1992
512	B336BGL	Leyland Tiger TRCTL11/3RH	Duple Caribbean 2	C48FT	1983	Ex Western National, 1992
513	B337BGL	Leyland Tiger TRCTL11/3RH	Duple Caribbean 2	C48FT	1983	Ex Western National, 1992
514	E675UNE	Leyland Tiger TRCTL11/3RZ	Plaxton Paramount 3200 III	C53F	1988	Ex Shearings, 1993
515	E677UNE	Leyland Tiger TRCTL11/3RZ	Plaxton Paramount 3200 III	C53F	1988	Ex Shearings, 1993
516	E771GNA	Leyland Tiger TRCTL11/3ARZA	Plaxton Paramount 3200 III	C53F	1989	Ex Shearings, 1993
517	J45SNY	Leyland Tiger TRCL10/3ARZM	Plaxton 321	C50F	1991	Ex Bebb, Llantwit Fardre, 1993
518	J46SNY	Leyland Tiger TRCL10/3ARZM	Plaxton 321	C50F	1991	Ex Bebb, Llantwit Fardre, 1993
519	J48SNY	Leyland Tiger TRCL10/3ARZM	Plaxton 321	C50F	1991	Ex Bebb, Llantwit Fardre, 1993
520	J54SNY	Leyland Tiger TRCL10/3ARZM	Plaxton 321	C50F	1991	Ex Bebb, Llantwit Fardre, 1993

701-722

Ford Transit 190 — Dormobile — B16F — 1985 — Ex Badgerline, 1991-92

701	C439BHY	706	C484BFB	711	B444WTC	715	C508BFB	719	C450BHY
702	C445BHY	707	C490BFB	712	C491BFB	716	C510BFB	720	C451BHY
703	C446BHY	708	C495BFB	713	C492BFB	717	C511BFB	721	C440BHY
704	C482BFB	709	C497BFB	714	C507BFB	718	C449BHY	722	C470BHY
705	C483BFB								

755	D755RWC	Ford Transit VE6	Dormobile	B16F	1986	Ex Eastern National, 1990
756	D756RWC	Ford Transit VE6	Dormobile	B16F	1986	Ex Eastern National, 1990

800-804

Mercedes-Benz 811D — Reeve Burgess Beaver — B23F — 1989 — Ex Eastern National, 1990

800	F800RHK	801	F801RHK	802	F802RHK	803	F803RHK	804	F804RHK

805-811

Mercedes-Benz 811D — Plaxton Beaver — B31F — 1992

805	K805DJN	807	K807DJN	809	K809DJN	810	K810DJN	811	K811DJN
806	K806DJN	808	K808DJN						

901-917

Dennis Dart 9SDL3016 — Plaxton Pointer — B35F — 1993

901	K901CVW	905	K905CVW	909	K909CVW	912	K912CVW	915	K915CVW
902	K902CVW	906	K906CVW	910	K910CVW	913	K913CVW	916	K916CVW
903	K903CVW	907	K907CVW	911	K911CVW	914	K914CVW	917	K917CVW
904	K904CVW	908	K908CVW						

1001	H101KVX	Leyland Olympian ON2R50C13Z4 Leyland	H47/31F	1990
1002	H102KVX	Leyland Olympian ON2R50C13Z4 Leyland	H47/31F	1990
1003	H103KVX	Leyland Olympian ON2R50C13Z4 Leyland	H47/31F	1990
1004	H104KVX	Leyland Olympian ON2R50C13Z4 Leyland	H47/31F	1990

1400-1424

Leyland Lynx LX112L10ZR1R Leyland — B49F — 1988 — Ex Eastern National, 1990

1400	E400HWC	1409	F409LTW	1412	F412MNO	1419	F419MWC	1422	F422MJN
1404	F404LTW	1410	F410MNO	1417	F417MWC	1420	F420MJN	1423	F423MJN
1405	F405LTW	1411	F411MNO	1418	F418MWC	1421	F421MJN	1424	F424MJN
1406	F406LTW								

1808-1871

Leyland National 11351A/1R — B49F — 1977-78 Ex Eastern National, 1990

1808	TJN507R	1823	VAR900S	1839	WJN559S	1849	YEV307S	1859	YEV317S
1810	TJN509R	1830	VNO732S	1840	WJN560S	1852	YEV310S	1864	YEV322S
1817	VNO740S	1835	VAR895S	1845	WJN565S	1853	YEV311S	1866	YEV324S
1821	VNO744S	1836	VAR896S	1846	WJN566S	1854	YEV312S	1871	YEV329S
1822	VNO745S	1837	VAR897S	1847	YEV305S				

1875-1922

Leyland National 11351A/1R — B49F — 1978-79 Ex Eastern National, 1990

1875	BNO665T	1884	BNO674T	1894	BNO684T	1903	DAR125T	1912	DAR134T
1876	BNO666T	1886	BNO676T	1895	BNO685T	1904	DAR126T	1913	JHJ139V
1878	BNO668T	1887	BNO677T	1896	DAR118T	1905	DAR127T	1915	JHJ141V
1879	BNO669T	1888	BNO678T	1897	DAR119T	1906	DAR128T	1918	JHJ144V
1880	BNO670T	1889	BNO679T	1898	DAR120T	1907	DAR129T	1919	JHJ145V
1881	BNO671T	1891	BNO681T	1900	DAR122T	1908	DAR130T	1920	JHJ146V
1882	BNO672T	1893	BNO683T	1902	DAR124T	1911	DAR133T	1922	JHJ148V
1883	BNO673T								

3110	XHK215X	Bristol VRT/SL3/6LXB	Eastern Coach Works	H43/31F	1981	Ex Eastern National, 1990
3113	XHK218X	Bristol VRT/SL3/6LXB	Eastern Coach Works	H43/31F	1981	Ex Eastern National, 1990
4000	XHK235X	Leyland Olympian ONLXB/1R	Eastern Coach Works	H45/32F	1981	Ex Eastern National, 1990
4001	XHK236X	Leyland Olympian ONLXB/1R	Eastern Coach Works	H45/32F	1981	Ex Eastern National, 1990
4002	XHK237X	Leyland Olympian ONLXB/1R	Eastern Coach Works	H45/32F	1981	Ex Eastern National, 1990
4003	B698BPU	Leyland Olympian ONLXB/1R	Eastern Coach Works	H45/32F	1984	Ex Eastern National, 1991
4004	B699BPU	Leyland Olympian ONLXB/1R	Eastern Coach Works	H45/32F	1984	Ex Eastern National, 1992
4004	C711GEV	Leyland Olympian ONLXB/1R	Eastern Coach Works	H45/32F	1984	Ex Eastern National, 1991
4006	C712GEV	Leyland Olympian ONLXB/1R	Eastern Coach Works	H45/32F	1985	Ex Eastern National, 1991
4009	C409HJN	Leyland Olympian ONLXB/1RH	Eastern Coach Works	DPH42/30F	1985	Ex Eastern National, 1990
4010	C410HJN	Leyland Olympian ONLXB/1RH	Eastern Coach Works	DPH42/30F	1985	Ex Eastern National, 1990

Livery: Canary yellow and maroon;
City Saver (yellow and orange): 501-16.

Previous Registrations:

278TNY	AFH192T, MKH487A, AEP253T, 999BCY, ATH58T				
MKH68A	A122XEP	MKH89A	A125XEP	MKH893A	RCY117Y

DAR118T is one of the 1979 delivery of Leyland Nationals with fleet number 1896. It is seen working to the Tesco superstore at Lakeside.
Michael Fowler

Most Thamesway double deckers work on LRT contracted routes. No.4009 (C409HJN), a Leyland Olympian with Eastern Coach Works body, is seen in Brentwood High Street bound for Walthamstow. This service has been served by Eastern National for a long time.
G R Mills

TOWLER

Alan C Towler, Esgate House, Friday Bridge Road, Elm, Wisbech, Cambridgeshire, PE14 0AS

131HUO	Bristol Lodekka FLF6B	Eastern Coach Works	H38/32F	1961	Ex Western National, 1977
EDV523D	Bristol Lodekka FLF6B	Eastern Coach Works	H38/32F	1966	Ex Western National, 1978
GNJ574N	Bristol VRT/SL2/6LX	Eastern Coach Works	H43/31F	1974	Ex Brighton & Hove, 1990
MRB806P	Bristol VRT/SL2/6LX	Eastern Coach Works	H43/34F	1975	Ex Trent, 1990
NFO198R	Bedford YMT	Duple Dominant	C53F	1976	Ex Johnson, Outwell, 1990
NPD690W	Bedford YNT	Plaxton Supreme IV	C53F	1981	Ex Safeguard, Guildford, 1986
PAY7W	Bedford YMT	Duple Dominant IV	C53F	1981	Ex Kinch, Mount Sorrel, 1984
TPM616X	Bedford YNT	Plaxton Supreme VI	C53F	1982	Ex Gastonia, Cranleigh, 1985
UFX629X	Bristol LHS6L	Plaxton Supreme V	C35F	1982	Ex Derby, 1987
D217OOJ	Freight Rover Sherpa 365	Carlyle	B18F	1987	Ex Bee Line Buzz, 1992
E686NNH	Leyland Tiger TRCL10/3ARZM	Jonckheere Jubilee P599	C51FT	1988	Ex Gillespie, Kelty, 1992

Livery: Cream, green and orange

Very few Bristol engined FLF models still exist, thus Alan Towler's pair, still on passenger carrying duties, are somewhat rare. EDV523D, the newer of the two, previously with Western National, is seen at Emneth and regularly performs on school contract journeys in the Wisbech area. *G R Mills*

UNITED COUNTIES

United Counties Omnibus Co Ltd, Rothersthorpe Avenue,
Northampton, NN4 9UT

Depots: St Johns, Bedford; Station Road, Corby; Stikeley Road, Huntingdon; Northampton Road, Kettering and Rothersthorpe Avenue, Northampton.

4	E645DCK	Renault S46	Dormobile	B25F	1987	Ex Fife Scottish, 1992
5	E638DCK	Renault S46	Dormobile	B25F	1987	Ex Fife Scottish, 1992
6	E639DCK	Renault S46	Dormobile	B25F	1987	Ex Fife Scottish, 1992
15	E635DCK	Renault S46	Dormobile	B25F	1987	Ex Fife Scottish, 1992
16	E641DCK	Renault S46	Dormobile	B25F	1987	Ex Fife Scottish, 1992
17	D411FRV	Iveco Daily 49.10	Robin Hood City Nippy	B19F	1987	Ex Ribble, 1991
18	D217NUR	Iveco Daily 49.10	Robin Hood City Nippy	B21F	1987	Ex Cumberland, 1992
19	D936EBP	Iveco Daily 49.10	Robin Hood City Nippy	B19F	1987	Ex East Midland, 1992

23-34

Iveco Daily 49.10 — Robin Hood City Nippy — B19F* — 1986-87 — *24 is DP21F

23	D23WNH	27	D27BVV	29	D29BVV	31	D31BVV	33	D33BVV
24	D24WNH	28	D28BNV	30	D30BVV	32	D32BVV	34	D34BVV
25	D25BVV							

45-50

Iveco Daily 49.10 — Robin Hood City Nippy — B23F — 1988

45	E45MRP	47	E47MRP	48	E48MRP	49	E49MRP	50	E50MRP
46	E46MRP							

51-56

Iveco Daily 49.10 — Robin Hood City Nippy — B25F — 1988 — Ex Hampshire Bus, 1988

51	F494NTR	53	F496NTR	54	F491NTR	55	F492NTR	56	F493NTR
52	F495NTR							

57-66

Iveco Daily 49.10 — Robin Hood City Nippy — B23F — 1989

57	F57AVV	59	F59AVV	61	G61JVV	63	G63JVV	65	G65JVV
58	F58AVV	60	F60AVV	62	G62JVV	64	G64JVV	66	G66JVV

67	G67LVV	Iveco Daily 49.10	Phoenix	B23F	1989

68-73

Iveco Daily 49.10 — Phoenix — B23F — 1990

68	G28PSR	70	G27PSR	72	G32PSR	74	G40SSR	75	G41SSR
69	G29PSR	71	G31PSR	73	G33PSR				

76	D612BCK	Iveco Daily 49.10	Robin Hood City Nippy	B21F	1986	Ex Ribble, 1992
77	E66BVS	Iveco Daily 49.10	Robin Hood City Nippy	B25F	1987	
81	C81PRP	Leyland Tiger TRCTL11/3RZ	Plaxton Paramount 3500 II	C46FT	1986	
82	C82PRP	Leyland Tiger TRCTL11/3RZ	Plaxton Paramount 3500 II	C46FT	1986	
84	C84PRP	Leyland Tiger TRCTL11/3RZ	Plaxton Paramount 3500 II	C46FT	1986	
85	C85PRP	Leyland Tiger TRCTL11/3RZ	Plaxton Paramount 3500 II	C46FT	1986	

92-96

Volvo B10M-60 — Plaxton Premiére 350 — C46FT — 1992 — Ex Parks, Hamilton, 1993

92	J430HDS	93	J439HDS	94	J445HDS	95	J446HDS	96	J450HDS

102	NBD102Y	Leyland Tiger TRCTL11/3R	Plaxton Paramount 3200 E	C53F	1983
103	NBD103Y	Leyland Tiger TRCTL11/3R	Plaxton Paramount 3200 E	C53F	1983
104	NBD104Y	Leyland Tiger TRCTL11/3R	Plaxton Paramount 3200 E	C53F	1983
105	83CBD	Leyland Tiger TRCTL11/3R	Plaxton Paramount 3200 E	C53F	1983

108-114

Leyland Tiger TRCTL11/3RH — Plaxton Paramount 3200 E — C50FT — 1983

108	A108TRP	110	A110TRP	112	A112TRP	113	A113TRP	114	A114TRP
109	A109TRP	111	A111TRP					

115	MSU465	Leyland Tiger TRCTL11/3RH	Duple 340	C46FT	1987	Ex Fife Scottish, 1992
116	VLT255	Leyland Tiger TRCTL11/3RZ	Duple Laser 2	C44FT	1985	Ex Stagecoach Malawi, 1993
120	C120PNV	Leyland Tiger TRCTL11/3RZ	Plaxton Paramount 3200 II	C53F	1986	
121	C121PNV	Leyland Tiger TRCTL11/3RZ	Plaxton Paramount 3200 II	C53F	1986	

122	C122PNV	Leyland Tiger TRCTL11/3RZ		Plaxton Paramount 3200 II	C53F	1986			
125	WLT908	Volvo B10M-61		Plaxton Paramount 3200	C50F	1983	Ex Stagecoach, 1988		
126	647DYE	Volvo B10M-61		Plaxton Paramount 3200	C50F	1983	Ex Stagecoach, 1988		

130-135

		Volvo B10M-61		Plaxton Paramount 3200 III	C53F	1988			
130	E130ORP	132	E132ORP	133	E133ORP	134	E134ORP	135	F135URP
131	E131ORP								

145	OUF66W	Leyland Leopard PSU3F/4R	Plaxton Supreme IV Exp	C48F	1981	Ex Southdown, 1989	
146	AVL746X	Leyland Leopard PSU3F/4R	Eastern Coach Works B51	C47F	1982	Ex Lincolnshire, 1987	

150-162

		Volvo B10M-60		Plaxton Premiére Interurban	DP53F	1993			
150	K150DNV	153	K153DNV	156	L156JNH	159	L159JNH	161	L161JNH
151	K151DNV	154	K154DNV	157	L157JNH	160	L160JNH	162	L162JNH
152	K152DNV	155	L155JNH	158	L158JNH				

171-177

		Leyland Leopard PSU3F/4R		Eastern Coach Works	C49F	1981			
171	CNH171X	173	CNH173X	174	CNH174X	176	CNH176X	177	CNH177X

Ten examples of the last coach body style built by Eastern Coach Works still exist in the United Counties fleet while many other former NBC subsidiaries have ousted the type. No.146 (AVL746X) as the odd-one-out in the set as it was new to RoadCar. It is seen still in good shape leaving Drummer Street, Cambridge.
G R Mills

The latest deliveries for the United Counties Coachlink fleet are Volvo B10Ms with Plaxton's Premiére Interurban, designed in conjunction with Stagecoach to their specification. No.152 (K152DNV) is an example of the new intake and is seen in Cambridge bound for Northampton and Bedford. *G R Mills*

178	EBD178X	Leyland Leopard PSU3G/4R	Eastern Coach Works B51	C49F	1982				
179	EBD179X	Leyland Leopard PSU3G/4R	Eastern Coach Works B51	C49F	1982				
184	JNH184Y	Leyland Leopard PSU3G/4R	Eastern Coach Works B51	C46F	1983				
185	JNH185Y	Leyland Leopard PSU3G/4R	Eastern Coach Works B51	C46F	1983				
187	NNH187Y	Leyland Leopard PSU3G/4R	Duple Dominant IV	C57F	1983				
191	NNH191Y	Leyland Leopard PSU3G/4R	Duple Dominant IV	C57F	1983				

301-313

		Iveco Daily 49.10		Robin Hood City Nippy	B19F	1987	Ex Ribble, 1990	
301	D406FRV	**304**	D728YBV	**307**	D735YBV	**310**	D610BCK	**312** D619BCK
302	D724YBV	**305**	D729YBV	**308**	D859FOT	**311**	D616BCK	**313** D725YBV
303	D726YBV	**306**	D731YBV	**309**	D613BCK			

314	D938ECR	Iveco Daily 49.10	Robin Hood City Nippy	B13F	1986	Ex Stagecoach, 1992
315	D22WNH	Iveco Daily 49.10	Robin Hood City Nippy	B13F	1986	Ex Bluebird Northern, 1991
316	D771MUR	Iveco Daily 49.10	Robin Hood City Nippy	B13F	1986	Ex Bluebird Northern, 1991
317	D26BVV	Iveco Daily 49.10	Robin Hood City Nippy	B13F	1986	Ex Bluebird Northern, 1991

Leyland Nationals have now been almost eliminated from the United Counties fleet with only nine mark 1s and five mark 2s remain. One of the latter, 584 (NRP584V) is seen in Bedford.
G R Mills

The Bedford Park and Ride service has recently seen the introduction of a pair of Leyland Nationals transferred from the Cumberland. No.502 (LFR864X) was new to Ribble and is one of the shorter, 10.6 metre, versions of the National 2. *G R Mills*

350-359   Mercedes-Benz 709D   Alexander AM   B25F   1992

350	K350ANV	**352**	K352ANV	**354**	K354ANV	**356**	K356ANV	**358**	K358ANV
351	K351ANV	**353**	K353ANV	**355**	K355ANV	**357**	K357ANV	**359**	K359ANV

500	LFR862X	Leyland National 2 NL106AL11/1R			B44F	1981	Ex Cumberland, 1993
501	LFR864X	Leyland National 2 NL106AL11/1R			B44F	1981	Ex Cumberland, 1993

543-576   Leyland National 11351A/1R   B49F   1978-79

543	BVV543T	**553**	ERP553T	**561**	KRP561V	**571**	MNH571V	**576**	MNH576V
552	ERP552T	**555**	ERP555T	**564**	KRP564V	**575**	MNH575V		

582-587   Leyland National 2 NL116L11/1R   B49F   1980

582	NRP582V	**583**	NRP583V	**584**	NRP584V	**585**	SVV585W	**587**	SVV587W

600	F110NES	Leyland Olympian ON6LXCT/5RZ Alexander RL	H66/44F	1989	Ex East Midland, 1992

601-611   Leyland Olympian ONLXB/1R   Eastern Coach Works   H45/32F*   1981   *601/2/5/6 are DPH45/27F

601	ARP601X	**604**	ARP604X	**606**	ARP606X	**608**	ARP608X	**610**	ARP610X
602	ARP602X	**605**	ARP605X	**607**	ARP607X	**609**	ARP609X	**611**	ARP611X

612	WLT528	Leyland Olympian ONLXB/1RV	Alexander RL	DPH43/27F	1987	Ex Bluebird Northern, 1991
613	D383XRS	Leyland Olympian ONLXB/1RV	Alexander RL	DPH43/27F	1987	Ex Bluebird Northern, 1991
614	WLT512	Leyland Olympian ONLXB/1RV	Alexander RL	DPH43/27F	1987	Ex Bluebird Northern, 1991
615	685DYE	Leyland Olympian ONLXB/1RV	Alexander RL	DPH43/27F	1987	Ex Bluebird Northern, 1991
616	GSO6V	Leyland Olympian ONLXB/1RV	Alexander RL	H47/30F	1986	Ex Bluebird Northern, 1991
617	GSO7V	Leyland Olympian ONLXB/1RV	Alexander RL	H47/30F	1986	Ex Bluebird Northern, 1991

The Leyland Olympian has become the standard Stagecoach vehicle for its double deck requirement, many with the Alexander high capacity body. Further Volvo Olympians are on order for next year. 627 (F627MSL) is a United Counties example dedicated to service 51 named 'The Great Eastern Line', operating on a regular frequency in Northampton. *G R Mills*

620-644

Leyland Olympian ONLXB/2RZ   Alexander RL   H51/36F*   1988-89   *645-9 are DPH51/31F
*635-644 are H51/34F

620	F620MSL	626	F626MSL	632	F632MSL	638	F638YRP	644	G644EVV
621	F621MSL	627	F627MSL	633	F633MSL	639	G639EVV	645	G645EVV
622	F622MSL	628	F628MSL	634	F634MSP	640	G640EVV	646	G646EVV
623	F623MSL	629	F629MSL	635	F635YRP	641	G641EVV	647	G647EVV
624	F624MSL	630	F630MSL	636	F636YRP	642	G642EVV	648	G648EVV
625	F625MSL	631	F631MSL	637	F637YRP	643	G643EVV	649	G649EVV

650-654

Leyland Olympian ON2R56G13Z4 Alexander RL   H51/34F   1990

650	H650VVV	651	H651VVV	652	H652VVV	653	H653VVV	654	H654VVV

655-670

Leyland Olympian ON2R50G13Z4 Northern Counties Palatine H47/29F   1992

655	K655UNH	658	K658UNH	661	K661UNH	664	K664UNH	668	K668UNH
656	K656UNH	659	K659UNH	662	K662UNH	665	K665UNH	669	K669UNH
657	K657UNH	660	K660UNH	663	K663UNH	667	K667UNH	670	K670UNH

701-714

AEC Routemaster 5RM   Park Royal   H36/28R   1961   Ex London Buses, 1988

701	HVS710	705	ABD892A	708	CUV192C	710	HVS935	714	BNK31A
703	HVS937	706	BNK32A	709	HVS936				

721-749

Bristol VRT/SL3/6LXB   Eastern Coach Works   H43/31F   1980   Ex Devon General, 1991

721	LFJ862W	727	LFJ879W	735	LFJ864W	740	FDV832V	745	LFJ885W
722	LFJ863W	731	FDV809V	736	LFJ865W	741	LFJ882W	746	LFJ859W
723	LFJ853W	732	FDV838V	737	FDV811V	742	LFJ883W	747	LFJ861W
724	LFJ852W	733	LFJ868W	738	FDV835V	743	LFJ858W	748	LFJ884W
725	LFJ854W	734	FDV812V	739	LFJ869W	744	LFJ878W	749	LFJ866W
726	LFJ855W								

Fifteen new Leyland Olympians with Northern Counties bodies were delivered to United Counties in 1992. Originally intended to replace older Bristol VRTs, the latter have been retained for school contract work. No.669 (K669UNH) is seen in Bedford bus station. *G R Mills*

750	FAO417V	Bristol VRT/SL3/6LXB	Eastern Coach Works	H43/31F	1978	Ex Cumberland, 1992
751	FAO418V	Bristol VRT/SL3/6LXB	Eastern Coach Works	H43/31F	1978	Ex Cumberland, 1992
752	FAO419V	Bristol VRT/SL3/6LXB	Eastern Coach Works	H43/31F	1978	Ex Cumberland, 1992
839	LBD839P	Bristol VRT/SL3/6LX	Eastern Coach Works	H43/31F	1975	

842-891

Bristol VRT/SL3/6LXB   Eastern Coach Works   H43/31F   1975-78

842	OBD842P	871	TNH871R	876	WBD876S	881	XNV881S	888	XNV888S
849	OVV849R	872	TNH872R	878	XNV878S	885	XNV885S	889	XNV889S
856	OVV856R	873	TNH873R	879	XNV879S	886	XNV886S	890	XNV890S
863	RRP863R	875	WBD875S	880	XNV880S	887	XNV887S	891	XNV891S
870	TNH870R								

900	BAU178T	Bristol VRT/SL3/6LXB	Eastern Coach Works	H43/31F	1978	Ex East Midland, 1993
901	BAU179T	Bristol VRT/SL3/6LXB	Eastern Coach Works	H43/31F	1978	Ex East Midland, 1993

902-967

Bristol VRT/SL3/6LXB   Eastern Coach Works   H43/31F*   1978-81   *919/61 are DPH40/28F

902	CBD902T	915	HBD915T	930	SNV930W	944	URP944W	954	VVV954W
903	CBD903T	916	HBD916T	931	SNV931W	945	URP945W	961	VVV961W
908	FRP908T	917	HBD918T	935	SNV935W	948	VVV948W	962	VVV962W
909	FRP909T	919	HBD919T	936	SNV936W	949	VVV949W	963	VVV963W
910	FRP910T	920	LBD920V	937	SNV937W	950	VVV950W	965	VVV965W
911	FRP911T	921	LBD921V	939	URP939W	952	VVV952W	966	VVV966W
912	FRP912T	923	LBD923V	940	URP940W	953	VVV953W	967	VVV967W
914	HBD914T	926	ONH926V	941	URP941W				

970-974

Bristol VRT/SL3/6LXB   Eastern Coach Works   H43/31F   1980   Ex Hampshire Bus, 1988

970	KRU843W	971	KRU845W	972	KRU846W	973	KRU847W	974	KRU852W

Previous Registrations:

647DYE	A320ANH	GSO7V	D387XRS	OUF56W	MAP344W, XLD244
685DYE	D379XRS	HVS710	WLT512	OUF66W	MAP352W, SYC852
83CBD	NBD105Y	HVS935	VLT255	VLT255	B357KNH, Malawi ?,
ABD892A	68CLT	HVS936	VLT51	WLT512	D384XRS
BNK32A	647DYE	HVS937	WLT682	WLT528	D382XRS
BNK31A	685DYE	MSU465	D525ESG	WLT908	A332ANH, 4009SC, A800TGC
GSO6V	D386XRS				

Liveries: Stagecoach white, red, orange and blue.
National Express: 92-6, 105.

The ranks of United Counties Routemasters have recently been halved, with operation of the veterans confined to route 101 in Bedford. Most, like 705 (ABD892A), have now lost the original registration mark to other vehicles. The lack of Stagecoach corporate livery is, perhaps, a further indication that the class is doomed to extinction.
G R Mills

UNIVERSITYBUS

University of Hertfordshire, Wall Hall Campus, Aldenham, Hertfordshire

OV303	XNK200X	Ford R1014	Plaxton Bustler	B47F	1981	Ex Arrow, Newgate Street, 1991
OV304	H748CBP	Mercedes-Benz 811D	Phoenix	B33F	1991	
OV305	H749CBP	Mercedes-Benz 811D	Phoenix	B33F	1991	
OV306	H840NOC	Dennis Dart 9.8SDL3004	Carlyle Dartline	B40F	1990	Ex Dennis demonstrator, 1991
OV307	H849NOC	Dennis Dart 9.8SDL3004	Carlyle Dartline	B43F	1990	Ex Carlyle demonstrator, 1991
OV308	KJD548P	Leyland National 10351A/2R		B36D	1976	Ex London Buses, 1992
OV309	THX204S	Leyland National 10351A/2R		B36D	1978	Ex London Buses, 1992
OV3	THX216S	Leyland National 10351A/2R		B36D	1978	Ex London Buses, 1992
OV3	THX261S	Leyland National 10351A/2R		B36D	1978	Ex London Buses, 1992

Livery: White

Successful operation of buses and coaches by education authorities is no new venture, but that by individual establishments in certainly innovative. Universitybus of Aldenham operate a pair of 9.8-metre Dennis Darts, both previously demonstrators, on services connecting the campus with local towns. H849NOC is seen in St Albans.
Colin Lloyd

VICEROY

F C Moore Ltd, 12 Bridge Street, Saffron Walden, Essex, CB10 1BU

RWC637K	Bedford YRQ	Plaxton Elite III	C43F	1972	Ex Wiffen, Finchingfield, 1982
HWB817N	Bedford YRT	Plaxton Elite III	C53F	1975	Ex Pepper, Thurnscoe, 1977
KJD520P	Leyland National 10351A/2R		B36D	1976	Ex London Buses, 1992
PWD842R	Bedford VAS5	Plaxton Supreme III	C29F	1977	Ex Clipson, Newton, 1986
TGW895R	Bedford YMT	Plaxton Supreme III	C53F	1977	Ex Tentrek, Sidcup, 1986
VJF472S	Bedford YMT	Caetano Cascais II	C53F	1977	Ex Victoria, Hutton, 1987
THX247S	Leyland National 10351A/2R		B36D	1978	Ex London Buses, 1992
FDU5T	Bedford YMT	Plaxton Supreme IV	C53F	1979	Ex Wainfleet, Nuneaton, 1985
FKX276T	Bedford YMT	Duple Dominant II	C53F	1979	Ex Cavalier, Hounslow, 1977
ECW65W	Bedford YMT	Plaxton Supreme IV	C53F	1980	Ex New Enterprise, Tonbridge, 1986
GFM663X	Bristol LHS6L	Plaxton Supreme III	C33F	1982	Ex James, Llangeitho, 1993
597AXF	Bova EL26/581	Bova Europa	C47FT	1982	Ex Hunter, Stockton, 1992
FKP554Y	Bedford CFL	Dormobile	M16	1983	Ex Wright, Brandon, 1989
B123ECS	Scania K112CRS	Plaxton Paramount 3500	C49FT	1984	Ex Dodds, Troon, 1991
C141KGJ	Bedford Ventura YNV	Duple Laser	C57F	1986	Ex McCormick, Belvedere, 1987
E693UEX	Leyland Tiger TRCTL11/3RZ	Plaxton Paramount 3200 III	C57F	1988	Ex Rosemary , Terrington, 1993
G23HKY	Scania K93CRB	Duple 320	C51FT	1989	Ex Grangeburn, Motherwell, 1993

Livery: White and blue

Previous Registrations:
597AXF   VWX370X

Viceroy has provide stage carriage services for a considerable span of time, but in recent years coach-based vehicles have been used. Operation of an Essex County Council tendered town service has prompted the arrival of a pair of former London Buses Leyland Nationals. THX247S is seen loading in High Street South, Saffron Walden *G R Mills*

VISCOUNT

The Viscount Bus and Coach Co Ltd, 351 Lincoln Road, Peterborough, Cambridgeshire, PE1 2PG

Depots: Wisbech Road, March and Station Road, Oundle. The fleet was once part of Cambus, those vehicles moving to Viscount were generally those vehicles already allocated to the depots.

B1	VEX291X	Bristol VRT/SL3/6LXB	Eastern Coach Works	DPH41/25F	1981	Ex Cambus, 1989
B2	E502LFL	Leyland Olympian ONLXCT/1RH	Optare	DPH47/31F	1988	Ex Cambus, 1989
B3	H473CEG	Leyland Olympian ON2R50G13Z4	Leyland	H47/31F	1990	
B4	H474CEG	Leyland Olympian ON2R50G13Z4	Leyland	H47/31F	1990	
B5	H475CEG	Leyland Olympian ON2R50G13Z4	Leyland	H47/31F	1990	

B6-B11

Leyland Olympian ONLXB/1R · Northern Counties · H45/30F · 1988 · Ex Cambus, 1989

B6	F506NJE	B8	F508NJE	B9	F509NJE	B10	F510NJE	B11	F511NJE
B7	F507NJE								

B33	DNG233T	Bristol VRT/SL3/6LXB	Eastern Coach Works	H43/31F	1979	Ex Cambus, 1989
B35	DNG235T	Bristol VRT/SL3/6LXB	Eastern Coach Works	H43/31F	1979	Ex Cambus, 1989
B36	DEX227T	Bristol VRT/SL3/6LXB	Eastern Coach Works	H43/31F	1979	Ex Cambus, 1989
B37	HAH237V	Bristol VRT/SL3/6LXB	Eastern Coach Works	H43/31F	1979	Ex Cambus, 1989
B38	YNG208S	Bristol VRT/SL3/6LXB	Eastern Coach Works	H43/31F	1979	Ex Cambus, 1989
B39	PWY39W	Bristol VRT/SL3/6LXB	Eastern Coach Works	H43/31F	1981	Ex York & District, 1990
B40	PWY40W	Bristol VRT/SL3/6LXB	Eastern Coach Works	H43/31F	1981	Ex York & District, 1990

B41-B52

Bristol VRT/SL3/6LXB · Eastern Coach Works · H43/31F · 1978-81 Ex Cambus, 1989

B41	WPW201S	B44	RAH264W	B47	KVF247V	B49	KVF249V	B51	VEX301X
B42	WPW202S	B45	KVF245V	B48	KVF248V	B50	KVF250V	B52	VEX299X
B43	VPW85S	B46	KVF246V						

The first double deckers supplied new to Viscount were a trio of all-Leyland Olympians. B4 (H474CEG), named 'John Clare', is seen returning to Queensgate in Perterborough from the service bus parking area. *G R Mills*

B55	MEL559P	Bristol VRT/SL3/6LXB	Eastern Coach Works	H43/31F	1976	Ex Wilts & Dorset, 1993
B57	BFX570T	Bristol VRT/SL3/6LXB	Eastern Coach Works	H43/31F	1979	Ex Wilts & Dorset, 1993
B58	VAH278X	Bristol VRT/SL3/6LXB	Eastern Coach Works	H43/31F	1979	Ex Cambus, 1989
B59	VAH279X	Bristol VRT/SL3/6LXB	Eastern Coach Works	H43/31F	1979	Ex Cambus, 1989
B60	VAH260X	Bristol VRT/SL3/6LXB	Eastern Coach Works	H43/31F	1979	Ex Cambus, 1989

B66-B73

Bristol VRT/SL3/6LXB · Eastern Coach Works · H43/31F · 1979-81 · Ex York & District, 1990

B66	LWU466V	B68	LWU468V	B70	LWU470V	B72	SUB792W	B73	SUB793W
B67	LWU467V	B69	FWR219T	B71	SUB791W				

B74-B80

Bristol VRT/SL3/6LXB · Eastern Coach Works · H43/31F · 1981 · Ex Keighley & District, 1990

B74	SUB790W	B76	PWY46W	B78	PWY48W	B79	PWY49W	B80	PWY50W
B75	PWY45W	B77	PWY47W						

FLF453	JAH553D	Bristol FLF6G	Eastern Coach Works	H38/32F	1966	Ex Cambus, 1989
VR615	JAH401L	Bristol VRT/SL/6LX	Eastern Coach Works	H43/31F	1972	Ex Millerbus, 1992
VR816	RKO816M	Bristol VRT/SL2/6LX	Eastern Coach Works	H43/31F	1975	Ex Cambus, 1993
S1	K391KUA	Optare MetroRider	Optare	B29F	1993	
S2	K392KUA	Optare MetroRider	Optare	B29F	1993	
S3	K393KUA	Optare MetroRider	Optare	B29F	1993	
S5	J805DWW	Optare MetroRider	Optare	B29F	1992	
S6	J806DWW	Optare MetroRider	Optare	B29F	1992	
S7	J807DWW	Optare MetroRider	Optare	B29F	1992	
S8	C518DYM	Iveco Daily 49.10	Robin Hood City Nippy	B21F	1986	Ex London Buses, 1991
S10	C510DYM	Iveco Daily 49.10	Robin Hood City Nippy	B21F	1986	Ex London Buses, 1991
S11	C521DYM	Iveco Daily 49.10	Robin Hood City Nippy	B21F	1986	Ex London Buses, 1991
S13	C513DYM	Iveco Daily 49.10	Robin Hood City Nippy	B21F	1986	Ex London Buses, 1991
S40	E40RDW	Volkswagen LT55	Optare City Pacer	B25F	1987	Ex Cambus, 1989
S41	E41RDW	Volkswagen LT55	Optare City Pacer	B25F	1987	Ex Cambus, 1989

S71-S77

Iveco 59-12 · Marshall · B25F · 1992

S71	K171CAV	S73	K173CAV	S75	K175CAV	S76	K176CAV	S77	K177CAV
S72	K172CAV	S74	K174CAV						

WM1-WM17

MCW MetroRider MF150 · MCW · B23F · 1987 · On loan from West Midlands Travel

WM1	E664RVP	WM7	D647NOE	WM10	E657RVP	WM13	D603NOE	WM16	D604NOE
WM2	D642NOE	WM9	D645NOE	WM12	D631NOE	WM15	D640NOE	WM17	D605NOE

Livery: White, yellow, blue and grey. The Peterborough Bus Company (PBC) is a division of Viscount using a red, cream and maroon livery.

Operating companies: PBC - B55/7, S2/3/10/3, VR615/816.

Six of the dozen Leyland Olympians with Northern Counties bodies, delivered to Cambus in blue and cream, were transferred to Viscount in September 1989. One of these, B11 (F511NJE), had been repainted into yellow, white and blue when photographed in Westgate, Peterborough.
G R Mills

The Optare City Pacer has found favour within the Cambus group with new, used and former demonstrators all taken into stock. S40 (E40RDW) is one of seven originally supplied to the Taff Ely operation at Pontypridd, and is seen at the Vancouver shopping centre, Kings Lynn. *G R Mills*

Viscount have patronised a local coachbuilder for the newest batch of midibuses, with seven from Marshall of Cambridge, built on Iveco chassis. S77 (K177CAV) was delivered in all white in order to receive advertising material and was seen operating thus at the Queensgate shopping complex at Peterborough. *G R Mills*

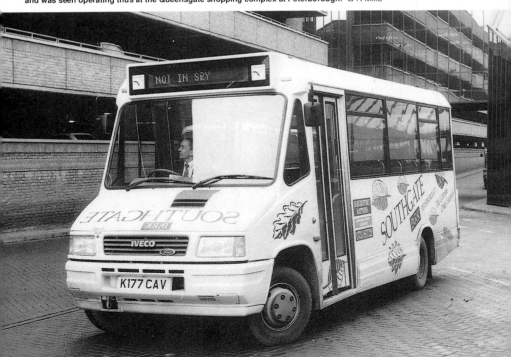

WEST'S

West's Coaches Ltd, 198/200 High Road, Woodford Green, Essex, IG8 8EF

JFP177V	Ford R1114	Duple Dominant II	C53F	1980	
LUE260V	Ford R1114	Duple Dominant II	C46F	1980	
KGA56Y	Bova EL26/581	Bova Europa	C53F	1982	Ex Crawford, Neilston, 1987
A15BUS	Bova EL28/581	Duple Calypso	C53F	1984	Ex Blue Iris, Nailsea, 1988
A14BUS	Bova EL28/581	Duple Calypso	C53F	1984	Ex Antler, Rugeley, 1988
D869NVS	Freight Rover Sherpa 374	Dormobile	B16F	1986	Ex London Country NW, 1988
E667YDT	MCW MetroRider MF150/88	MCW	B23F	1988	
F711CWJ	MCW MetroRider MF150/97	MCW	B23F	1988	
F712CWJ	MCW MetroRider MF150/97	MCW	B23F	1988	
F713CWJ	MCW MetroRider MF150/110	MCW	B23F	1988	
F714CWJ	MCW MetroRider MF150/110	MCW	B23F	1988	
F715CWJ	MCW MetroRider MF150/110	MCW	B23F	1988	
F718CWJ	MCW MetroRider MF150/110	MCW	B23F	1988	
F719CWJ	MCW MetroRider MF150/110	MCW	B23F	1988	
F367CHE	MCW MetroRider MF150/110	MCW	B23F	1988	
A10BUS	DAF SB220LC550	Optare Delta	B47F	1989	
A12BUS	DAF SB2305DHS585	Caetano Algarve	C53F	1989	Ex Traject, Halifax, 1991
A13BUS	TAZ D3200	TAZ Dubrava	C53F	1989	
A16BUS	Volvo B10M-60	Plaxton Paramount 3500 III	C53F	1989	Ex Parks, Hamilton, 1992
A19BUS	Leyland Swift LBM6T/2RA	Wadham Stringer Vanguard II	B39F	1991	
J6BUS	Dennis Dart 9SDL3011	Wright Handy-bus	B35F	1992	
J9BUS	Dennis Dart 9.8SDL3012	Wright Handy-bus	DP40F	1992	
J12BUS	Dennis Dart 9.8SDL3017	Wright Handy-bus	B40F	1992	
K2BUS	Dennis Dart 9.8SDL3017	Wright Handy-bus	B40F	1992	
K5BUS	DAF SB220LC550	Optare Delta	B49F	1993	

Previous Registrations:

A10BUS	G259EHD	A14BUS	B127DHL	A16BUS	F972HGE
A12BUS	F233RJX	A15BUS	A321HFP	A19BUS	H550AMT
A13BUS	F788TBC				

Livery: Red and white

Wests of Woodford Green has used private index marks for all the larger buses in the fleet with distinctive BUS index marks. Latest is the use of Select marks, such as K2BUS which has been carried from new. It is a Dennis Dart with Wright of Ballymena body and is seen at the Two Brewers terminus in Ongar. *G R Mills*

Outside Epping Station, on the Central line of the Underground, is where Wests K5BUS was seen in early 1993, shortly after delivery. It is one of two Optare Deltas now operating in thefleet. *Colin Lloyd*

West's front-line coaches comprise Volvo and DAF powered units. Most of the latter are power units for the Bovas, and the only DAF chassis is A12BUS, a SB2305 fitted with a Caetano Algarve bodywork. It is seen at Wembly during a Schoolboys International Football event.
G R Mills

WHIPPET

Whippet Coaches Ltd, Cambridge Road, Fenstanton, Cambridgeshire

KJD268P	MCW Metropolitan BR111DH	MCW	H43/29D	1976	Ex London Transport, 1984
KJD271P	MCW Metropolitan BR111DH	MCW	H43/32F	1976	Ex London Transport, 1984
KJD272P	MCW Metropolitan BR111DH	MCW	H43/29D	1976	Ex Reading, 1989
LEW971P	Leyland Atlantean AN68/1R	Roe	H43/34F	1976	
OCU781R	MCW Metropolitan BR111DH	MCW	H45/29D	1976	Ex Reading, 1989
ORD108R	MCW Metropolitan BR111DH	MCW	H45/28D	1976	Ex Reading, 1989
OUC95R	MCW Metropolitan BR111DH	MCW	H43/32F	1976	Ex London Transport, 1983
OUC109R	MCW Metropolitan BR111DH	MCW	H43/32F	1976	Ex London Transport, 1983
OUC110R	MCW Metropolitan BR111DH	MCW	H46/32F	1976	Ex London Transport, 1983
OUC123R	MCW Metropolitan BR111DH	MCW	H43/29D	1976	Ex London Transport, 1985
OUC124R	MCW Metropolitan BR111DH	MCW	H43/32F	1976	Ex London Transport, 1983
OUC144R	MCW Metropolitan BR111DH	MCW	H43/29D	1976	Ex London Transport, 1985
OUC152R	MCW Metropolitan BR111DH	MCW	H43/29D	1976	Ex Reading, 1989
SGM129S	MCW Metropolitan BR111DH	MCW	H45/28D	1976	Ex Reading, 1989
RCU481S	MCW Metropolitan BR111DH	MCW	H46/30F	1977	Ex Hart, Cleveland, 1992
RCU482S	MCW Metropolitan BR111DH	MCW	H46/30F	1977	Ex Irvine, Law 1989
WKH424S	MCW Metropolitan BR111DH	MCW	H44/30F	1977	Ex Camm, Nottingham, 1989
WKH426S	MCW Metropolitan BR111DH	MCW	O44/30F	1977	Ex Camm, Nottingham, 1989
WKH427S	MCW Metropolitan BR111DH	MCW	H44/30F	1977	Ex Camm, Nottingham, 1989
EAV811V	Leyland Atlantean AN68A/2R	Northern Counties	H47/36F	1980	
EAV812V	Volvo B58-56	Duple Dominant	B63F	1980	
RDS82W	Volvo B58-56	Duple Dominant	B53F	1980	Ex Skill, Sheffield, 1991
FCY290W	Bedford YMQ	Duple Dominant	B43F	1981	Ex Hedingham, 1992
FCY291W	Bedford YMQ	Duple Dominant	B45F	1981	Ex Hedingham, 1992
FCY292W	Bedford YMQ	Duple Dominant	B53F	1981	Ex Hedingham, 1992
FCY293W	Bedford YMQ	Duple Dominant	B53F	1981	Ex Hedingham, 1992
REG870X	Volvo B58-56	Duple Dominant	B63F	1981	
KYN283X	Leyland Titan TNLXB2RRSp	Leyland	H44/29F	1981	Ex London Buses, 1993
KYN296X	Leyland Titan TNLXB2RRSp	Leyland	H44/29F	1981	Ex London Buses, 1993
VAV161X	Volvo B10M-61	Plaxton Supreme IV Exp	C57F	1982	
VAV163X	Volvo B10M-61	Plaxton Supreme IV Exp	C53F	1982	
EEW113Y	DAF MB200DKFL600	Plaxton Paramount 3200 E	C57F	1983	
FEW224Y	DAF MB200DKFL600	Plaxton Paramount 3200 E	C57F	1983	
FEW225Y	DAF MB200DKFL600	Plaxton Paramount 3200 E	C57F	1983	
FEW226Y	DAF MB200DKFL600	Plaxton Paramount 3200 E	C53F	1983	
FEW227Y	DAF MB200DKFL600	Plaxton Paramount 3500	C53F	1983	
A807REW	DAF MB200DKFL600	Duple Caribbean	C55F	1984	
B102EFL	DAF SB2300DHS585	Plaxton Paramount 3500 II	C53F	1985	
B103EFL	DAF SB2300DHS585	Plaxton Paramount 3500 II	C53F	1985	
GIL2968	Volvo B10M-61	Plaxton Paramount 3200 II	C57F	1985	Ex Reliance, Gravesend, 1991
C189MFL	DAF MB230DKFL615	Plaxton Paramount 3500 III	C53F	1986	
C43NEW	DAF MB230DKVL615	Plaxton Paramount 3500 III	C57F	1986	
D850AAV	Leyland Atlantean AN68/2L	Willowbrook	H49/33F	1987	
E893HEG	DAF SB2305DHS585	Plaxton Paramount 3500 III	C53F	1987	
E441ADV	Volvo Citybus B10M-50	Alexander RH	DPH47/35F	1988	Ex Filer, Ilfracombe, 1990
E176OEW	Volvo Citybus B10M-55	Alexander RH	DPH47/35F	1988	
E177OEW	DAF SB2300DHS585	Duple 340	C55F	1988	
E178OEW	DAF SB2300DHS585	Duple 340	C55F	1988	
F693PAY	Volvo B10M-61	Plaxton Paramount 3200 III	C53F	1989	
F694PAY	Volvo B10M-61	Plaxton Paramount 3200 III	C53F	1989	
G823UMU	Volvo Citybus B10M-50	Northern Counties	DPH45/35F	1989	
G824UMU	Volvo Citybus B10M-50	Northern Counties	DPH45/35F	1989	
H303CAV	Volvo Citybus B10M-50	Northern Counties	DPH45/35F	1990	
J722KBC	Volvo B10M-60	Plaxton Paramount 3200 III	C53F	1992	
J723KBC	Volvo B10M-60	Plaxton Paramount 3200 III	C53F	1992	

Livery: Two-tone blue and cream

Previous Registration:
GIL2968   B169WKO

EAV812V is one of a pair of Duple Dominant buses based on the Volvo B58 chassis. It is seen in Cambridge, one of its regular haunts. *G R Mills*

Whippet's own one of the largest fleets of Scania powered Metropolitan double decker. Having had over two dozen pass through the fleet, many of these still remaining in stock. WKH426S, new to Kingston-on-Hull, is a unique member as the only open-top version, and is seen at Fenstanton while working the main line service from Cambridge on a summer Saturday. *G R Mills*

Whippet's operate five Volvo Citybus, of which four were delivered new. All are fitted with high-back seating making the quintet suitable for excursion and private hire duties. The newest of these, H303CAV, is seen in Parkside, Cambridge before working a journey to Huntingdon. *G R Mills*

Standard MCW Metropolitan is OCU781R, one of many acquired from the various Metropolitan fleets now working in Cambridgeshire. New to Tyne and Wear pte, this example has retained its dual-doored configuration. *Michael Fowler*

YELLOW BUS

Motts Coaches (Aylesbury) Ltd, 15 Station Road, Stoke Mandeville,
Buckinghamshire, HP22 5UL

No	Reg	Chassis	Body	Seating	Year	Notes
1	JHE141W	MCW Metrobus DR104/6	MCW	H45/31F	1980	Ex Stevensons, Spath, 1991
2	JHE142W	MCW Metrobus DR104/6	MCW	H45/31F	1980	Ex South Yorkshire, 1991
3	JHE143W	MCW Metrobus DR104/6	MCW	H45/31F	1980	Ex South Yorkshire, 1991
4	JHE139W	MCW Metrobus DR104/6	MCW	H45/31F	1980	Ex South Yorkshire, 1991
5	C52HDT	Dennis Domino SDA1202	Optare	B33F	1985	Ex South Yorkshire, 1991
6	OWG368X	Leyland Leopard PSU3F/4R	Plaxton Bustler	DP53F	1982	Ex South Yorkshire, 1991
8	UKE830X	Leyland Leopard PSU3G/4R	Eastern Coach Works B51	DP53F	1982	Ex South Yorkshire, 1991
9	JHE163W	MCW Metrobus DR104/6	MCW	H45/32F	1980	Ex East Kent, 1991
10	JHE164W	MCW Metrobus DR104/6	MCW	H45/32F	1980	Ex South Yorkshire, 1991
11	LOA834X	Leyland Leopard PSU3F/4R	Willowbrook 003	DP53F	1982	Ex Stevensons, Spath, 1992
12	DDM33X	Leyland Leopard PSU3F/4R	Willowbrook 003	C47F	1982	Ex Stevensons, Spath, 1992
13	KON323P	Leyland Fleetline FE30ALR(6LXG) MCW		H43/33F	1976	Ex West Midlands Travel, 1989
15	OJD365R	Leyland Fleetline FE30ALRSp	Park Royal	H44/24D	1977	Ex London Buses, 1992
16	OJD446R	Leyland Fleetline FE30ALRSp	Park Royal	H44/24D	1977	Ex London Buses, 1992
17	OJD463R	Leyland Fleetline FE30ALRSp	Park Royal	H44/24D	1977	Ex London Buses, 1992
18	THX545S	Leyland Fleetline FE30ALRSp	Park Royal	H44/27D	1977	Ex London Buses, 1992
19	GGM96W	Leyland Leopard PSU3E/4R	Willowbrook 003	C46F	1981	Ex Cyril Evans, Senghenydd, 1992
20	LCY101W	Leyland Leopard PSU3E/4R	Willowbrook 003	C49F	1981	Ex Wealden, Five Oaks,Green, 1992
21	D809MNY	Renault-Dodge S56	East Lancashire	DP24F	1987	Ex Windsonian, 1992
22	OJD247R	Leyland Fleetline FE30ALRSp	Park Royal	H44/24D	1977	Ex London Buses, 1992

Reg	Chassis	Body	Seating	Year	Notes
MUS151P	Leyland Leopard PSU3C/4R	Duple Dominant	B53F	1976	Ex Williams, Cross Keys, 1993
MUS152P	Leyland Leopard PSU3C/4R	Duple Dominant	B53F	1976	Ex Williams, Cross Keys, 1993
TGD219R	Leyland Leopard PSU3C/4R	Duple Dominant	B53F	1977	Ex Williams, Cross Keys, 1993
SUR283R	Leyland Leopard PSU3C/4R	Plaxton Supreme III	C53F	1977	Ex Clarke, Southall, 1987
EHS107T	Leyland Leopard PSU3E/4R	Duple Dominant	B55F	1978	Ex Williams, Cross Keys, 1993
CSU960	Volvo B10M-61	Plaxton Paramount 3500 III	C49FT	1988	Ex Selwyn, Runcorn, 1989
WSU472	Volvo B10M-61	Plaxton Viewmaster IV	C49F	1982	
4442MT	Volvo B10M-61	Jonckheere Jubilee P90	CH46/12FT	1984	
5705MT	Volvo B10MT-53	Van Hool Astral	CH55/12FT	1985	Ex Harris, Armadale, 1988
5812MT	Volvo B10M-61	Jonckheere Jubilee P50	C51FT	1987	
6601MT	Volvo B10M-61	Jonckheere Jubilee P50	C51FT	1983	Ex Telling, Byfleet, 1987
6957MT	Volvo B10M-61	Jonckheere Jubilee P99	C51FT	1988	Ex Morriston Cs, Swansea, 1991
9920MT	Mercedes-Benz 0303	Mercedes-Benz	C51FT	1985	
4932PH	DAF SB2305DHS585	Plaxton Paramount 3200 II	C53FL	1985	
272CFC	Volvo B10MT-53	Jonckheere Jubilee P95	CH55/12FT	1986	Ex Flight's, Birmingham, 1989
YJO957X	Volvo B10M-61	Plaxton Paramount 3500	C49FT	1982	
JBW68Y	Volvo B10M-61	Plaxton Paramount 3500	C53F	1983	Ex Bebb, Llantwit Fardre, 1985
C782MVH	DAF SB2305DHS585	Plaxton Paramount 3200 II	C53F	1986	Ex Smith, Alcester, 1987
C725VLW	Iveco 35-8	Elme	C16F	1985	Ex Golynia, Long Melford, 1989
D289XCX	DAF SB2305DHS585	Plaxton Paramount 3200 III	C53F	1987	Ex Smith, Alcester, 1988
F103CBD	Volvo B10M-60	Jonckheere Deauville P599	C48FT	1989	Ex Middleton, Rugeley, 1992
F648PLW	Mercedes-Benz 609D	Reeve Burgess	C22F	1989	Ex Advance, Hemel Hempstead, 1991
F952RNV	Volvo B10M-60	Jonckheere Deauville P599	C51FT	1989	Ex Hillingdon, Southall, 1991
F902YNV	Volvo B10M-60	Jonckheere Deauville P599	C47FT	1989	
F903YNV	Volvo B10M-60	Jonckheere Deauville P599	C47FT	1989	
G380RNH	Volvo B10M-60	Jonckheere Deauville P599	C51FT	1990	
H65XBD	Volvo B10M-60	Jonckheere Deauville P599	C51FT	1991	
K184GDU	Mercedes-Benz 814D	Wright	B31F	1993	

Livery: Yellow

Previous Registrations:

278CFC	C712GOP	6957MT	E209GNV
4442MT	A384UNH	9920MT	B493CBD
4932PH	C460JCP	CSU960	E486BFM
5705MT	B421CGG	JBW68Y	RDW27Y, 6957MT
5812MT	D100BNV	WSU472	YBW472X
6601MT	ONV649Y	YJO957X	XBW473X, 5812MT

South Yorkshire Transport has now supplied many of the vehicles to the Motts/YellowBus fleet, including six Metrobuses, though one example came from Stevensons. Seen passing through Cowley, Oxfordshire, while bound for Risinghurst and nearby Risinghurt is 10 (JHE164W)
G R Mills

Yellow Bus number 21 typifies the East Lancashire body design for the Renault-Dodge S56s. Built in 1987 it is fitted with high-back seating and joined the Yellow Bus fleet from Windsonian.
Colin Lloyd

ISBN 1 897990 02 2
Published by *British Bus Publishing*
The Vyne, 16 St Margarets Drive, Wellington,
Telford, Shropshire, TF1 3PH

Printed by Graphics & Print
Unit A13, Stafford Park 15
Telford, Shropshire, TF3 3BB